FOUCAULT'S PHILOSOPHY OF ART

Philosophy, Aesthetics and Cultural Theory
Series Editor: Hugh J. Silverman, Stony Brook University, USA

The *Philosophy, Aesthetics and Cultural Theory* series examines the encounter between contemporary Continental philosophy and aesthetic and cultural theory. Each book in the series explores an exciting new direction in philosophical aesthetics or cultural theory, identifying the most important and pressing issues in Continental philosophy today.

Also available:
Derrida, Literature and War, Sean Gaston

Forthcoming:
The Literary Agamben: Adventures in Logopoeisis, William Watkin
Philosophy and the Book, Dan Selcer

Series contact information:
Prof. Hugh J. Silverman, Philosophy, Stony Brook University
Stony Brook, New York 11794-3750 USA
hugh.silverman@stonybrook.edu
http://ms.cc.sunysb.edu/~hsilverman/

FOUCAULT'S PHILOSOPHY OF ART

A GENEALOGY OF MODERNITY

JOSEPH J. TANKE

Alexander,
Thanks for your
participation in our
symposium, and your
work on behalf of
beauty.

continuum

Continuum International Publishing Group
The Tower Building   80 Maiden Lane
11 York Road   Suite 704
London SE1 7NX   New York NY 10038

www.continuumbooks.com

British Library Cataloguing-in-Publication Data
A catalogue record for this book is available from the British Library.

ISBN-10: HB: 1-8470-6484-1
PB: 1-8470-6485-X
ISBN-13: HB: 978-1-8470-6484-4
PB: 978-1-8470-6485-1

Library of Congress Cataloging-in-Publication Data
Foucault's philosophy of art : a genealogy of modernity /
Joseph J. Tanke.
p. cm.
Includes bibliographical references and index.
ISBN-13: 978-1-84706-484-4 (HB)
ISBN-10: 1-84706-484-1 (HB)
ISBN-13: 978-1-84706-485-1 (pbk.)
ISBN-10: 1-84706-485-X (pbk.)
1. Foucault, Michel, 1926-1984. 2. Art Philosophy.
I. Title.
B2430.F724T36 2009
701'.17092–dc22   2008038913

Typeset by Newgen Imaging Systems Pvt Ltd, Chennai, India
Printed and bound in Great Britain by the Cromwell Press Group

To
Molly

CONTENTS

CONTENTS

ACKNOWLEDGMENTS

This book was begun in the Philosophy Department at Boston College and was completed at California College of the Arts in San Francisco and Oakland, California with the generous support of the Chalsty Initiative in Aesthetics and Philosophy. Conversations with faculty, friends, colleagues, and students in both institutions have no doubt contributed to what I have done well in these pages. I would like to thank David Rasmussen, Kevin Newmark, and Richard Kearney for years of intense conversation and instruction. I would also like to thank the numerous friends whose passionate pursuit of wisdom encouraged me to devote myself fully to this project. In particular, I have profited from my friendships with Ed McGushin, Colin McQuillan, Brenda Wirkus, Dan Russell, Mat Foust, Pete DeAngelis, Leslie Curtis, Adam Konopka, and Julia Legas. This book has benefited greatly from Jim Bernauer's expertise, reading, and advice. His legendary seminars on Foucault provided the initial inspiration, and his good judgment saw that my interest in Foucault and visual art could form the basis of fruitful research. A special thanks is owed to my colleagues and students at CCA. Your creativity, collegiality, and commitment to interdisciplinary production and study are daily reminders of art's importance and potential. I hope that you will see traces of our mutual inquiry in these pages. Finally, I would like to thank Hugh Silverman, Series Editor, as well as Sarah Campbell and Tom Crick at Continuum for their enthusiasm for this project.

None of this work would have been possible without my family, especially my mother, who has supported my education and encouraged my work for many years. Above all, my partner Molly Slota, to whom this book is dedicated, deserves my undying gratitude for all that she has done to ensure its completion. You have done more for me than I can enumerate here, so I will simply say that you continue to make of your life a work of art and demonstrate how the care of the self is deeply rooted in the concern for others. One can offer no higher tribute in a Foucaultian context.

ILLUSTRATIONS

ABBREVIATIONS

To facilitate reference, the following abbreviations were adopted throughout:

MICHEL FOUCAULT

AME   *Aesthetics, Method, and Epistemology: Essential Works of Foucault, 1954–1984, Volume Two*, ed. James D. Faubion (New York: The New Press, 1998).

AK   *The Archaeology of Knowledge and The Discourse on Language* (1969), trans. A. M. Sheridan Smith (New York: Pantheon Books, 1972).

BC   *The Birth of the Clinic: An Archaeology of Medical Perception* (1963), trans. A. M. Sheridan Smith (New York: Vintage Books, 1994).

CP   *Ceci n'est pas une pipe* (1968) (Paris: Fata Morgana, 1973).

DE1   *Foucault: Dits et écrits I, 1954–1975*, ed. Daniel Defert, François Ewald, and Jacques Lagrange (Paris: Éditions Gallimard, 2001).

DE2   *Foucault: Dits et écrits II, 1976–1988*, ed. Daniel Defert, François Ewald, and Jacques Lagrange (Paris: Éditions Gallimard, 2001).

EST   *Ethics: Subjectivity and Truth: Essential Works of Foucault, 1954–1984, Volume One*, ed. Paul Rabinow (New York: The New Press, 1997).

FF   'La force de fuir' (1973), in *DE1*, 1269–1273.

FL   *Foucault Live*, ed. Sylvère Lotringer (New York: Semiotext(e), 1996).

FLib   'Fantasia of the Library,' in *LCMP,* 87–109.

FN   'The Father's "No,"' in *LCMP,* 68–86.

ABBREVIATIONS

FS	*Fearless Speech*, ed. Joseph Pearson (Los Angeles: Semiotext(e), 2001).
GSA1	*Le gouvernement de soi et des autres: Cours au Collège de France (1982–1983)* (Paris: Seuil/Gallimard, 2008).
GSA2	'Le Gouvernement de soi et des autres: le courage de la vérité' (1984), unpublished transcript of course at the Collège de France, prepared by Michael Behrent.
GSA2: 1 Feb.	1 February 1984 Lecture at the Collège de France.
GSA2: 8 Feb.	8 February 1984 Lecture at the Collège de France.
GSA2: 29 Feb.	29 February 1984 Lecture at the Collège de France.
GSA2: 7 Mar.	7 March 1984 Lecture at the Collège de France.
GSA2: 14 Mar.	14 March 1984 Lecture at the Collège de France.
GSA2: 21 Mar.	21 March 1984 Lecture at the Collège de France.
HEM	'L'homme est-il mort?,' in *DE1*, 568–572.
HER	*The Hermeneutics of the Subject, Lectures at the Collège de France, 1981–1982* (2001), ed. Frédéric Gros and trans. Graham Burchell (New York: Palgrave Macmillan, 2005).
HM	*History of Madness* (1972), trans. Jonathan Murphy and Jean Khalfa (London: Routledge, 2006).
IP	'Intellectuals and Power' (with Gilles Deleuze), in *FL*, 74–82.
LCMP	*Language, Counter-Memory, Practice: Selected Essays and Interviews*, ed. Donald F. Bouchard (Ithaca, New York: Cornell University Press, 1977).
LMC	*Les mots et les choses: Une archéologie des sciences humaines* (Paris: Éditions Gallimard, 1966).
LJF	'Le jeu de Michel Foucault,' in *DE2*, 298–329.
LMI	'Les mots et les images,' in *DE1*, 648–651.
NGH1	'Nietzsche, Genealogy, History,' in *LCMP*, 139–164.
NGH2	'Nietzsche, la généalogie, l'histoire,' in *DE1*, 1004–1024.

OGE	'On the Genealogy of Ethics,' in *EST*, 253–280.
OT	*The Order of Things: An Archaeology of the Human Sciences* (1966) (New York: Vintage Books, 1994).
PB	'Pierre Boulez, Passing Through the Screen,' in *AME*, 241–244.
PM	*La Peinture de Manet*, ed. Maryvonne Saison (Paris: Éditions du Seuil, 2004).
PP	'Photogenic Painting' (1975), ed. Sarah Wilson and trans. Dafydd Roberts in *Gérard Fromanger: Photogenic Painting* (London: Black Dog Publishing Limited, 1999), 81–104.
PE	'La pensée, l'émotion' (1982), in *DE2*, 1062–1069.
QRP	'À quoi rêvent les philosophes?,' in *DE1*, 1572–1575.
QV	'Qui êtes-vous, professeur Foucault?,' in *DE1*, 629–648.
SP	'Structuralism and Post-Structuralism,' in *AME*, 433–458.
SSS	'Sade, sergent du sexe,' in *DE1*, 1686–1690.
ST	(Sans titre), in *DE1*, 321–353.
TNP	*This is Not a Pipe* (1968), trans. James Harkness (Berkeley: University of California Press, 1983).
TP	'Theatrum Philosophicum,' in *LCMP*, 165–196.
UP	*The Use of Pleasure: Volume 2 of The History of Sexuality* (1984), trans. Robert Hurley (New York: Vintage Books, 1990).
WE	'What is Enlightenment?,' in *EST*, 303–319.

ADDITIONAL REFERENCES

19CA	Robert Rosenblum and H. W. Janson, *19th-Century Art* (New York: Harry N. Abrams, Inc., 1984).
AP	Aaron Scharf, *Art and Photography* (London: Allen Lane, The Penguin Press, 1968).
ARI	John T. Paoletti and Gary M. Radke, *Art in Renaissance Italy* (New York: Harry N. Abrams, Inc., Publishers, 1997).

AV	Gary Shapiro, *Archaeologies of Vision: Foucault and Nietzsche on Seeing and Saying* (Chicago: The University of Chicago Press, 2003).
DR	Gilles Deleuze, *Difference and Repetition*, trans. Paul Patton (New York: Columbia University Press, 1994).
HMA	H. H. Arnason, *History of Modern Art*, 3rd edn. Revised and updated by Daniel Wheeler (New York: Harry N. Abrams, Inc., Publishers, 1986).
LM	Ana Martín Moreno, *Las Meninas*, trans. Nigel Williams (Madrid: Aldeasa, 2003).
LMF	David Macey, *The Lives of Michel Foucault: A Biography* (New York: Pantheon Books, 1993).
MF	Didier Eribon, *Michel Foucault*, trans. Betsy Wing (Cambridge: Harvard University Press, 1991).
PMLO	Charles Baudelaire, *The Painter of Modern Life and Other Essays*, trans. Jonathan Mayne (New York: Phaidon Press Inc., 2005).
RM	Jacques Meuris, *René Magritte*, trans. Michael Scuffil (Los Angeles: Taschen, 2004).
SAP	Gilles Deleuze, 'The Simulacrum and Ancient Philosophy,' appendix to *The Logic of Sense*, trans. Mark Lester and Charles Stivale. (New York: Columbia University Press, 1990), 253–279.

INTRODUCTION

A GENEALOGY OF MODERNITY

Towards the end of his spectacular if all-too-short career, Michel Foucault made many efforts to clarify his positions and to link his intellectual preoccupations with the exigencies of the present. Reading his late interviews, occasional texts, and methodological asides, it is striking the degree to which it became increasingly urgent for him to sketch the potential import of his research, especially as he veered deeper into specialized discussions of ancient philosophy. One senses the desire on Foucault's part to be transparent about his motivations and explicit about the contemporary relevance of these investigations. One of the most forceful formulations he provided for his work was that it could be understood as the 'ontology of ourselves.' Such a pursuit, he explained, would be conducted not by reflecting upon the nature of the human being, but by reconstructing the history of the present, that is, the series of discourses, practices, events, and accidents that shape our modernity.

Constantly searching out the historical conditions for his own point of view, Foucault located it in a short text by Kant, 'What is Enlightenment?' In his 1983 lecture course, *Le gouvernement de soi et des autres*, and his essay, the title of which repeats Kant's own, Foucault offered something of a self-portrait. Kant's text offers, he tells us, a historically distinctive way of posing the question of who we are in our being, marking one of the first times philosophical thought was brought explicitly into contact with the events surrounding it. In his reading, Foucault distinguished between two philosophical currents issuing from Kant, both of them 'critical.' The first tradition analyzes the conditions according to which something can be recognized as true, performing the type of investigations common to analytic philosophy. The second, in which Foucault situates himself, provokes, diagnoses, and attempts to transfigure the present. It is a form of thought that analyzes how fields of experience are historically constituted, giving rise to certain values and possible positions within them. The essential thing about this second 'critical' tradition is that it brings philosophy to bear upon the present (*l'actualité*), and achieves this without inserting the present into a teleological framework. As Foucault explained, in the text on the *Enlightenment*, Kant was able to pose the problem of his present not, as was frequently done, by comparing it with other periods, the immortal ancients or a future on the horizon, but through a direct investigation of the present. Foucault: 'In the text on *Aufklärung*, he deals with the question of contemporary reality alone.'[1]

Modernity was the guise under which this new mode of philosophizing was instantiated, one that made it possible for philosophy to problematize the world in which it found itself. 'Philosophy as the surface of emergence of an actuality (*une actualité*), philosophy as the interrogation of the philosophical sense (*le sens philosophique*) of the present to which it belongs, . . . it is that . . . which characterizes philosophy as a discourse of modernity, as a discourse on modernity' (*GSA1*, 14). For this reason, Foucault conceives of modernity less as a period and more as an *ethos* or attitude: it is a relationship with one's present that allows for that present to be punctured, rendered alien, and subjected to philosophical analysis. It is also for this reason that Foucault points to the notion of modernity as essential for understanding the forms of analysis that he attempted. Attaching himself to the second critical tradition, Foucault explains: 'It is not a question of an analytic of the truth, but . . . a question of what one could call an ontology of the present, an ontology of actuality, an ontology of modernity, and an ontology of ourselves' (*GSA1*, 22). In his response to the question, What is Enlightenment?, Foucault proposed transforming this Kantian question into a genealogical endeavor, one that would not simply recount the story of who we are, but intervene at strategic points to facilitate the elaboration of new configurations. 'The point, in brief, is to transform the critique conducted in the form of necessary limitation into a practical critique that takes the form of a possible crossing-over [*franchissement*]' (*WE*, 315). This history, Foucault explained, would be truly 'critical,' both an analysis of the historical limitations that have formed us *and* the experimentation necessary to surpass them.

It is noteworthy that in seeking to go beyond Kant, Foucault invoked the work of Charles Baudelaire (1821–1867), specifically his laudatory essay on Constantin Guys (1802–1892), the 'painter of modern life.' In discussing Baudelaire's text, Foucault astutely notes the role the notion of modernity plays in advancing the analysis. This 'ironic heroization' of the present is first and foremost the attempt to transfigure it. For Baudelaire, 'modernity' functions, as it did for Kant, as the device by means of which one can take leave of oneself in order to initiate the process of reconfiguration. Foucault here deploys a distinction, so integral to his late investigations, between the hermeneutics of desire and the creation of the self as a work of art:

> Modern man, for Baudelaire, is not the man who goes off to discover himself, his secrets and his hidden truth; he is the man who tries to invent himself. This modernity does not 'liberate man in his own being'; it compels him to face the task of producing himself. (*WE*, 312)

For Baudelaire, this dynamic modernity is created not within the realm of politics but the sphere of art. In his elegy, Baudelaire praises Guys' engagement with his moment in history, ridiculing artists who continue to shroud their subjects in mytho-historical garb. Guys' genius, according to Baudelaire, is to have abstracted pure visual poetry from the fluctuations of modern life. In his vignettes, Guys refuses the false promises of academic form and the pompousness of Salon painting, favoring careful observation of the place and time in which he finds himself. As Baudelaire explains, Guys has 'sought after the fugitive, fleeting beauty of present-day life, the distinguishing character . . . we have called "modernity."'[2] The portrait of Guys is itself an exhortation for others to break with the artistic conventions of the past. 'It is . . . excellent . . . to study the old masters in order to learn how to paint; but it can be no more than a waste of labour if your aim is to understand the special nature of present-day beauty' (*PMLO*, 13). Baudelaire encourages artists to attend to their surroundings, sharpen their powers of observation, and to find beauty in the ephemeral. Baudelaire's essay can be read as a break with the rule-governed system of beaux-arts classicism in favor of a Romantic aesthetics predicated upon the reconciliation of the eternal and the transitory.[3] But it is also, as Foucault explains, a reminder that the transfiguration of self and society integral to the notion of modernity 'can only be produced in another, a different place, which Baudelaire calls art' (*WE*, 312).

While Foucault no doubt rejects the exclusive priority Baudelaire granted to art in changing the world, its use here is indicative of the place that art would have occupied within a more complete historical-ontology of ourselves. It is striking that in a brief, methodological sketch of genealogical critique Foucault devotes so many lines to what has been called 'aesthetic experience.' It is the realization—and Foucault is by no means the first to have had it—that art is an essential component in understanding who we are, what constitutes our present, and how both might be transformed. These reflections on Baudelaire, however, also tell us much about Foucault's overall approach to art. Foucault understood art, modern art in particular, as an anticultural force, one that harbored the capacity to oppose unwarranted consensus, question our habits, and posit new values. For Foucault, art is just as inseparable from the ethical-political actuality in which it finds itself, as is the modern form of philosophizing he isolates in Kant. As I argue throughout this work, Foucault's thinking on the subject, as it can be gleaned from those occasional essays that are at last coming to scholarly attention, attempts to analyze the modern image from such a genealogical perspective. This means that it is the attempt to think and analyze art in terms of its historical uniqueness, to point to the moments of rupture within the history of art that gave shape to an assemblage of art that came to be known as modern.

This study follows Foucault's thought as it engages with the work of visual artists from the seventeenth century through to the contemporary period in order to reconstitute something of a lost genealogy, or more precisely, another strand in the historical ontology of ourselves. It reads Foucault's discussions of Diego Velázquez's (1599–1660) *Las Meninas* and René Magritte's (1898–1967) *The Treason of Images* (*Ceci n'est pas une pipe*), from the standpoint of his final lecture courses. This perspective, the concern with the emergence of the being of modernity, allows us to open up a systematic perspective on Foucault's writings on art, by highlighting their genealogical character. It also introduces Anglophone readers to some unknown recesses of the Foucaultian corpus, for example, his recently published lecture on Édouard Manet (1832–1883) and his remarks on modern art in his final course, *Le gouvernement de soi et des autres: le courage de la vérité*. Throughout, I do not attempt to defend Foucault's taste in culture. As is often the case, many of these opportunities came to him by chance, and in some instances conflict with his preferences. Instead, I argue that when viewed together, we can see in these essays the emergence of a form of thinking that can serve as a necessary corrective to the ahistorical tendencies of philosophical aesthetics.

This genealogical project attempts to explain how modern vision, primarily in the sphere of 'fine art,' has been formed by means of an exchange with the cultural products of the past few centuries. It is my hope that this strategy not only provides us with an understanding of one European thinker's approach to visual art, but that it enables us to discover and contest the boundaries of our own experiences. It seeks to make a contribution to that field of contemporary thought concerned with the analysis of and reflection upon visual art, through an exploration of the methods Foucault forged in his studies of madness, clinical medicine, the human sciences, the prison, and the history of sexuality. Like many, I see no repudiation of the tools Foucault formulated under the banner of archaeology, even as he began to expand his fields of analysis, complicate his sense of historical transmission, and modify his form of presentation through the invocation of genealogy. This study employs both methods in tandem, according to Foucault's recommendation that the critique of our modernity should be 'genealogical in its design and archaeological in its method' (*WE*, 315). It reads these essays and views these artists not, perhaps, as an art historian would. It is not a question here of recounting a history of forms or describing the logic of influence and stylistic development. Nor does Foucault's approach compel us to reconstruct the network of historical-social values from which these works emerged. These essays tell the story of how art sheds its traditional vocation in order to become modern. It observes individual works of art as they operate upon a received system of values, practices, and distributions in order to excavate a new form of being for themselves.

This genealogical enterprise attempts to explain not only how the modern work of art is unique in terms of its formal, ontological, ethical, and epistemological properties, but seeks to facilitate its transformation. In this sense, genealogy is opposed to both the pursuits of metaphysics, and the supposed neutrality of the historian. It is, as Foucault puts it in his essay on Nietzschean genealogy, a knowledge 'made for cutting.'[4] Genealogy breaks apart the conceptual, linguistic, and visual sedimentations that assume 'self-evident' status. It seeks to restore to thinking the field of forces, events, and contingencies from which our being has been abstracted. Genealogy's historical sense is a type of vision, or as one might say, following Foucault, the 'acuity of a look (*regard*) which distinguishes, separates, and disperses' the customary groupings of the historian and the fixed essences of the metaphysician. Genealogy is, to a large degree, a visual practice, a 'dissociating look' (*regard dissociant*) that makes surprising discoveries possible and puts them to use in the transformation of ourselves (*NGH1*, 153; *NGH2*, 1015; The translation has been modified slightly). The genealogy of art's modernity does not, therefore, confirm traditional chronologies, nor does it subscribe to teleologies of historical development. It seeks to immerse us in the field of historical contingencies that have fashioned us, to in turn make it possible to think and see otherwise.

The purpose of history, guided by genealogy, is not to discover the roots of our identity but to commit itself to its dissipation. It does not seek to define the unique threshold of where we come from, the homeland to which metaphysicians promise a return; it seeks to make visible (*faire apparaître*) all of those discontinuities that traverse us. (*NGH1*, 162; *NGH2*, 1022; The translation has been modified slightly)

The history and theory of art remains pious to the extent that its practices partake of a search for origins, treating the past as containing the meaning of future forms, styles, and configurations in a nascent state. Whereas the metaphysician and traditional historian see the origin as a single and univocal direction, later to become fully developed in the history of art, the genealogist sets sights upon the 'numberless beginnings whose faint traces and hints of color are readily seen by an historical eye' (*NGH1*, 145). In contrast to the customary strategy of recounting the facts of art in order to weave a tale of evolution and progress, genealogy sees art's history as a web of entangled events, whose chance combination has yielded a contingent configuration of production, display, reception, and discourse. In thinking its emergence, genealogy seeks to intervene in its smooth transmission, that is, it makes it possible to create, practice, and view art in a new light. As we have seen through Foucault's reflections on Kant, the genealogy of modernity is at once its critique. This means that we must not take for an endorsement Foucault's historical analysis of what art has temporarily congealed into. In Foucault's philosophy of art, the reserves of theory are directed into a diagnostic role, one that enables us to grasp how the regularities of one period are fundamentally dissimilar from those of another. This disparity strips the present of its seeming necessity. Genealogy's goal is thus the systematic elaboration of an eccentric point of view.

In creating such a dissociating view, Foucault's genealogy employs the resources of archaeology, a comparative method that places in sharp relief the heterogeneity separating two periods of discursive and/or visual practice. In Chapter 2, I argue that familiarity with this method is essential for understanding Foucault's rather idiosyncratic approach to art, and that facility can provide philosophical discussions of art with a much-needed concreteness. More specifically, the method of archaeology, in its application to visual culture, shows how certain exemplary visual products—those that generate discursive, pictorial, emotional, and economic investment—displace the conventions of those that have preceded them. It asks of works that are moments of transition, how they supply new rules for the distribution of painting's formal elements, how they maintain different relationships with truth, and how they in turn necessitate changes in the comportment of producers and viewers. Accordingly, we see throughout our discussion of Foucault's writings on art that the hermeneutic question, what does this work mean?, has been supplanted by the archaeological question: what does this work of art do? The archaeological analysis of art seeks to make explicit the ways in which a work either confirms or contests the historical conventions that precede it. As such, it attempts to make thought sensitive to how a given work actively carves out its place within a historical-visual tapestry.

Throughout this study, I refer to works of art, images, and visual arrangements as events, or extrapolating from Foucault's discussions of discursive events in the *Archaeology of Knowledge*, statements and statement-events. The event is the target of both archaeology and genealogy, whose singularity and specificity they are charged with preserving. In considering discourse as a series of events, Foucault was attempting to isolate moments of historical rupture, that is, turning points after which it became impossible to practice a knowledge in the same manner. Statements, be they discursive or visual, do not occur in a vacuum; they operate upon a field of other statements. In describing works of art as events, we are—following Foucault's usage—attempting to restore existence to these cultural products.

Rather than treating the history of art as a stagnant repository of forms, styles, practices, and theoretical codifications, the archaeological point of view attempts to reconstitute the fields upon which these works operated in order to examine the changes carried in their wake. Art works are not simply objects that have their place in museums, galleries, and private collections. They are responses to a field that conditions their appearance, and which, in some instances, they serve to transform. Treating works of art as events is the attempt to keep in mind the fact that we are dealing with something which, at the level of its existence, is unique in that it, as Foucault explains in his essay devoted to the painter Paul Rebeyrolle (1926–2005), 'causes a force to pass.'[5] This formulation is not by chance, for this is one of the very specific senses that Foucault gives to the event. The essay on genealogy explains: 'An event . . . is not a decision, a treaty, a reign, or a battle, but the reversal of a relationship of forces . . .' (*NGH1*, 154). Treating works of art as events, not as riddles to be deciphered by the philosopher, means that interpretation is subordinated to the analysis of the work's visual properties, its exchanges with the archive of Western art, and its displacement of previous arrangements. It means, above all else, that the work of art is a dynamic, active, and, in some instances, aggressive being. It is at once thoroughly conditioned by its historical place, and the means by which history is made and transformed. It is hoped that the formulation of the event allows us to see the rather specific type of causality carried by certain works, along with how modernity was constructed through their rivalry.

When we take a genealogical look at Western art, we see that modernity is fundamentally incompatible with representation, and indeed that it emerges through a displacement of its values and distributions. Our first chapter develops Foucault's discussion of *Las Meninas*, reading the canvas with Foucault's arguments in *The Order of Things* about the epistemological mutations that took place at the end of the eighteenth century, giving shape to our modernity. *Las Meninas* serves as a guiding image throughout *The Order of Things* because it enables Foucault to present in visual form the transformations taking place within Western knowledge as it approaches the threshold of modernity. Here, I read the larger work for clues about the changes carried into the field of vision by the discursive operations of the burgeoning sciences of modernity and the subsequent collapse of the representative grids of the Classical age. Taken together, both *The Order of Things* and *Las Meninas* enable us to see the emergence of some of the major themes that characterize modern art: finitude, an interest in the invisible, and the insistence upon the materiality of painting. In short, this chapter examines the epistemological and aesthetic conditions common to both science and painting in its post-representational modernity.

In order to explore how painting in particular removes itself from the dictates of representation, Chapter 2 reconstructs Foucault's abiding interest in the work of Édouard Manet. It explains how his canvases rupture centuries-old visual conventions, heralding a new ontological condition for the work of art. By reading Foucault's lecture in the light of the *Archaeology of Knowledge*, this chapter explains, develops, and defends Foucault's overall approach to art. It demonstrates how archaeology enables philosophy to become more sensitive to historical-visual experience, and points to the methodological advantages of conceptualizing works of art as events.

For Foucault, Manet fundamentally alters Western pictorial conventions by incorporating into the tableau its conditions of representation. Manet thereby calls attention to painting's construction as an object, making the painting's materiality an inescapable part of the viewing experience. This chapter provides a concrete example of how, by means of a subtle discourse upon itself, the representative element of painting is thrown off. A subtle reading of this lecture allows us to understand it not simply as a 'naïve' rediscovery of Clement Greenberg's (1909–1994) influential thesis on modern painting.[6] Foucault, although insistent upon the flatness of Manet's canvases, never attempted to transmute it into the essence of painting in the way that Greenberg did. For him, it was simply one of the means by which the representative function was bent in order to comment upon itself, thereby functioning as a moment in the movement by which representation was able to surpass itself. As we will see, there are two other major ways (lighting and the positioning of the viewer) in which Manet's canvases call attention to the representative space they are in the process of leaving behind. The notion of the 'tableau-object' is Foucault's way of indicating that modern art, at the archaeological level, is fundamentally dissimilar from what it had been throughout the Renaissance and Classical age, in that the material conditions of representation form an inescapable part of the viewing experience. From here, we follow the rupture inaugurated by Manet into the work of Paul Rebeyrolle. We examine a little-known essay in which Foucault contends that it is necessary to think post-representational art in a post-representational fashion: attuned to the passing of forces, sensitive to the function of a canvas' materiality, and aware of the energy created by changes of perspective.

Chapter 3 reads Foucault's celebrated analysis of René Magritte's *Ceci n'est pas une pipe* for what it has to tell us about the status of art within modernity. For Foucault, Magritte's work silences painting's referential function, i.e., the fact that for a large part of its history, painting, despite its separation from language, ultimately pointed to something outside of itself. We gain a further understanding of the voyage undertaken by modern painting in its critique and displacement of representation. In this sense, the essay should be viewed as complementing Foucault's discussion of Manet, despite the obvious stylistic differences between the two. Visually, it is hard to imagine two more dissimilar artists: Manet emphasizes the material properties sustaining painting's representative capacity, whereas Magritte traces exacting similitudes. When viewed from the archaeological level, however, we see that both artists created operations that altered the received principles of painting. Both create paintings designed to flout the patterns of seeing established by representation. Their canvases removed painting from the type of affirmation entailed in representation, and inaugurated two countervailing tendencies within the arts of modernity. Whereas Manet's canvases were an excavation of representation's conditions of possibility, the post-representational art issuing from the event 'Magritte' opens up a completely fictive space, one where the vision supplied by the art object can no longer be subordinated to questions about its relationship with the world. According to Foucault, Magritte achieves this by detaching resemblance from affirmation, that is, through the creation of the similitude. As Foucault understands it, the simulacral image, despite its unreality, is not without consequence, and requires a form of thought that allows its unique causality to come into view.

In order to develop the capacities for assessing this new type of art image, I place in constellation Foucault's writings on Gilles Deleuze (1925–1995), Andy Warhol (1928–1987), Gérard Fromanger (b. 1939), and Duane Michals (b. 1932). In Chapter 4, we see that Foucault provides us with a deeply ethical thinking of the simulacrum, one that is sensitive to the immaterial causality of the modern image and its ability to reconfigure our relationships with ourselves. Such an approach is predicated upon the refusal of Platonism, that 'archaic morality' which prevents us from reveling in the multiple events that burst forth from the image. In contrast to the tradition-bound discourses of aesthetics, Foucault develops a philosophy of art that celebrates the irreality of images. Such an analysis of the changing conventions of culture must also reckon with the development and diffusion of photography, so integral to the being of these images. I take Foucault's short history of the amateur practices of the image—the culture that emerged in the years 1860 to 1900 that Foucault sees as essential for understanding Fromanger's practice—as the occasion to consider the relationship between photography and painting. By means of Foucault's analysis, we are able to point to the centrality of their interaction for the emergence of pictorial modernity. Here it is asked, what are the new forms of seeing that the photographic approach to reality makes possible? And, what are its consequences for the practice of painting? We explore the ways in which their historical interactions have given us new, hybrid images that refuse stable identities. We also look to Foucault's essay on the American photographer Duane Michals to complete a discussion of his ethical assessment of the modern image's 'incorporeal materiality,' that is, its ability to form us in the wake of the 'thought-emotions' arriving from distant places.

This ethical analysis of art is deepened in Chapter 5 through a presentation of Foucault's final lecture course. These late investigations show how the notion emerges in the Western tradition that the subjectivity of the artist serves as a guarantee for the truthfulness of the work. According to Foucault, modern art is the reactivation of a classical form of truth, one that holds that the attainment of truth carries a certain price. Through a presentation of his reading of the Hellenistic Cynics, I show how the form of truth unique to modern art is the redeployment of the connection between *askēsis* and *parrhēsia* (frank speech). *Parrhēsia* is an ancient modality of speech that cements the connection between truth and belief on the basis of ethical practices, that is, through the self-transformation of the would-be speaker of truth. With Foucault, I trace this form of truth-telling from its formulations in Ancient philosophy, through to the practices of contemporary art. This allows us to understand how modern art—despite the fact that in many cases it no longer affirms anything exterior to itself—can nevertheless remain a vehicle for critique. These final reflections are important, if all too brief, in that they allow us to discern something of Foucault's overall conception of modern art. For him, the artistic products of modernity are in no way held to be self-secluding and removed from larger cultural concerns, as so many histories have convinced us that they were. What is distinctive about modern art, for Foucault, is that it is an anticultural form of truth-speaking that requires some sort of ethical labor on the part of its practitioners in order to be endowed with this capacity. Through this exercise, art gains the right to play an active role in the transformation of culture.

Across these five chapters, I argue that what we witness when we consider Foucault's writings on art together is the effort to distill some lessons about the status of art in modernity. Unlike Gary Shapiro, whose impressive study of Nietzsche and Foucault, *Archaeologies of Vision*, places some of the artists considered by Foucault within a fourth archaeological space, one called 'postmodern,' I argue that Foucault was continually advancing his analysis of these disparate manifestations under the heading of modernity. For Shapiro, the arts of similitude, those works by Magritte, Warhol, Fromanger, and Michals that, according to Foucault, derealize the image through its repetition and circulation, escape from the modern *episteme*—that of man and the analytic of finitude—described in *The Order of Things*. As Shapiro explains, ' . . . Foucault discerns on the horizon a successor epoch to this last one . . . to be replaced by the return of language and the ascendancy of the simulacrum.'[7] For Shapiro, works such as Magritte's *The Treason of Images* and Warhol's *Brillo Boxes* (1964) usher in this new era: they are 'the factors that will destabilize the reign of man and the representational image.'[8] Shapiro builds his case by observing the prophetic tone that ties together Foucault's notorious prediction of the 'death of man' at the end of *The Order of Things*, and the prophecy of an art liberated from the identity of the image at the end of *This is Not a Pipe*. He remarks the affinity between Foucault's claim that if certain events of thought *were* to occur, 'of which we can at the moment do no more than sense the possibility . . . then one can certainly wager that man would be erased, like a face drawn in the sand at the edge of the sea,'[9] and the proposition that 'A day will come when, by means of the similitude . . . the image . . . will lose its identity.'[10] Here, I suggest that we need to note Foucault's own reticence about how to gauge contemporary thought, art, and experience. As we will see in Chapters 1 and 2, one of archaeology's negative limits is its ability to analyze its own discursive formation. This means that any analysis of the present was, for Foucault, always tentative, pointing to tendencies within the present that differed from those of the past and which *might* instantiate a new configuration. Despite many of the promises that Foucault found through his analysis of literature, the torsions of the human sciences, and the uniqueness of our moment, I do not think he ever saw contemporary thought as having definitively 'advanced' beyond the modern *episteme*. To be clear, I do not think that Shapiro and I disagree about the importance of Foucault's discussions of Magritte, Warhol, Fromanger, and Michals for the philosophy of art. For my part, however, I argue that Foucault viewed these works as belonging to a space called modernity, which he was attempting to measure and critique. For him, the simulacral cultural products of Magritte, Warhol, Fromanger, and Michals were simply some of the ways in which art opened up its post-representational destiny. This means that these artists, for Foucault, would be cut of the same archaeological cloth as Manet, even if their strategies of production and outward appearances were appreciably different. They design operations that force art, painting, and/or photography to throw off the heavy burdens of representation.

I am not unaware of how unconventional this thesis sounds to those reared on the historical and theoretical accounts that posit two distinct phases within twentieth-century art.[11] Already one can hear the voices of consternation, lining up their expert opinions, chronologies, and narratives of progress. 'Warhol, a modern artist? Wouldn't we all be better off without all this *theory*?' It is precisely here that we must be most careful about smuggling in what we think we know about the notion of modernity and the art of the past two centuries, as it is precisely these assurances that Foucault was testing. If Foucault was interested in these works, it was because he saw something of ourselves, our actuality, contained within them. In a late interview, Foucault confessed (or feigned?) ignorance of the so-called postmodernism debates, uttering 'I've never clearly understood what was meant in France by the word "modernity."'[12] He described his project in many of the Kantian terms that were important for him in his 1983 lecture course:

> We must . . . have the modesty to say . . . that . . . the time we live in is very interesting; it needs to be analyzed and broken down, and that we would do well to ask ourselves, 'What is today?' I wonder if one of the great roles of philosophical thought since the Kantian '*Was ist Aufklärung?*' might not be characterized by

saying that the task of philosophy is to describe the nature of today, and of 'ourselves today.' (*SP*, 449)

Modernity, as it was for Kant and Baudelaire, was a notion supple enough to allow him to take distance from the immediate and subject it to a 'dissociating look.' In his writings on art, it enabled him to fit together different types of work, submit them to analysis, and demonstrate how they were points of historical departure. For Foucault, the historical ontology of ourselves is inseparable from its critique and, one can hope, its transformation. Continuing his train of thought in the interview quoted above, Foucault immediately added:

I would like to say something about the function of any diagnosis concerning what today is. It does not consist in a simple characterization of what we are but, instead—by following lines of fragility in the present—in managing to grasp why and how that which is might no longer be that which is. In this sense, any description must always be made in accordance with these kinds of virtual fracture which open up the space of freedom understood as a space of concrete freedom, that is, of possible transformation. (*SP*, 449–450)

Throughout, I do not attempt to defend Foucault's unconventional chronologies against the charges that he plays fast and loose with art's history, but show how these genealogical descriptions can illuminate and transform a space that is still largely our own. It is the attempt, one might say, to see to what extent the effort to think the history of art can free it from what it silently thinks and enable it to be practiced otherwise. More than marking a place of possible transition within the history and production of art, I argue that Foucault's historical methods create a point of departure for philosophical aesthetics. One should not expect to find here an account of a how a subject can experience certain pleasurable sensations before a given arrangement, how one can be justified in making certain judgments, or even a discussion of the nature of art. Foucault's contribution consists of having bequeathed to philosophy certain strategies that can aid in developing its powers of perception. As I have been arguing in this brief introduction, genealogy is a type of historical vision, one whose companion, archaeology, can make us ever more sensitive to what we find before us. I hope to have shown that Foucault's unique approach to vision will enable philosophy to see more of the world in which it finds itself.

In his essay on the unclassifiable 'Monsieur G.,' whose practice, forms of observation, and mode of life Baudelaire is at pains to capture, he laments that ultimately the label 'philosopher' is impracticable. Constantin Guys is too attached to the sensuous, Baudelaire explains, to be given that honor. 'I would bestow upon him the title of philosopher, to which he has more than one right, if his excessive love of visible, tangible things condensed to their plastic state, did not arouse in him a certain repugnance for the things that form the impalpable kingdom of the metaphysician' (*PMLO*, 9). It is debatable whether or not, upon acquaintance with contemporary thought, Baudelaire would reverse his judgment. If, however, we can be said to have turned a blind eye to the chimeras to which historically we have been beholden, credit is due to thinkers like Foucault. It is through him that we might once again learn to love the visible.

CHAPTER 1

THE STIRRINGS OF MODERNITY

INTRODUCTION

Any consideration of Foucault's philosophy of art would do well not only to begin with the dense analysis of *Las Meninas* (Figure 1), which opens *The Order of Things* (henceforth cited as *OT*), but to read the larger work for what it tells us about the particular shape of modern experience. In this chapter we mine both for insights into the nature of our visual modernity. It will be shown how these investigations mark out the contours of the area in which we see, think, and create. This approach has the methodological advantage of allowing us to isolate the properly historical dimension of Foucault's rather unique way of looking. *Las Meninas* forms the starting point of our journey, as it is situated on the near side of Foucault's genealogy. For him, the canvas announces the end of two periods preceding our modernity: the Renaissance and the Classical age. Painted during the heart of the latter, the period that begins in the middle of the seventeenth century and extends to the end of the eighteenth century, *Las Meninas* is untimely. In Foucault's analysis, it reveals the seeds of a nascent modernity, the point at which representation begins to break down. Paradoxically, it also contains some of the values associated with the Renaissance experience of the world, one that haunts the Western imagination throughout modernity. This chapter advances a reading of *Las Meninas* and *OT* whereby the canvas can be seen, alternatively, as belonging to the three historical periods under examination within the larger text. To be clear, I am not claiming *Las Meninas* is a 'modern work.' I argue that, because of its visual feints, formal complexity, and historical references, Foucault exploits it as shorthand for the transformations witnessed in the excavation of Western thought.

Figure 1 Diego Velázquez, *Las Meninas*, 1656. Museo del Prado, Madrid. Scala/Art Resource, New York.

Another word of caution is in order. Foucault's ruthless excavation of the human sciences treats three distinct historical periods: the Renaissance, the Classical age, and modernity. His genealogical account of modernity in art, however, tends to conflate the previous two periods. He understands modern art as coming into being through a displacement of a previous system of rules that he refers to, at different points, as *quattrocento* painting and Classical painting, periods that obviously cut across what *OT* defined as two distinct historical phases. It is clear that Foucault views modernity as a rupture with the conventions that structure painting from the Renaissance, roughly the middle of the fifteenth century, to approximately the end of the nineteenth. My chronological presentation of Foucault's work does not bury these differences, instead reading each work for what it contributes to an emerging picture of art within modernity. In this chapter we examine the three periods of *OT* for the different valuations they ascribe to *Las Meninas*, as well as for what they, in spite of their heterogeneity, contribute to the shape and practice of modern art. In later chapters, we follow Foucault's approach, presenting modern art as a displacement of the *quattro-cento* conventions and Classical painting.

1.1 SETTING THE STAGE AROUND THE CENTRAL ABSENCE

After some hesitation about its appropriateness, Foucault placed the memorable discussion of *Las Meninas* at the start of his book under the chapter title *Les suivantes* (Maids of Honor), the French name for the canvas.[1] The analysis is notoriously elliptical, shirking much of the information available about the painting, leaping across the canvas, to leave behind a trail of insights—but only a vague sense as to what the painting is about. Not only does Foucault's treatment avoid many traditional approaches, at one point he even insists it is necessary to feign ignorance about the historical personages represented in the canvas in order to keep the visual dance going. 'We must therefore pretend (*feindre*) not to know who is to be reflected in the depths of that mirror, and interrogate that reflection according to its own existence' (*OT*, 10; *LMC*, 25; The translation has been modified slightly). Indeed, what follows is an analysis of the space that can be created as the historical figures of King Philip IV, Queen Maria Anna, and the Infanta Margarita Teresa are forced to loosen their hold over the viewer's eye to the advantage of the philosopher's discourse.

Las Meninas serves Foucault well as a guiding image for *OT* because the painting is structured around a central absence in which he places the three opposed forms of experience unearthed in the larger work. Exterior to the canvas, right in front of the canvas, there is a blank space that quickly becomes crowded as three symbolically loaded figures jockey for position and the right to configure this work. It is that place, the place of the king, as Foucault terms it, which allows Foucault to read the tableau in such a way that the three periods covered by *OT* can simultaneously be located within. This contested position, we can say with Foucault, is sovereign and what-ever occupies it—resemblance, representation, or man—assumes the powers formerly invested in the king. Foucault:

> In the realm of anecdote, this centre is symbolically sovereign, since it is occupied by King Philip IV and his wife. But it is so

above all because of the triple function it fulfils in relation to the picture. For in it there occurs an exact superimposition of the model's gaze as it is being painted, of the spectator's as he contemplates the painting, and of the painter's as he is composing his picture. (*OT*, 14–15)

These figures—King Philip IV and Queen Maria Anna, i.e., the models, Velázquez as he paints this representation, and ourselves, the spectators as we observe it—are stand-ins for the different historical orders detailed in *OT*. Foucault instantiates strife between these three figures who, by occupying this sovereign position, would temporarily stabilize the painting's meaning. This illustrates the incompatibility of these three ways of ordering the world, as this painting takes on three very different senses depending upon who has assumed the position before it. To usurp the place of the king, as both representation and man will do throughout the course of the book, is to take over the task of fixing the mobility of the visual panoply. It is to assume the constructive role of giving beings their truth, words and things their relationship, and gazes their first principle. This is why the adjective 'sovereign' is used throughout *OT* to describe the ordering principle of a given *episteme*: resemblance throughout the Renaissance, discourse during the Classical age, and man in modernity. What we observe in *Las Meninas*, then, is what we witness when we take an archaeological look at our thought: there is a succession of three distinct ways of ordering our knowledge of the world that succeed one another in that place that is just prior to and yet constitutive of experience.

Throughout the discussion of *Las Meninas*, Foucault's own discourse moves on an ambiguous terrain, dissecting the canvas into its component parts and reassembling them before the reader/viewer's eyes. This movement exploits, as we have been describing it, the essential absence in front of the canvas, but it also depends upon a fundamental heterogeneity that characterizes the relationship between seeing and saying. As Foucault will announce at many points in his writings on art and vision, what we see never resides in what we say and *vice versa*. It is not that words fall short of their counterpart in the painted image or that sight lacks the precision of carefully chosen words. Rather, each resists our efforts to translate one into the idiom of the other, and it is only through a shuffling of the presuppositions of each that they begin to approximate one another. In the midst of the discussion of *Las Meninas*, Foucault offers this important insight into his own efforts before the canvas:

> But the relation of language to painting is an infinite relation. It is not that words are imperfect, or that, when confronted by the visible, they prove insuperably inadequate. Neither can be reduced to the other's terms: it is in vain that we say what we see; what we see never resides in what we say. And it is in vain that we attempt to show, by the use of images, metaphors, or similes, what we are saying; the space where they achieve their splendour is not deployed by our eyes but that defined by the sequential elements of syntax. (*OT*, 9)

This is one of those rare moments in which Foucault offers his readers a general insight into his understanding of the challenges entailed in writing about visual art. Words and images, for Foucault, each obey different spatial and temporal assumptions that must be analyzed. They carry different rules that make decipherability possible. It is not that language is inadequate to the image, or that the visible exceeds what can be said about it. The 'grammars' of both seeing and saying are irreducible, meeting up only after they have been fitted to each other.

The *History of Madness* sees this divergence emerging from the breakup of the medieval world's tightly knit symbolism. There was once a time, Foucault explains, when images communicated directly. They were charged with speaking unambiguously according to codes drawn up by the Church Fathers. But gradually, the image grew 'overburdened with supplementary meanings.'[2] These additional significations increased the image's complexity, and freed associations no longer directly translatable into language. This process removed the image's meaning from the realm of immediate perception. As Foucault explains, at the start of the Renaissance,

> The beautiful unity between word and image, between that which was figured in language and said by plastic means, was beginning to disappear, and they no longer shared a single, unique signification that was immediately discernable. Although it was still the case that the vocation of the Image was essentially to *say*, and its role was to transmit something that was consubstantial with language, the time had nonetheless come when it no longer said

exactly the same thing. By its own means painting was beginning the long process of experimentation that would take it ever further from language, regardless of the superficial identity of a theme.[3]

The Renaissance image thus 'underwent a fundamental change,' such that its power was 'no longer that of instruction but . . . fascination' (*HM*, 18). These images are, as Foucault indicates, still meaningful, but subject to increased complexity, one which resists the image's assimilation to discourse. As we will see in Chapter 3, modern art is the place where painting finally severs this link with meaning.

In the discussion of *Las Meninas*, Foucault's own discourse serves as a performative illustration of this gap separating seeing from saying.[4] What we see in *Las Meninas*, as we stand before it with Foucault's text, never quite materializes without being transformed. He exploits this heterogeneity, demonstrating that all assignments are temporary and likely to come undone. With this notion of an unbridgeable gap between language and vision, we arrive at the bedrock of the archaeological project. The history presented in *OT* is the story of how this gap has been temporarily closed down to constitute different forms of experience. Although these investigations carry us beyond the domain of art, the work's broader visual concerns, primarily the experience and critique of representation, introduce many of the values, themes, and practices we encounter as we sort through the fragments of modernity.

1.2 THE HISTORICALITY OF VISUAL AND PHILOSOPHICAL EXPERIENCE

The thesis of *OT* is actually quite simple: since the Renaissance, Western culture has had three fundamentally different ways of ordering its knowledge. That is, it has undergone two complete rearrangements in the way it relates what is seen to what is said. These rearrangements are so all-encompassing that it makes sense to speak of them as 'ruptures' and to describe them in their heterogeneity. The last of these events forms the threshold of modernity, the space in which we think, speak, and see today, and it is the being of this modern experience that Foucault was attempting to analyze.

Experience, Foucault tells us, is never immediately given but mediated by the 'fundamental codes of . . . culture' (*OT*, xx). These codes, which it is the job of archaeology to describe, form a 'hidden network' structuring the ways in which objects, words, concepts, practices, and perceptions can be linked within a given period. Given the trajectory we are following, we would do well to note the distinctly visual thrust of Foucault's project and his insistence that perception is never simply neutral but always already coded. Percepts, as Kant knew, are dependent upon both concepts and the schematizing operations of the imagination. Seeing is never unencumbered, but produced in tandem with operations that give structure to vision. While Foucault rejects Kant's transcendental account, looking to history rather than the properties of the subject, he is in general agreement with the guiding insight: experience as it is perceived, spoken off, practiced, and reflected upon results from perceptual, linguistic, and practical grids already laid down within culture with the status of historical *a prioris*. Foucault explains that his research is directed at 'The fundamental codes of a culture—those governing its language, its schemas of perception, its exchanges, its techniques, its values, and the hierarchy of its practices' (*OT*, xx). Experience can never be described directly, for these systems 'establish for every man . . . the empirical order with which he will be dealing and within which he will be at home' (*OT*, xx).

The notion of the 'already coded eye' (*le regard déjà codé*) was explored through Foucault's engagements with clinical medicine and *avant-garde* literature. The archaeology of the *regard médical, The Birth of the Clinic*, explored the fundamental reorganizations carried out in medical discourse as well as the general conceptions of life, death, and disease. These transformations at the beginning of the nineteenth century provided the historical preconditions for a modern medical experience, one in which perception could meet its objects in a space discursively prepared for it. The doctor's 'loquacious gaze' is not the result of an empiricism unencumbered from superstition; it is the product of 'a new alliance between words and things, enabling one *to see* and *to say*.'[5] Likewise, Foucault's literary reviews, in particular his book on Raymond Roussel, detailed the power of language to weave space, form novel relations between words and things, and to redistribute the rapport between the visible and the invisible.[6] In both cases, these investigations led Foucault to repudiate all forms of philosophical reflection that would describe visual experience directly without first examining the historical networks forming such an experience.

It is not, however, inappropriate to look to philosophical figures such as Descartes and Kant to gain insight into the status of knowledge within a given period. As Foucault explains, in addition to empirical grids, there are, within a given period, theoretical reflections that explain why these experiential codes exist. 'At the other extremity of thought, there are . . . philosophical interpretations which explain why order exists in general . . . [and] why this particular order has been established and not some other' (*OT*, xx). Philosophical discourse is revealed to have more in common with the empirical domains of life, labor, and language than is commonly supposed. What Foucault demonstrates is that philosophy is in many instances subordinate to the empirical sciences studying living beings, economic facts, and the laws of language. The point, therefore, is not that philosophical reflection is unimportant, but that we need to be humble about its supposed independence from the order of things. Theoretical reflection is not a rock that we can grab onto, but is itself swimming downstream in the *episteme*.

OT thus traces the complicated paths linking empirical experience and theoretical reflection. It exposes the naïveté of supposing the purity of either, demonstrating how a 'middle region' maintains them. This archaeological level has a number of names throughout *OT*: positive unconscious of knowledge, historical *a priori*, general space of knowledge, *episteme*, or simply order. The resources of archaeology are developed more fully in Chapter 2 through a consideration of its applicability to painting. For now, however, the archaeological level can be understood as that which is contained within culture, prior to experience, which makes it possible to join things and words together in a meaningful way (*OT*, xxi). There are three such phases of the history of order: the Renaissance, the period in Western history that spans the fifteenth to the start of the seventeenth century; the Classical age, the seventeenth century through the end of the eighteenth; and the modern age, which, for Foucault, begins at the end of the eighteenth century and continues to our own day. Each age assigns to thought a particular direction that it must follow. Foucault attempts to summarize each organizing principle, assigning a synonymous designation indicative of the way in which the era orders its knowledge. The Renaissance is the age of resemblance, the Classical age that of representation, and modernity the age of man. In each case, this means that, respectively, similitude, discourse, and the finitude of man—understood in a technical sense that is explained in what follows—play a 'constructive role' in the ordering of thought (*OT*, 17). It is important to understand these three periods in their specificity, for they contribute to the distinctive character of our modernity. As we examine each, we will be looking to *Las Meninas* to see how Foucault locates it within the visual dance before the canvas.

1.3 THE EXPERIENCE OF RESEMBLANCE

Throughout the Renaissance, knowledge consisted of linking things to one another by relations of *resemblance*. Resemblance is primarily a visual category, thought to form the hinge between different types of beings. According to the Renaissance cosmology, entities in the universe echo one another ontologically. Foucault explains of this configuration: 'In the vast syntax of the world, the different beings adjust themselves to one another; the plant communicates with the animal, the earth with the sea, man with everything around him' (*OT*, 18). It is therefore knowledge's task to discover and make explicit these *similitudes*.[7] Knowledge thus consists of uncovering likenesses among things and making their connections apparent. Relationships of similitude, for example, enable us to speak of the human torso as a 'stump,' a 'head' of lettuce or a tree's 'limbs.' For the Renaissance mind, these examples are more than turns of phrase, but indicative of the play of resemblances animating the universe. For the Renaissance, things are what they are because of the way in which they are like other things.

Resemblance manifests itself in four ways. It is first located among spatially *convenient* (*convenientia*) things. The entities of world, it is thought, form a chain in which points of contact are instantiated on the basis of similitude. Like things have spatial proximity, for resemblance imposes upon things adjacencies at the same time as adjacency guarantees resemblance. Things can nevertheless be said to resemble one another, even when they are not proximately joined (*OT*, 18–19). *Emulation* (*aemulatio*) is the second form of resemblance, and enables it to overcome its first law of place. It abolishes distance, allowing one to discover things imitating one another from one end of the universe to the other (*OT*, 19). We operate, for example, on the basis of resemblance when we speak of human eyes as stars, for both entities bring light to what would otherwise be dark (*OT*, 28). Thirdly, Renaissance knowledge is *analogical*, meaning that relations of analogy allow knowledge to move from entity to entity in spite of obvious differences. The power of analogy is immense and its field of application is universal. 'Through it, all the figures in the whole universe can be drawn together' (*OT*, 22). The human being occupies a privileged position in the Renaissance world, charged with discovering these analogies and knitting them together into a meaningful whole. This personage is not the same as modern man, whose finitude will be investigated ceaselessly. Our Renaissance man is the 'privileged point' within a 'space of radiation' (*rayonnnement*) where analogies are discovered and transmitted (*OT*, 23). Finally, resemblance is founded upon the *sympathies* at play in the depths of the universe. Sympathy refers to a power of assimilation inherent within things. 'Sympathy is an instance of the *Same* so strong . . . that it will not rest content to be merely one of the forms of likeness; it has the dangerous power of . . . rendering things identical to one another (*OT*, 23; The italics reflect those in the original French text). The world would indeed be quickly reduced to a homogenous mass were sympathies not counterbalanced by *antipathies*, which enable things to maintain their identities. The Renaissance world is thus construed as a competition between forces of sympathy and antipathy, and this final form of resemblance is what, ontologically speaking, grounds the other three (*OT*, 23–25).

Despite all this overlapping, the Renaissance world is not completely closed in upon itself. Knowledge is able to discover similitudes because entities are accompanied by a system of signatures. These signatures render resemblance visible and endow it with the power of speech. How else would knowledge find its way into the resemblances that compose the universe were it not for a secondary system that brings them to attention? 'These buried similitudes must be indicated on the surface of things; there must be visible marks for the invisible analogies' (*OT*, 26). It is, for example, the visual resemblance of the walnut to the brain that tells us that when crushed and mixed with spirits it will remedy a headache (*OT*, 26). Signatures are thus signs that indicate to knowledge the presence of a resemblance. But signatures are themselves resemblances, i.e., relations of convenience, emulation, analogy and sympathy. 'The signature and what it denotes are of exactly the same nature [i.e., resemblance]; it is merely that they obey a different law of distribution; the pattern from which they are cut is the same' (*OT*, 29). This means that the Renaissance system of signatures that renders nature knowable is itself a system of resemblances, but one that operates on a different level. This is significant because, as Foucault explains, for the Renaissance, language has real being, a 'raw, historical sixteenth-century being,' that sharply distinguishes it from the Classical age's discourse (*OT*, 35). According to the position assigned to it by the Renaissance, language is substantial, not yet having retreated to that arbitrary and neutral place of signification it will occupy during the Classical age. Renaissance language 'partakes in the world-wide dissemination of similitudes and signatures. It must, therefore, be studied itself as a thing in nature' (*OT*, 35). Signatures perform something like the functions of signification to the extent that they resemble or, in one of Foucault's formulations, *mirror* that which they indicate.

> The great untroubled mirror in whose depths things gazed at themselves and reflected their own images back to one another is, in reality, filled with the murmur of words . . . . And by the grace of one final form of resemblance, which envelops all the others and encloses them within a single circle, the world may be compared to a man with the power of speech. (*OT*, 27)

Thus, by means of signatures, Renaissance knowledge is endowed with an order of resemblances that mirrors the primary resemblances found among things. Understanding the mirroring function of signatures throughout the Renaissance is important in that it helps to make sense of some of Foucault's cryptic comments about the place of the mirror in his discussion of *Las Meninas*. More precisely, it links King Philip IV, the 'man of resemblance,' and his wife Maria Anna, reflected in the mirror at the back of the room, with the age of resemblance. It is their presence in the mirror that turns them, in the space of Foucault's discourse, into stand-ins for the Renaissance age. As Foucault asks in another context, 'Is it not the role of resemblance to be the sovereign that makes things appear?' (*TNP*, 46).

1.4 THE MAN OF RESEMBLANCE IN THE PLACE OF THE KING

This mirror does not obey the laws of perspective. It bypasses what is in the room—the painter, his studio, the giant canvas, the Infanta and her attendants—providing a look at a space incompatible with representation. The presence of Philip and Maria Anna in the room at the Alcázar Palace is implied by every aspect of this representation—the attention of all the personages in the room focuses upon them—yet their hold over the scene is tenuous. Foucault explains of their shadowy presence: 'In the midst of all those attentive faces, all those richly dressed bodies, they are the palest, the most unreal, the most compromised of all the painting's images: a movement, a little light, would be sufficient to eclipse them' (*OT*, 14). They are present in the representation only by virtue of the mirror, a mirror that could very well be the site of a perfect duplication, were that its purpose. The mirror, however, is not a space of representation. It was insinuated into the representation to hold what cannot belong to representation.

Instead of surrounding visible objects, this mirror cuts straight through the whole field of the representation, ignoring all it might apprehend within that field, and restores visibility to that which resides outside of all view. But the invisibility that it overcomes in this way is not the invisibility of what is hidden: it does not make its way around any obstacle, it is not distorting any perspective, it is addressing itself to what is invisible both because of the picture's structure and because of its existence as painting. (*OT*, 8)

Velázquez's mirror contains what is structurally absent from this canvas and archaeologically incompatible with the painting's existence as representation. In the section 'The Place of the King,' Foucault describes the mirror as 'showing us what is represented, but as a reflection so distant, so deeply buried in an unreal space . . . that it is no more than the frailest duplication of representation' (*OT*, 308; *LMC*, 318–319). The mirror in fact contains those figures represented by the fictional painter interior to *Las Meninas* itself. It is significant, as Foucault's words indicate, that the mirror 'shows' (*montre*) what is represented, without representing it. According to the dictates of Renaissance thought, it mirrors, that is, it resembles what has been represented on the canvas. Thanks to its addition, we gain a glimpse of what is fundamentally at odds with representation, in archaeological terms, in the same way that it is impossible for both King Philip IV and Velázquez to occupy the same position before the canvas.

This deflection is necessary because the royalty are incompatible with the age of representation to which this painting belongs. Foucault explains, 'the king appears in the depths of the looking-glass to the extent that he does not belong in the tableau' (*OT*, 15; *LMC*, 30; The translation has been modified). In a tableau in which 'representation is represented at every point,' the man of resemblance has no place (*OT*, 307). The representative capacity of *Las Meninas* is predicated upon the displacement of the royal order as the actual painter Velázquez, the physical embodiment of representation, steps to the canvas. The mirror thus contains what is excluded from the representation by dint of the new configuration shaped by the painter's move into the sovereign position. What we are witnessing in this representation is, as Foucault describes it, the 'necessary disappearance of that which is its foundation—of the person it resembles and the person in whose eyes it is only a resemblance' (*OT*, 16). As Velázquez places brush to canvas to represent Philip and Maria Anna, for whom the world is only resemblance, he steps on their toes and ushers them aside. In doing so, he usurps the power previously vested in resemblance, just as representation brings to a close the reign of resemblance within Western knowledge. This elision of the king by the painter means that 'representation, freed finally from the relation that was impeding it, can offer itself as representation in its pure form' (*OT*, 16).

This is more than just an epistemological mutation that brings an older ordering of the world to a close. It is an event that has repercussions for our artistic modernity. In this displacement of the royal order, we have the beginnings of a mode of being that will characterize the modern artist. It is of no little significance to us that the artist steps into the place occupied by the king and queen. Fundamentally, this means that the majesty once accorded to resemblance will be invested in the capacity for representation. As we will see, both here and in Chapter 5, what Foucault calls the 'artistic life,' the heroic estimation of the artist that continues into our own day, has roots in this breakup of the Renaissance *episteme*. To understand this point, however, we need to look more closely at this transference of sovereignty from resemblance to representation.

1.5 THE EXPERIENCE OF REPRESENTATION

The Classical age is born when the painter assumes the position of the king and representation the role of sovereign. At the archaeological level, representation can be understood as the introduction of a system of signs—be they linguistic or visual—that allow for the analysis and ordering of knowledge. For the Classical age, the sign no longer resides in the world as a signature stamped upon things.

Signs are arbitrarily established tools that facilitate measurement, classification, and order. Arising on the ruins of the world of resemblance, the project of Classical thought is to translate the contents of knowledge into a neutral language stripped of its intrinsic affinity with the things of the world. Whereas Renaissance knowledge arranged things on the basis of hidden similarities, the Classical sign separates entities according to differences (*OT*, 50). Representation can be thought of as a grid placed over the Renaissance experience of the same, a taxonomic network dictating a new direction for the mind. No longer is it the job of knowledge to discover hidden similitudes animating the universe; the task is to classify beings in their differences (*OT*, 53–55).

This rupture is not simply a change of worldviews, the improvement of observational methods, or the progressive liberation of reason from superstition. It is a wholesale cultural transformation carried out at the level of the *sign*, one with far-reaching consequences for Classical knowledge and, as will be explained, the creative enterprises of modernity. Negatively, the sign is no longer, as the signature once was, something substantive. 'Language has withdrawn from the midst of beings themselves and has entered a period of transparency and neutrality' (*OT*, 56). As tools of *analysis*, signs are arbitrary, founded not upon any internal relationship with what they designate, but designed for maximum clarity. For the Classical age signs are no longer pre-established meanings pulled from a hidden depth, but fabricated to facilitate the sorting of a visual field, and they are always judged in terms of their *function* (*OT*, 58–62). The sign's job is to *translate* what is known and allow different representations to be drawn together in an act of knowledge. Finally, representation must also be represented within the sign. *Reduplication* is thus the 'indispensable condition' by which a sign can be taken as a sign (*OT*, 64; *LMC*, 78; The translation has been modified slightly). Simply put: it is necessary that we know we are dealing with a sign, and the sign must, therefore, mark within itself its signifying function. Within the binary system of Classical signs, the signifier must be easily recognized if it is to represent the signified.

This conception of the sign as redoubled, functional, and arbitrarily established gives Classical knowledge its unique configuration. As Foucault makes clear, we are dealing with an entirely new direction for thought.

It is no longer the task of knowledge to dig out the ancient Word from the unknown places where it may be hidden; its job now is to fabricate a language, and to fabricate it well—so that, as an instrument of analysis and combination, it will really be the language of calculation. (*OT*, 62–63)

Whereas in the Renaissance it was necessary to collect every fathomable resemblance before attaining complete knowledge of an entity, the Classical sciences of order allow for a being's identity to be defined with recourse to a few simple properties. What differentiates general grammar, natural history, and the analysis of wealth from anything that existed during the Renaissance is that they identify a thing by highlighting its differences from other proximate objects.[8] The study of language in general grammar, the classification of plants and animals in natural history, and the examination of needs in the analysis of wealth construct systems of representations that bring clarity and distinctness to the natural disorder of things. Knowledge is thus the attempt to compose a discourse, a *taxonomic* system of names, which allocates representations in an orderly fashion. It is no longer necessary—as it was for the Renaissance—to collect everything said about a thing in order to know it. It suffices to analyze it carefully, define its *differences*, establish its *identity*, and locate it within a *table* of representations. 'The essential problem of Classical thought lay in the relations between *name* and *order*: how to discover a *nomenclature* that would be a *taxonomy*' (*OT*, 208; The italics reflect those in the original French text). Language, no longer that ambiguous being it was throughout the Renaissance, is structured by the task of representing what is known. The Classical age substitutes *discourse* for the sixteenth-century experience of language's density. Discourse's essential function is, at once, to name beings and to enter into a relationship with itself, permitting continual refinement and clarification.

Such a conception of language, and the analytical task it imposes upon thought, have tremendous consequences for the distribution of the visible and invisible in the Classical age. We would do well to take note of these changes, as it is this experience of representation that was repudiated so dramatically by modernity, particularly in the domain of art. Our discussion of natural history below serves as a contrast with the new relations between the visible and the invisible woven by the modern science of biology (Section 1.11), and enables us to understand the visual implications of representation.

1.6 THE VISUALITY OF REPRESENTATION

For natural history, Foucault demonstrates how the perceptions of plants and animals are carefully filtered so the visible fits into the project of order. Far from being a simple form of observation, natural history is a 'new field of visibility . . . constituted in all its density' (*OT*, 132). Its gaze results from a series of operations ensuring that what is seen can be represented in an easily recognizable description. It is no longer necessary to collect all traces of animals and plants left in languages and legends, as it was for the Renaissance historian Ulisse Aldrovandi (1522–1605), who included an animal's various manifestations in mythology, travelers' reports, and local cuisine, alongside of his anatomical descriptions. The Renaissance understanding of signatures forced this undertaking on Aldrovandi and his students.[9] 'To know an animal or a plant . . . is to gather together the whole dense layer of signs with which it . . . may have been covered. . . . For Aldrovandi was meticulously contemplating a nature which was, from top to bottom, written' (*OT*, 40).

The Classical age creates a different rapport between words and things, allowing for a different distribution of the visual. Natural history's new observational space is predicated upon the removal of signs from the world and the introduction of the representative sign. No longer is it necessary to collect everything said about a salamander; it suffices to designate its essential properties. In this sense, Jonston's *Natural History of Quadrupeds* (1657) orders empirical observation according to a different plan. 'The essential difference lies in what is *missing* in Jonston. The whole of animal semantics has disappeared, like a dead and useless limb' (*OT*, 129). Now only observations that facilitate definition in terms of identity and difference are recorded.

Rather than view natural history as the advance of a new empiricism, Foucault explains how this science's form of observations was constituted by a series of discursive operations. Representation's taxonomic project forces natural history to institute a number of systematic exclusions, thus limiting what becomes visible. Others' observations are, of course, excluded at the level of the sign, but so too are the experiences of taste and smell (*OT*, 132). Touch is given sovereignty over a simple distinction—texture—verifiable in visual analysis (*OT*, 132–133). Sight is therefore the privileged form of experience, but it is a very specialized type of seeing that we are dealing with by the time that we have passed through these exclusions. 'The area of visibility in which observation is able to assume its powers is thus only what is left after these exclusions: as visibility freed from all other sensory burdens and restricted, moreover, to black and white' (*OT*, 133). The observations that pass through the sieve form the guiding concepts of natural history: structure and character. These are the properties of an organic entity that, when defined in their differences, allow us to assign a name to a plant or animal. Structure performs a pre-linguistic sorting of the visible, such that what becomes observable can be translated into a discursive representation. Character is a secondary sorting that allows for these descriptions to be constituted as a language that defines differences, placing entities within a taxonomic network. Visual experience, as defined by these grids, is highly regimented. 'To observe . . . is to be content with seeing—with seeing a few things systematically' (*OT*, 133). The look is no doubt limited, but in a way that permits the natural historian to traverse the gap between what is seen and said. Natural history is a visibility thoroughly prepared by the archaeological space of representation. Visual representations are experiences that have been worked over so that they can be easily translated directly into linguistic representations.

This, in outline form, is the *episteme* of the Classical age. Its fundamental experience is Order, a direction that shapes the visible. To see according to representation is to see the world through a network of identities and differences, which intensify certain facets of experience by excluding others. It is to see only a few things, but to see them very well and to speak with confidence about what one sees. At the archaeological level, this results from a new regime of signs. Language, understood as representation (i.e., discourse), has assumed the place of the king. It is the sovereign, which from the middle of the sixteenth century until the start of the nineteenth, assigns entities their place and momentarily stabilizes the flux of visual experience.

> [I]n the Classical age, discourse is that translucent necessity through which representation and beings must pass—as beings are represented to the mind's eye, and as representation renders beings visible in their truth. The possibility of knowing things and their order passes . . . through the *sovereignty* of words. (*OT*, 311; *LMC*, 322; The translation has been modified slightly. The italics are my own)

Within the Classical age, language, more precisely, language practiced as representation, is sovereign. Classical visual experience too is defined by this omnipresence of representation, and the exclusions and intensifications it entails. With this archaeological rupture, resemblances, once the focus of Renaissance science, are banished from the kingdom of knowledge, just as that impertinent painter forces the king and queen from the space before the canvas.

1.7 REPRESENTATION ASSUMES THE PLACE OF THE KING

In that space before *Las Meninas*, that place where 'the painter and the sovereign alternate, in a never-ending flicker,' representation now wears the crown (*OT*, 308). The archaeological upheaval is embodied in Velázquez, the actual painter, who displaces his models, ambiguously present in the mirror, as he puts brush to canvas.

> In the depth that traverses the picture, hollowing it into a fictitious recess and projecting it forward in front of itself, it is not possible for the pure felicity of the image ever to present in a full light both the master who is representing and the sovereign who is being represented. (*OT*, 16)

Quite simply: it is physically impossible for both the models implied by the painting and Velázquez himself to occupy the same position before the canvas. Foucault exploits this formal device, calling attention to the heterogeneity between two ways of observing the world, that of resemblance and representation. It allows us to read *Las Meninas* as a reflection upon the relationship between painting (representation) and the aristocratic political order (resemblance). Art historians interested in the social history surrounding this work view it as an 'astute attempt on Velázquez's part to bring respectability to the painter's trade.'[10] They point to the status accorded to the profession within Spain, which, despite Philip IV's patronage, lagged behind the rest of Europe. Anecdotes about Velázquez's own struggle to improve his social position suggest the pairing of representation and nobility is more than a visual ploy. It is unusual for a tableau of this period to feature someone, in essence a craftsperson, albeit one held in high regard by Philip, on par with members of the royal family. With help from Philip, Velázquez was eventually made a member of the aristocracy shortly before his death. His chest here proudly bears the insignia of the Knights of Santiago, a detail added at least two years after the painting's completion (*LM*, 20–22). There is thus a well-worn line of interpretation, starting with court painter Luca Giordano's judgment that *Las Meninas* is 'the theology of painting,' which views this scene as an argument for the advancement of the painter's craft.[11] In more formal terms, however, what we witness is the moment at which the order of representation triumphs over resemblance, assuming the sovereign right to assign meaning to this scene. To represent representation, as Velázquez does here, is to call attention to the necessary conflict between these two ways of ordering the world. Resemblance is incompatible with the new values of representation, and thus consigned to the shadows.

1.8 THE PERSISTENCE OF RESEMBLANCE AND THE DEIFICATION OF THE ARTIST

The displacement of resemblance by representation has two major consequences for the art of the period. The first pertains to what we can call the 'persistence of resemblance,' and the second, the 'deification of the artist.' It is not frequently noted that despite the fundamental heterogeneity between the Classical age and the Renaissance, a continuous 'murmur' of resemblance haunts both *OT* and Western consciousness: the king does, after all, remain in the picture. This murmur is essential for understanding certain key points within *OT*. For example, what might be called 'creativity' is established in the space of resemblance once knowledge resides exclusively in representations. When language becomes ordered by differences, the poet and painter are the untimely ones who continue to view the world with the eyes of resemblance. To see and speak according to the bygone era of similitude is to inhabit a shadowy realm at the borders of knowledge. It is to work against the fundamental cultural codes of an era, discovering instances of the same against the grid of differences. It is also, as Foucault points out, to confront the affinity between creativity and madness.

> Once similitude and signs are sundered from each other, two experiences can be established and two characters appear face to face. The madman, understood not as one who is sick but as an established and maintained deviant, as an indispensable cultural function, has become, in Western experience, the man of primitive

resemblances. . . . He inverts all values and all proportions, because he is constantly under the impression that he is deciphering signs: for him, the crown makes the king. (*OT*, 49).

Poiēsis, too, from the start of the Classical age, joins things on the basis of similitudes, against the grain of representation.

> At the other end of the cultural area . . . the poet is he who, beneath the named, constantly expected differences, rediscovers the buried kinships between things, their scattered resemblances. Beneath the established signs . . . he hears another, deeper, discourse, which recalls the time when words sparkled in the universal resemblance of things: the Sovereignty of the Same, so difficult to express, effaces in its language the distinction between signs. (*OT*, 49; *LMC*, 63; The translation has been modified)

It is clear from this archaeology that madness is not a route to creativity. The poet passes through representation, bringing relations of similitude to bear upon the grid of established knowledges. Madness, on the other hand, remains deaf to representation, trapped within resemblances. 'The poet brings similitude to the signs that speak it, whereas the madman loads all signs with a resemblance that ultimately erases them' (*OT*, 50). Thus, even though madness and poetry presuppose the same rupture in Western experience, the former does not weave similitude into representation the way the latter does. Madness remains trapped in the figure of the Same, whereas poetry exploits it, cutting across fields of knowledge. *La folie, l'absence d'oeuvre.*

Creative production—this theme returns throughout our study— consists of a movement of destructuring, one that passes by way of representation. For Foucault, *poiēsis*, generally speaking, is the introduction of a foreign element into a new domain. It is a type of crossing of registers whereby something—an idea, an image, a practice, a word—is introduced into a different field, destabilizing the new field and the element itself. This usually takes place by historical admixture. Writing of his friend the composer/conductor Pierre Boulez (b. 1925), Foucault presents creative practice as a 'combative' relationship with history, where history is the history of one's own medium or discipline. 'I think his object, in this attention to history, was to make it so that nothing remains fixed, neither the present nor the past. He wanted them both to be in perpetual motion relative to each other.'[12] Boulez forges a volatile relationship between the present and the past, not to destroy our understanding of either of them but to encourage new possibilities to spring forth in a 'new free space' (*PB*, 244; Translation modified). Within the Classical age, something similar occurs when the persistent forms of resemblance, those located within Western consciousness but beneath the established order of knowledge, are introduced into grids of representation. These similitudes undermine the established orders, opening up new trajectories for thought. It is no accident that in the Preface to *OT*, Foucault cites a poetic image from Lautréamont so dear to the Surrealists: the chance encounter between a sewing-machine and an umbrella on an operating table.[13] Underscoring the historical-epistemological significance of this image, that is, the way in which Lautréamont cuts across language's representative capacity with the analogical groupings of resemblance, Foucault takes delight in playing on two senses of the word 'table': the one, the medical object where the encounter takes place, and the other, the *tabula*, which 'permits thought to operate upon beings, put them in order, divide them into classes, group them by names designating their similarities and their differences' (*OT*, xvii. *LMC*, 9; Translation modified). At the archaeological level, Surrealism becomes possible at the moment when analogical pairings are excluded from the domain of knowledge.

This interplay of resemblance and representation, in Foucault's mind, accounts for the distinctive features of Baroque painting. If historians distinguish it from Renaissance and Mannerist styliza-tions on the basis of verisimilitude, this is because representation has fully flowered. In the canvases termed 'baroque,' the presentation of man and nature is marked by a naturalism bordering on the scientific.[14] Even religious figures are humanized, with their flesh, blood, perspiration, and tears rendered in exacting detail. These images are, however, art and not representations of knowledge. This is because, as Foucault points out, resemblance insinuates itself into these representations through illusion, analogy, and visual traps. Primarily, this happens at the level of space and lighting. Baroque images, such as *Las Meninas,* surpass the Renaissance's system of perspective, attempting to erase the separation of viewer from scene. In Velázquez's composition, light masks the tableau's surface, creat-ing the illusion that we occupy the space of the painter, Infanta

Margarita, and the court attendants. The illusion is the visual experience of resemblance finding its way into representation.

The age of resemblance is drawing to a close. It is leaving nothing behind it but games. Games whose powers of enchantment grow out of the new kinship between resemblance and illusion: the chimeras of similitude loom up on all sides, but they are recognized as chimeras; it is the privileged age of *trompe-l'oeil* painting. (*OT*, 51)

Resemblance now resides on the side of creativity, and this accounts for the two poles around which Baroque painting revolves: the heightened exactness of representation and the illusionistic artifices of similitude. The painter moves through the grid of seeing established by the order of the Classical age, in order to uncover the visions that reside below it.

The second major artistic consequence of this epistemic shift is that it bestows upon the artist a heroic status. This notion of the 'artist's life'—familiar to us in modernity as the idea that the life of the artist must somehow be different and that this subjectivity should serve as a guarantee for art's truth—will be considered in Chapter 5. While we are accustomed to the myths of artistic genius, Foucault shows that this notion has its condition of possibility in the rupture that brings the Classical age into being. This ability to isolate resemblances beneath the grid of representations transfers powers previously vested in resemblance to the one still capable of speaking its language. In a substantial review of Jean Laplanche's *Hölderlin et la question du père* (1961), Foucault details the historical appearance of this life, demonstrating how it took root when Western knowledge ceased to occupy itself with resemblance. He traces the history by which the heroic quality, once reserved for the epic's characters, was transferred to the artist. 'The heroic dimension passed from the hero to the one whose task it had been to represent him at a time when Western culture itself became a world of representations.'[15] This transformation has consequences not only for the subjectivity of the artist but also for the being of the work.

A work no longer achieved its sole meaning as a monument, a memory engraved in stone which was capable of surviving the ravages of time; it now belonged to the legend it has once commemorated; it became itself an 'exploit' because it conferred eternal truth upon men and upon their ephemeral actions and also because it referred to the marvelous realm of the artist's life as its 'natural' birthplace. (*FN*, 73–74)

It is interesting that in an essay occupied with literary themes, Foucault recounts this history with references to painters:

The painter was the first subjective inflection of the hero. His self-portrait was no longer merely a marginal sign of the artist's furtive participation in the scene being represented, as a figure hidden at the corner of the canvas; it became, at the very center of the work, the totality of the painting where the beginning joins the ending in the absolute heroic transformation of the creator of heroes. (*FN*, 74)

This movement of the artist from the corner to the center of the canvas needs to be understood in two senses. First, from the start of Classical age until the end of the nineteenth century, we witness an increased production of self-portraits, as well as an increased privilege accorded to painters within these representations. Again, one thinks of the place reserved for Velázquez in *Las Meninas*. A comparison with the position of Jan van Eyck (1395–1441), barely visible in a mirror at the back of the *Arnolfini Wedding Portrait* (1434), a similar scene from the early Renaissance, makes the displacement explicit. More importantly for our purposes, however, the movement Foucault is discussing refers to the process by which, from the Classical age onward, the artist is linked with his or her work and forced to serve as its ground of truth. Foucault is here sifting the soil by which the life, the psychology, and the intentions of the artist form a shadow, exterior to the work itself, which must be traversed if one is to access to the work. Foucault is indeed critical of the resulting forms of biographical criticism, chiding their practitioners for a lack of historical sense: 'The psychological dimension in our culture is the negation of epic perceptions' (*FN*, 75). As we will see in Chapter 5, however, despite reservations about this pairing of life and work, he insists upon its centrality within a genealogy of modern art. Setting aside the question of whether such a paradigm provides us with a fully satisfying means of analysis, Foucault explains how this combination of art and life was introduced and maintained within Western culture by a historical category called Cynicism.

What is essential about Foucault's account of the transition from the Renaissance to the Classical age is that it provides us with an understanding of *why* this heroization of the artist takes place. Rather than viewing this exaltation of the artist as the outgrowth of Renaissance humanism, or an improvement in the profession's status, the transition should be located at the archaeological level. Given that the artist of the Classical age to some degree still inhabits the world of resemblance, properties associated with that period attach to his or her subjectivity. Specifically, it is the *magical* aspect inherent in the Renaissance way of knowing that is carried over to the one capable of discovering resemblances.

If, as Foucault explains of Renaissance knowledge, 'magic was inherent in this way of knowing,' this is not because it suffered from a lack of rigor, but because our division between divination and erudition did not yet exist (*OT*, 33). Both were accorded equal dignity by the Renaissance *episteme*, with the mind construing both nature and the written word as signs instituted by God. Foucault recounts that, 'God, in order to exercise our wisdom, merely sowed nature with forms for us to decipher (and it is in this sense that knowledge should be *divinatio*)' (*OT*, 33). In both divination and erudition, one pursues resemblances in the same way: as instances of the same to be brought from hiding and restored to speech. Both sciences maintain the same hermeneutic relationship with the world, itself an immense text to be deciphered and given voice. Knowledge in the Renaissance is essentially interpretive, but it is a hermeneutics for which every thing holds, provided one knows how to listen, the word of God.

With the dawn of the Classical age the artist is the one who establishes these relationships of similitude. When, in the seventeenth century, resemblances ceased to be the basis of knowledge, they became the occasion for art. To cut across the grid of representations is to commit an error within the order of knowledge, at the same time as it is to rediscover a more primordial voice. Despite the fact that thinking the things of this world according to the patterns of resemblance is, for the science of the Classical age, erroneous, this pattern of thought nevertheless retains its connection with the divine. In the Classical age, the artist inserts—be it in poetry or paint—resemblances into the space of representation. Similitudes banished from the realm of knowledge are rediscovered in the domain of *poiēsis*, according to a logic that defies cultural codes. The corresponding divinization of the artist, carried to new heights by modernity and the discovery of man's finitude, is predicated upon this persistence of resemblance within the Western archive. Only with this persistence can an artist like Bruce Nauman (b. 1941) proclaim, in the neon language of metaphysics and motel signs, 'The True Artist Helps the World by Revealing Mystic Truths.'[16]

1.9 THE EXPERIENCE OF MAN

The third epistemic mutation, analyzed in *OT* and encapsulated in Foucault's treatment of *Las Meninas,* is one that forms the ground from which we still see, speak, and think—that of modernity.

This event, probably because we are still caught inside it, is largely beyond our comprehension. Its scope, the depth of the strata it has affected, all the positivities it has succeeded in disintegrating and recomposing, the sovereign power that has enabled it, in only a few years, to traverse the entire space of our culture, all this could be appraised and measured only after a quasi-infinite investigation concerned with nothing more nor less than the very being of our modernity. (*OT*, 221)

Despite all that is said about Foucault's postmodernism, it is clear that in *OT,* he treats the modern *episteme* as both the target of his investigations and the occasion for his own thought. He explains of the new sciences of economics, philology, and biology, and philosophy's inheritance of the Kantian critique that 'all that still forms the immediate space of our reflection. We think in that area' (*OT*, 384). Modernity and the analysis of finitude that it proscribes is a form of thinking nearing an end, but one which nevertheless continues to be our own. As we will see in Chapter 2, there is a very precise indication that archaeology can analyze only what has been left behind. Nevertheless, I maintain Foucault viewed it as a powerful tool for the critique of the present. In an interview given shortly after the publication of *OT*, he explained: 'In trying to diagnose the present in which we live, we can isolate as already belonging to the past certain tendencies which are still considered to be contemporary.'[17] Archaeology measures the distance separating who we are in the present by comparing it with past conventions, practices, and divisions. The rich picture of artistic modernity Foucault supplied is an indication that it is late in the day for modernity, with a new space coming into view. I contend that in his writings on art, Foucault used the notion of modernity as a device for reflecting upon how works of his time departed from past visual conventions, most significantly, the space of representation.

Across Foucault's work there develops a form of questioning that continually pushes at the limits of that modernity, but one reluctant to claim for itself a new plane. It measures the distance separating our way of seeing and thinking from what has come before it, pointing to tendencies that may yield new configurations. It nevertheless remains hesitant to proscribe these as directions for thought. Throughout our study we see that Foucault's methods have enabled him to present a powerful diagnosis of our artistic modernity, one that grasps the significance of a work of art by sharply distinguishing it from what has come before. For now, however, we should watch closely as representation is beginning to crumble under the influence of forces that once again assign to words, things, and visual experience a new mode of being. The breakup of representation is the most profound and thoroughgoing reorganization that Western thought has undergone. Not only does this event supply the ground from which we think, it heralds the arrival of a new figure in *Las Meninas*.

The mode of being assigned to words and things, from the start of the nineteenth century onward, is History. Just as Order had been the site of classification throughout the Classical age, History provides modernity with the space upon which beings are thought, viewed and linked. This is not simply a narrative history, but a fundamental orientation toward things in the world. It means that beings enter the order of knowledge only on the condition that they are grasped in their temporality, presented in their relations of succession, and construed in terms of their imminent death. For modernity, History is

the fundamental mode of being of empiricities, upon the basis of which they are affirmed, posited, arranged, and distributed in the space of knowledge . . . . [I]t is equally the depths from which all beings emerge into their precarious, glittering existence. Since it is the mode of being of all that is given us in experience, History has become the unavoidable element in our thought . . . . (*OT*, 219)

This mode of historical being, by definition, exceeds the grids of representation. Concretely, the analysis of wealth is replaced by a political economy discovering the time of labor and the scarcity that renders it necessary; philology displaces general grammar by taking as its object the struggles, desires, and actions of people fossilized in words; and the taxonomies of natural history are undercut by a biology that exposes death, slowly gnawing away at living beings. Together, their appearance means that the Western mind is no longer content to order the empirical contents of knowledge into the identities and differences of representation, but unfolds as a reflection upon the forces underneath representation. The modern *episteme* is thus distinguished by the appearance of an unfamiliar being in whom it will attempt to unify these forces. That being is man.

To say, as Foucault does, that 'man is an invention of recent date' is obviously not to deny the importance of the species prior to the start of the nineteenth century. Nor is it to neglect humanistic themes or the place occupied by the *cogito* within Classical thought. What this formulation points out is that prior to the nineteenth century, there was no epistemological consciousness of man as such. Meaning, human beings were indeed recognized as occupying a significant position within the order of creation, but that they were not systematically investigated in their being. Modernity's discourse on man's finitude did not arise because the physicality of man as he lives, labors, and speaks finally imposed itself upon thought. Man was born of the forces that overwhelmed representation. Life, labor, and language thus herald the coming of man in the modern *episteme*, shaping the discourses in which he is born.

The role that man plays within modern thought is, historically speaking, unique. Man is that 'strange empirico-transcendental doublet' who, it is thought, can unify these sciences and supply their justification. In modern thought man has a dual role, alternately serving as the empirical *object* of knowledge, and the transcendental *subject* in whom its legitimating conditions can be found. The point that often gets overlooked—perhaps because it goes without saying—is that this is a bizarre project inasmuch as knowledge is something with pretensions to be more than finite, while its foundations, in this case man, are revealed by that same knowledge as finite at every step of the way. Modern thought is thus a radical departure from the Classical age, setting for itself the task of apprehending man in his being as that which both makes possible and exceeds representation. The threshold of modernity is, in philosophical terms, marked by the Kantian critique of representation. No longer does human nature permit representations to be joined easily in the neutral space of discourse, as was the case with the *cogito*. Knowledge, henceforth, entails knowledge of what makes representation possible. The Kantian investigation marks the place, within European culture, where the table of the Classical age was bypassed with knowledge forced to reside outside of representation. Thus, epistemological projects from Kant onward no longer attempt the clarification of representations; they unfold as discourses of the transcendental variety, quickly assuming an anthropologizing bent, attempting to locate the conditions for knowledge in a discourse on man himself. Modern science provides thought with a strange imperative: man, in his knowledge, must continually work backwards to that which renders knowledge possible. At bottom what he discovers will not please him. All his sciences are reminders that he is finite, for the three great transcendentals that herald his birth—life, labor, and language—also sketch his finitude. Knowledge, alas, is not to be detoured. And modern epistemology will, through an interminable back and forth, attempt to make the empirical contents of this finitude serve as its foundation.

Modern thought's analytic of finitude is of course fundamentally different from the way finitude was conceived throughout the Classical age. There, the finite was uncovered as occupying a space within the infinite, that is, by means of a comparison with its opposite. From the nineteenth century onward, however, Western thought no longer accords itself this luxury. Foucault explains, 'our culture crossed the threshold beyond which we recognize our modernity when finitude was conceived in an interminable cross-reference with itself' (*OT*, 318). Modern thought has the difficult task of thinking the finite on its own terms, and then configuring this finitude as a foundation for empirical knowledge. The infinity of the task is why Foucault refers to the analytic as 'interminable,' 'repetitive,' and 'endless.' The 'analytic of finitude' is thus the general name Foucault assigns to philosophical enterprises in which man functions as both object and subject. It characterizes those forms of philosophy that confuse the empirical with the transcendental by having, at various points, one stand for the other. The anthropological necessity of modern thought stems from this 'doubling over dogmatism,' that shuttles between two levels of thought: 'the pre-critical analysis of what man is in his essence' and the 'analytic of everything that can, in general, be presented to man's experience' (*OT*, 341). This is simply a way of saying that modern man has a dual destiny: to be the object of knowledge and the subject who knows.

1.10 THE PLACE OF MAN AND THE POSITION OF THE VIEWER

With the arrival of man, the dance in front of *Las Meninas* is halted once again. As the spectator (i.e., man) brushes aside the painter (i.e., representation), he assumes all the privileges associated with this sovereign space. Just as the painter, the actual painter Velázquez, had displaced the king and queen, man, personified by the viewer, the actual viewer standing there in the Velázquez room of the *Museo del Prado*, overcomes the age of representation. Henceforth, it will be the viewer who, in a sovereign act, fixes the relationships between the tableau's various elements. This man before the tableau, it will be difficult to force him to relinquish this position, for he is well fabricated to perform all the tasks demanded by it. In fact, we might even say, with Foucault, that the canvas has heralded his coming from the beginning. Who else besides man can play so well the role of the subject who looks and the object observed? Who but the viewer can serve as the scene's foundation, its object, as well as the subject for whom it is a representation?

The opening paragraph of the 'The Analytic of Finitude,' which is not as celebrated as the first discussion of *Las Meninas*, is essential for understanding man's arrival and the advent of the modern:

When natural history becomes biology, when the analysis of wealth becomes economics, when, above all, reflection upon language becomes philology, and Classical *discourse*, where being and representation found their common locus, fades, then, in the profound movement of such an archaeological mutation, man appears with his ambiguous position as an object for knowledge (*savoir*) and as a subject who knows (*connaît*): enslaved sovereign, observed spectator, he appears in the place of the king, which was assigned to him in advance by *Las Meninas*, but from which his real presence had been excluded for such a long time. As if, in that vacant space towards which Velázquez's whole painting was directed, but which it was nevertheless reflected only by the coincidence of the mirror and by a break-in, all the figures whose alternation, reciprocal exclusion, interweaving, and fluttering one imagined (the model, the painter, the king, the spectator) suddenly stopped their imperceptible dance, congealed into one substantial figure, and demanded that the entire space of representation finally be related to one fleshy gaze. (*OT*, 312; *LMC*, 323; The translation has been modified)

This passage succinctly encapsulates the reasons for man's privileged position—both within modern knowledge and the space before the tableau. In man there is a unity—fragile, as we have seen—of the various functions of modern knowledge. He is at once subject *and* object, at once capable of apprehending the scene before him *and* serving as its model. As we saw, modern thought's strange destiny forces man to serve as the foundation for representation through an action of doubling that transforms empirical knowledge of his finitude into its justification at the transcendental level. The viewer standing before *Las Meninas* plays the same role. He serves the represented painter, contained within the scene, as a model, i.e., as an object of representation. The viewer thereby founds the visual game that unfolds within the canvas. At the same time, however, the entire representation is for him an object of contemplation, i.e., he is the viewing subject for whom this representation exists. With the viewer serving as both model and observer, we have in *Las Meninas* the same contortions that Foucault located in modern knowledge. In the space before *Las Meninas*, the viewer transforms into a doublet. The painting is a representation for the viewer only because the viewer, placed before it, stands at its foundation. By his empirical presence as object/model before the tableau, the viewer provides the transcendental condition for the painting's meaning, of which he is nevertheless the beneficiary.

For man finally to assume this sovereign space, it is essential for two things to take place within the orders of knowledge. First, as we have seen, representation is predicated upon the effacement of the king. With Philip IV commanding the lines of sight, the picture contains a radically different meaning: it is the image of royal power, of a world in which everything accommodates itself to a sovereign before whom it is obligatory to curtsey. All present in the scene belong to an ordering of the world in which the man of resemblance assigns them their place. The viewer and the painter are incompatible with this order and have no rights within it. In the realm of historical anecdote, we know that after its completion this tableau was taken directly from Velázquez's studio and sequestered in Philip's private study. Until the time of his death, Philip was, in the estimation of one historian, 'virtually the only person allowed to gaze upon it' (*LM*, 28). Not only was the viewer temporarily deflected by the obstinate presence of the king and queen in the mirror, but for a time, by fiat. Representation was, however, already chipping away at the supposed rights of this ancient privilege. It was Velázquez who insinuated himself into the place of the king, thereby asserting the rights of representation. With the effacement of Philip and Maria Anna, Western culture ceased to be ordered by resemblance. Power was thereby transferred to the one capable of joining elements of knowledge together according to the dictates of representation. The lucidity proffered by representation is, however, a false clarity that leaves more in the dark than it illuminates. As the Western mind begins to inquire into what makes representation possible, we recognize the debut of our modernity. The second event, which thus anticipates the coming of man within the space of knowledge, is the subsequent breakdown of the Classical age's grid of visuality. It is worth developing this in more detail, as much of our modernity is composed of its falling shards.

1.11 MODERN VISUALITY AND THE BREAKDOWN OF REPRESENTATION

The modern *episteme* came into being as the grids of representation established by the Classical age began to crack up at the end of the eighteenth century. Foucault presents this event as having unfolded in two decisive stages. In both cases, across the domains of natural history, the analysis of wealth, and general grammar, thought begins to be deployed at a level that surpasses representation. Within these empirical knowledges, thought sets itself the task of describing what exceeds the table. The first assault occurs in the years of 1775–1795. Although the regularities of the Classical age are not fundamentally altered during this first phase, elements are introduced into each of the empirical domains that make it increasingly difficult for representation to function as it had since the close of the Renaissance. Taking again an example from natural history, we find that during this first phase, character remains the primary means by which living beings are classified; however, in the works of Jussieu, Lamarck, Vic d'Azyr, character ceases to be an exclusively visual category. It begins to refer instead to an invisible domain opening up beneath what is immediately observable about a plant or animal. After the introduction of the notion of *organic structure*, it is incumbent upon the natural scientist to determine how characters are related to functions within the organism, how those functions compose the organism into a hierarchy of characters, and how functions and characters are themselves supported by the broader notion of life. A deeper space presents itself to thought, with character serving as merely one sign for the processes, systems, and functions at work in the organism. Thought, within the field of natural history, has begun to overflow the table of representations, meaning that there will no longer be a direct correspondence between the visible and its name. Explaining the complications introduced, Foucault writes:

> To classify, therefore, will no longer mean to refer the visible back to itself, while allotting one of its elements the task of representing the others; it will mean, in a movement that makes analysis pivot on its axis, to relate the visible to the invisible, to its deeper cause, as it were, then to rise upwards once more from that hidden architecture towards the more obvious signs displayed on the surfaces of bodies. (*OT*, 229)

The task of assigning beings a place within the configuration of what is known has not yet changed, and Foucault reiterates that we are still operating within the parameters of representation. A fateful detour has been introduced, however, one that complicates and deepens the visual field. Describing a process common to the sciences of this period, Foucault explains:

> Thus, European culture is inventing a depth for itself in which what matters is no longer identities, distinctive characters, permanent tables . . . but great hidden forces developed on the basis of their primitive and inaccessible nucleus, origin, causality, and history. From now on things will be represented only from the depths of this density withdrawn into itself, perhaps blurred and darkened by its obscurity, but bound tightly to themselves, assembled or divided, inescapably grouped by the vigor that is hidden down below, in those depths. Visible forms, their connections, the blank spaces that isolate them and surround their outlines—all these will now be presented to our gaze only in an already composed state,

already articulated in that nether darkness that is fomenting them with time. (*OT*, 251–252)

The European sciences are beginning to discover the invisible or, more precisely, that the visible order or representation is sustained by a play of forces that it will henceforth be the task of knowledge to capture. In this first phase of modernization, the visible order that the Classical age worked so hard to establish is continually exposed as nothing more than 'a superficial glitter above an abyss' (*OT*, 251).

In the second phase, the years 1795–1825, words, vision, and thought acquire a mode of being completely incompatible with the Classical age. This second movement is an intensification of the first, such that it will no longer be possible to speak of these sciences as belonging to representation. The tables of rigorously established identities are ripped open by thought as it refuses to stick with the visible surfaces of taxonomy. Knowledge operates instead in a space where connections are formed on the basis of invisible relationships. Following up on our example from natural history, we see that by the time we get to the work of Cuvier, we are no longer dealing with the same animal. The project of taxonomy has given way to the task of apprehending *life* in and of itself. Cuvier strengthens the notion of function such that, unlike in the works of Jussieu, it is no longer subordinated to structure, character, and the space of the table. Approaching the threshold of modern biology, thought no longer seeks to classify beings according to their differences. It apprehends them upon the basis of the invisible homogeneity that sustains them all: life. 'From Cuvier onward, it is life in its non-perceptible, purely functional aspect that provides the basis for the exterior possibility of a classification' (*OT*, 268).

Two important consequences follow from this. The first, as has already been suggested, is that biology constitutes itself as a science of the nonperceptible, whose aim is to render visible the invisible unity sustaining beings in their being. The second is a related point, but pertains to the broader existential dimensions the notion of life introduces into scientific and philosophical thought more generally. No longer are entities construed as connected to each other in a tabular space. As a result of the discoveries tearing apart the table of representations, beings are forced into a new rapport with their individuality. 'From Cuvier onward, the living being wraps itself in its own existence, breaks off its taxonomic links of adjacency, tears itself free from the vast, tyrannical plan of continuities . . .' (*OT*, 274). This disintegration of the table introduces historicity and finitude into nature, that is, it makes it possible to conceive of life according to those conditions that sustain and eventually force it to expire. Thus, at the same time as thought discovers the living being in its singularity, it discloses the forces exhausting it from within.

For life—and this is why it has a radical value in nineteenth-century thought—is at the same time the nucleus of being and of non-being: there is being only because there is life, and in that fundamental movement that dooms them to death, the scattered beings, stable for an instant, are formed, halt, hold life immobile—and in a sense kill it—but are then in turn destroyed by that inexhaustible force. The experience of life is thus posited as the most general law of beings, the revelation of that primitive force on the basis of which they are; it functions as an untamed ontology, one trying to express the indissociable being and non-being of all beings. (*OT*, 278)

Foucault is here highlighting and, on a certain reading, poking fun at the various philosophies of existence that, throughout the twentieth century, return to this pairing of individuality and death as though it held the key to ontological knowledge. He demonstrates how those forms of reflection that fashion death as the timeless ground of meaning are themselves recent epistemic appearances made possible by rearrangements in the sciences of life. Being, as it is *given to* philosophy, is that which exceeds representation and hence must be thought according to the forces that animate and eventually overwhelm the individual. It is perhaps a sign of discretion that no proper names are mentioned at this point in the text; however, it is not difficult to recognize the themes that dominate existential phenomenology as Foucault pulls them from the archives of the nineteenth century. The *Birth of the Clinic* is more explicit, arguing that Bichat's transformations in the clinical experience of life, looked upon from the vantage point of death, supplied modern philosophical thought with an 'anthropological structure' from which 'we have not yet escaped' (*BC*, 198).

In this rupture of representation, we can witness the emergence of the space into which man will step, thereby configuring our modernity. It is man who will be the prime subject and object of this form of thought, the being who, it is hoped, can redeem this finitude. *Las Meninas* encapsulates this transition so well because we locate ourselves within it so easily. There we are, standing before it, receiving all the attention and respect reserved for the king. There we are, discoursing about our finitude, wondering how it might stand as the foundation for this representation. As man overtakes the place of the king, he reinterprets the canvas according to his own image, and it is common to hear people describe their experience of the tableau in decidedly modern terms. Detailing Velázquez's expressionistic handling of paint, his exploitation of its materiality, and his tendencies toward abstraction effaces its status as representation. These categories were planted in the soil of Western experience once thought began to function outside of representation, finding a fragile unity in that strange doublet. With man's arrival on the scene of Western knowledge, painting itself embodies the positivities that characterize the modern *episteme*: finitude, individuality, materiality, the invisible—in short, all those themes that one recognizes as belonging intimately to philosophy and art within modernity. With man now controlling the lines of sight, painting comes to mirror the existence laid down by that rupture which inaugurates our modernity.

CONCLUSION

It would be a mistake not to take account of how deeply our artistic modernity was shaped by this rupture that shook Western knowledge at the start of the nineteenth century. This is precisely what Foucault's researches in *OT* enable us to think. Starting from the conclusions reached in this book, Foucault will attempt to understand the direction of modern art, in particular the work of Édouard Manet, in accordance with this rupture and the post-representational direction that it prescribes. Painting, starting with Manet, ceases to concern itself with its traditional representational task, instead undertaking the interrogation of its own finitude in much the same way as the sciences of man. Primarily, this manifests itself in painting's exploration of its own materiality, that is, those material properties that underlie and sustain its capacity for representation. This critique of representation is not, as is sometimes thought, a narcissistic turn on the part of a medium attempting to purify itself. It is a direction that was laid down in the archive long ago.

In Chapter 2, we see that, for Foucault, the art of Manet is nothing if not the point at which representation, within the cultural practice of painting, begins to surpass itself. Leaving behind its Classical vocation, painting invents a space beyond representation in much the same way as the sciences of the nineteenth century. From Manet onward, the experience of painting will be fundamentally altered along the same lines as the rest of Western culture: modern painting no longer prizes the visual clarity and truth assumed to reside in representation. In its post-representational modernity, painting seeks a deeper truth, interrogating the conditions that make representation possible. As such, it will necessarily be occupied with that which resides outside of representation. There, painting discovers its own finitude, occupying itself with those movements of force at work beneath the visibility supplied by representation. This insistence upon materiality that we find throughout the long life of artistic modernism has much to do with the way being began to be conceived at the start of the nineteenth century. And, just as the European sciences discover a new depth beyond representation, one that accords a new privilege to the invisible, Manet's canvases occupy themselves with those forces operating beneath representation. Invisibility, materiality, finitude, and force—all of these themes traverse modern painting in accordance with the rupture that separates modern culture from the Classical age. Modernity: the great quest beyond representation.

CHAPTER 2

RUPTURE

INTRODUCTION

There is something about travel that partakes of transgression. As Foucault once described it in his essay on Georges Bataille (1897–1962), transgression is an action that crosses a threshold, and in doing so allows us to think about that limit, its relationship with the outside, and the inside that it defines. 'Perhaps it is like a flash of lightning in the night which . . . gives a dense and black intensity to the night it denies . . . yet owes to the dark the stark clarity of its manifestation.'[1] Transgression is not, strictly speaking, negative. The act does not simply do away with the boundary; it affirms it, illuminating its contours. '[I]ts role is to measure the excessive distance that it opens at the heart of the limit and to trace the flashing line that causes the limit to arise.'[2] Travel is an action of testing that invites one to open up a distance within oneself. The journey enables one to trace the fragile boundaries that compose one's habits, language, and field of vision. Foucault once remarked about the curious sense of freedom that we feel when 'As foreigners we can ignore all those implicit obligations which are not in the law but in the general way of behaving.'[3] In taking distance from habitual ways of relating to ourselves via our cultural traditions, both become transparent for first having become strange. Put simply, with the transgression that travel entails, one's own becomes unfamiliar, and in becoming unfamiliar becomes the object of a new curiosity. Foucault's time in Tunis provided such an opportunity. Upon arrival he explained one of the reasons for his voyage: 'After having remained in the French University . . . long enough to be what one must be, I wandered abroad to give my myopic gaze the exercise of distance.'[4] Indeed, it seems as though this distance further stimulated Foucault's excavation of Western pictorial conventions, and was an essential move in the creation of genealogy's 'dissociating look.'

It is generally accepted that Foucault left for Tunis in September of 1966 seeking to expand his intellectual horizons and dodge some of the attacks prompted by the publication of *OT* in April of the same year. According to Rachida Triki, Foucault's experiences in Tunisia should be understood as threefold. It afforded him the opportunity to clarify theoretical issues associated with archaeology, culminating in the publication of the *Archaeology of Knowledge* (henceforth cited as *AK*) in March of 1969. Secondly, the distance provided the opportunity for the investigation of the pictorial conventions of Western art. In 1968 Foucault gave a course on Italian art of the fifteenth century. This was no doubt intended to serve as a backdrop for Foucault's explanation of the ways in which the work of French painter Édouard Manet (1832–1883) proved to be a definitive rupture with *quattrocento* pictorial conventions. Finally, Foucault became immersed in the local political struggles waged between university students and Habib Bourguiba's Destour party. While we do not wish to downplay the significance of the Tunisian political events of the years 1967–1968, we here focus on the first two points, as they are essential for understanding a crucial component of Foucault's genealogy of modern art.[5] In this chapter, we develop the language and resources of archaeology in the effort to clarify Foucault's lecture on Manet. I argue that familiarity with that method is essential for understanding the historical comparisons generated by his discussion, and that it enables us to gauge the distance separating modern art from the history of painting. Foucault speaks of Manet's canvases as operations that rupture the practices that have governed painting since the Renaissance. They are the place where painting first becomes reflective about its representative capacity, and where, through the incorporation of representative elements into representation itself, painting inaugurates the movement that enables it to surpass representation. At the end of this chapter, we follow Manet's rupture into the work of Paul Rebeyrolle, examining Foucault's short essay 'The Force of Flight' in order to explore possibilities of discussing art from a nonrepresentational point of view.

This chapter is largely reconstructive, following the scattered fragments of Foucault's lifelong interest in Manet in order to imagine a book that unfortunately never came to pass. Capitalizing upon the success of *OT,* Foucault signed a contract with Éditions de Minuit for a study of Manet that he tentatively titled *Le noir et la couleur*. A fair amount of mystique surrounds this project, prompted in large part by Deleuze's easy familiarity with the endeavor, tantalizing references to a 'destroyed manuscript,' and the hope that a copy might one day come to light.[6] Unfortunately, no such text exists, and any sketches from September and October of 1970 have been lost and/or destroyed. 'Daniel Defert assures it,' Maryvonne Saison explains in her introduction to *La peinture de Manet*.[7] Foucault compiled many notes, extensively examined Manet's oeuvre, and even investigated possible links with Manet's teacher Thomas Couture (1815–1879), with the only results a series of public lectures, all delivered outside of France. We are fortunate to have at our disposal a transcript of the last of these lectures, along with a couple of signposts scattered across the Foucaultian corpus that enable us to reconstruct Foucault's preoccupation with the work of Manet.[8]

2.1 FOR A DISSOCIATING POINT OF VIEW: THE AIMS OF ARCHAEOLOGY

Near the end of the *AK*, Foucault asks the following: 'could one conceive of an archaeological analysis that would reveal the regularity of a body of knowledge, but which would not set out to analyze it in terms of epistemological figures and sciences?'[9] Can one trace the regularity of a field that does not claim to be scientific but which nevertheless manifests the rule-like consistency of knowledge? That is, can the resources developed to describe discursive regularities be applied to fields that are nondiscursive? Foucault hesitates, ultimately responding in the affirmative. He sketches three possible directions, one of which is the use of archaeology for the analysis of painting.[10]

As we have seen, Foucault opposed analyzing the visual according to models borrowed from linguistics. He thought that art could not be reduced to a form of language, arguing that it has a distinct history, follows its own rules, and thus requires an analysis of its own 'logic.' This is not to say, however, that for Foucault vision is completely free of discursive attachments. In a 1967 review of two works by Erwin Panofsky, '*Les mots et les images*,' the title itself a reference to Magritte's illustration for the periodical *La Révolution surréaliste* (1929), Foucault claimed Panofsky's methods constituted an important new form of seeing, one which might allow analysis to surmount the limits of language. According to Foucault, Panofsky's iconology, as opposed to classical iconography, teaches us how to be more sensitive to the complex relationships between images and discourse. Whereas the latter method treats images as mute texts to which speech must be restored, Panofsky's method 'lifts the privilege of discourse.' As Foucault insists, this is not simply 'to claim the autonomy of the plastic universe, but to describe the complexity of their connections (*rapports*).' In presenting iconology, Foucault describes Panofsky's method much as he would his own project, namely, that of analyzing all the intertwinings of 'the *visible* and the *sayable* which characterize a culture at a moment in its history.'[11] Speaking, therefore, of an archaeology of painting, despite some of the language borrowed from archaeology proper—e.g., statement, discursive formation—should not be understood as equating the visual with the discursive. It is the attempt to use notions formed in the analysis of discursive regularities to describe patterns found in the history of art. Foucault himself warned against referring plastic forms to a discourse that would be an 'interpretive base common to all phenomena' (*LMI*, 650). Both discourse and figure have unique yet historically intertwined modes of being that archaeology must recount.

The first movement of archaeology is designed to rid thought of notions that block an engagement with the concrete functioning of texts, documents, and images. While Foucault's 'negative work' is primarily concerned with operations of discursive unification, a quick look at some of the 'obscure forces' that 'must be driven out from the darkness in which they reign,' demonstrates the importance of this move for discussions of visual art (*AK*, 22). The arguments found in the first chapter of the *AK* are designed to free thought—and one could equally say vision—of the 'ready-made syntheses' that enter analysis without examination. Notions such as influence, tradition, development and evolution, spirit and *oeuvre*, present us with an easily unified historical field, one that neglects the accidents, contradictions, discontinuities, and emergences that genealogy seeks out. These notions are themselves a type of unthought, haphazardly formulated and unwieldy in their demands. They mollify the troubled sea of historical becoming, substituting calm and simple transmission for clashes of force and the reversal of an event. In defining its level of analysis, archaeology inspects these notions to show how, once freed from them, vision might function differently.

Foucault's arguments show that rather than simply describing the functioning of a text, document, or image, these notions link them together in a manner outlined in advance by these procedures. These groupings retain an unjustified explanatory power to the extent that they defy rational presentation. Their repudiation carries us to the heart of archaeology's aspirations: to describe directly the historical function of a discourse without introducing any unexamined forms of synthesis. Influence, for example, is 'too magical . . . to be very amenable to analysis,' because it relies on a highly speculative notion of causality (*AK*, 21). Likewise, tradition constructs a homogenous field below the surface of actual events, allowing them to be linked together. It rounds off differences, giving discourse false forms of continuity, while attributing decisive changes to flimsy notions such as originality and genius (*AK*, 21). Operations like development and evolution derive explanatory power from a focus on a single aspect of an artist's work, interpreting other works as progression toward or deviation from this standard. Spirit plays a similar role on a larger scale, linking disparate phenomena through appeals to a collective unconsciousness, *Zeitgeist*, or worldview. The danger, of course, is that such narratives blind one to the actual, material existence of a work, its historical uniqueness and its recalcitrant properties. *Oeuvre* is the principle, thought to be the most self-evident, upon which these other notions depend, and to which Foucault directs most of his critical attention. What could be more sacrosanct than a collection of works protected by the proper name? To this interpretative faith, Foucault asks us to consider how, within a body of work, the name does not always function in the same way. 'Does the name of an author designate in the same way a text . . . published under his name, a text . . . presented under a pseudonym, another found after his death . . . and . . . a notebook?' (*AK*, 23–24). Foucault's fear is not wrongful attribution, but blunting the contradictory directions opened up within the *oeuvre* itself, and he therefore warns against treating it as a starting point for analysis. Even though in his lecture Foucault deals almost exclusively with the work of Manet, he avoids treating it as a stable entity, preferring comparisons between individual canvases and the historical conventions from which they depart.

The archaeological point is that these unities are far from immediately given, resulting instead from interpretive commitments whose logic is difficult to define. In formulating the resources of archaeology, Foucault hopes to break up habitual ways of thinking and looking. The archaeological treatment of painting avoids these pitfalls, speaking not of style, genius, evolution, or development, but the operations carried out by individual works of art upon the received conventions of painting. Archaeology places a premium on seeing difference, heterogeneity, and divergence, and the Manet lecture attempts to show how certain canvases take their place within the archive by breaking with previous artistic conventions.

2.2 TOOLS OF ARCHAEOLOGY

Foucault's *AK* severs all ties with a hermeneutic conception of signs and traditional forms of logical analysis. He proposes instead to follow the effects generated by the statement (*énoncé*), his term for that most basic element of a discourse considered at the level of its historical functioning. Throughout *AK*, he fights off attempts to reduce the statement to the sentence or the proposition. A statement is always more than its meaning, or what can be said about it from a logical point of view. It is 'a function that cuts across a domain of structures and possible unities, and which reveals them with concrete contents, in time and space' (*AK*, 87). Treating it either as something to be interpreted or considered in terms of its logical formation neglects its unique level of existential causality. The statement is anterior to both the grammatical unity of the sentence and the logical unity of the proposition, and its functioning, in its historical specificity, is what makes it possible to join signs together in meaningful and logical ways. Instead of reconstituting the lost meaning of a sentence, or dissecting a proposition in terms of its internal, formal relationships, Foucault proposes to describe statements that have taken place and that, to a greater or lesser degree, continue to function.

Conceiving of the statement as an event (*l'événement*) is Foucault's attempt to restore to discourse and, as we will see, artistic works, the character of existence. In construing discourse as a series of events, archaeology attempts to consider discourses on par with other happenings, be they ethical, political, social, economic, or institutional. Foucault argues that in order to restore the event to thought we need to free analysis from questions of truth and falsity as well as the requirements of validity. The archaeologist attends instead to the functions that a given discourse carries out, the conditions that must be supplied for the discourse to function, and the effects generated by that discourse. In both his inaugural lecture at the *Collège de France* and his essay '*Theatrum Philosophicum*,' Foucault describes the event as having an 'incorporeal materiality' (*matérialité incorporelle*), that is, the ability to cause effects in reality despite the fact that, strictly speaking, discourses are not embodied.

> Of course, an event is neither substance, nor accident, nor quality nor process; events are not corporeal. And yet, an event is certainly not immaterial; it takes effect, becomes effect, always on the level of materiality. Events have their place; they consist in relation to, coexistence with, dispersion of, the cross-checking accumulation and the selection of material dispersion. Let us say that the philosophy of the event should advance in the direction, at first sight paradoxical, of an incorporeal materialism.[12]

Failure to consider the effects of a statement is what Foucault terms the 'elision of the reality of discourse.' Philosophy mishandles this existential dimension by converting the discursive event into something to be interpreted or evaluated from a logical point of view. In his writings on images, models borrowed from linguistics are insufficient, for the simple reason that they neglect the historical functioning of works of art. They close down on images, construing them as signs to be interpreted. Formalisms are equally suspect, in that they concern themselves with rules of possible combination, rather than actual historical occurrences. The archaeological formulation of the statement, therefore, restores to thought the possibility of thinking images as events with unique historical existences.

The important thing about the statement is its relational quality, the fact that it brings into play collateral spaces upon which it operates. The sum of these directions is known as the discursive formation (*formation discursive*), divisible into four domains. These include: the circumscription of objects, or the ways in which diverse phenomena are grouped into categories for investigation; the formation of enunciative modalities or subject positions—institutional, social and otherwise—that must be occupied if someone is to be the author of a statement; the delineation of concepts, or the rules of relation and separation that govern the formation of distinctions and orderings; finally, the demarcation of a field of strategies, or the rules that make it possible to take up a theoretical position within a given discourse. As the statement functions, it brings these different spaces into play, and it is defined in its historical specificity by how it is positioned with respect to these domains. The task, therefore, of archaeological description is to start with the statement and describe how it simultaneously operates in each of these fields.[13] Wherever a regularity of practices can be described in the formation and combination of statements, one is dealing with a discursive formation.

The rules governing what can or cannot be said within a discursive formation, as well as how statements can be related, are known as the rules of formation (*règles de formation*). When one has grasped the rules of formation, i.e., when one describes the conditions that must be fulfilled for a series of signs to constitute a statement, then one has mapped a discursive formation. Regularity is the watchword, for it is the indication that we are in the presence of a knowledge, that is, a field of statements that are formed and transformed according to a system of rules. The archive (*l'archive*) is the totality of discursive practices that govern the appearance of statements within a culture. Foucault is very specific that he does not have in mind the sum total of texts or institutions dedicated to preserving them, but the systems of enunciability that establish and preserve statements as events (*AK*, 129). It is at once the first rule of what can be said and the laws that govern the accumulation, inscription, appearance, grouping, and maintenance of statements. It is their place in the archive that gives to discourses their historical uniqueness, differentiates them in their functioning, and specifies their duration.

Modesty imposes two limits on archaeology: 'the archive cannot be described in its totality; and in its presence it is unavoidable' (*AK*, 130). In the first place, this means that one cannot exhaustively describe the archive of a culture. One must attempt to stick to areas in which similar statements are clustered. Even with this precaution, however, the findings of archaeology remain provisional. Secondly, and more significant for our purposes, Foucault contends that it is not possible to discover one's own archive, that is, the rules of formation from which we speak. As we saw in Chapter 1, Foucault was reluctant to claim that contemporary trends definitively marked a new position for thought. Archaeology is able to describe the rules of formation only to the extent that they are beginning to be left behind. This does not mean, however, that archaeology is unable to contribute to the diagnosis of our present. On the contrary, it tests, sorts, and attempts to map the field of the recently said by comparing it with what is definitively no longer our own. Foucault explains:

> The analysis of the archive . . . involves a privileged region: at once close to us, and different from our present existence, it is

the border of time that surrounds our presence, which overhangs it, and which indicates it in its otherness; it is that which, outside ourselves, delimits us. The description of the archive deploys its possibilities . . . on the basis of the very discourses that have just ceased to be ours . . . . In this sense, it is valid for our diagnosis. (*AK*, 130–131)

Said differently, Foucault's investigations of the present unfold indirectly, that is, by defining in its separateness the rules of an art from which modernity has departed. This limitation is essential for understanding my claim that Foucault viewed the arts of the simulacrum, those works by Warhol, Magritte, Fromanger, and Michals, as belonging to the space of modernity. He charts this space by contrasting it with what he at various points calls representation, the *quattrocento*, and classical painting. For Foucault, we discover the being of the art of our time by opening up a dissociating view on it, one secured by the analysis of prior conventions.

2.3 ARCHAEOLOGY AND PAINTING

The archaeological analysis of painting eschews some of the usual devices of art historical research. Above all, commentary is avoided. As a methodology, commentary remains allegorical, setting itself up as capable of restoring meaning by referring to a concealed level. 'In analyzing a painting, one can reconstitute the latent discourse of the painter; one can try to recapture the murmur of his intentions, which are not transcribed into words, but into lines, surfaces, and colours; one can try to uncover the implicit philosophy that is supposed to form his view of the world' (*AK*, 193). One might likewise attempt to describe how a work is a product 'of its time.' 'It is also possible to question science, or at least the opinions of the period, and to try to recognize to what extent they appear in a painter's work' (*AK*, 193). Both varieties of commentary are rejected, depending as they do upon constructing a level, 'as deep as it necessary to imagine,' upon which to reconcile contradictory directions (*AK*, 24). It must be possible, commentary holds, to discover the truth of what the artist was trying to say or to read the cultural *Zeitgeist* from his works. This method, according to Foucault, animates literary and artistic criticism of the nineteenth century. As the century unfolded, critics related to works less as objects requiring taste, and 'more and more as a language that had to be interpreted and in which the author's tricks of expression had to be recognized' (*AK*, 42). What Foucault points to here is a transition from an aesthetics of judgment to one of interpretation. For the former, the aesthetic question is one of fixing in scope the conditions to be fulfilled before one can accurately say that a composition is beautiful. For the latter, the challenge is to explicate the work's undisclosed content. Commentary thus functions by attempting to arrive at the 'true' intentions of the painter or author. It posits an ever-deeper, more truthful level of expression, supposedly restored in the activity of criticism.

Archaeology is designed to take leave from this approach. By way of contrast, the archaeology of painting 'would not set out to show that the painting is a certain way of "meaning" or "saying" that is peculiar in that it dispenses with words' (*AK*, 194). We see here the import of the lesson Foucault attributed to Panofsky: it is methodologically specious to translate between plastic forms and the discursive register without first attending to what is unique about each. He continues, explaining archaeology's positive task: 'It would try to show that, at least in one of its dimensions, it is a discursive practice that is embodied in techniques and effects' (*AK*, 194). Again, we must be careful about how we understand 'discursive practice' in this context, as we risk being pulled back into habits of commentary if we construe these as another form of meaning. We have few problems if we understand this phrase in its properly archaeological sense: archaeology treats painting as a practice or as a practical knowledge that has its own rules, sequences, and transformations. It attempts to show how the distribution of painting's formal elements occurs with a describable regularity in a given period. That is, it recounts how color, space, depth, lighting, distance, and volume appear as a result of certain rules of formation. One does not attempt to restore language to what is nonverbal or to recreate the intention of the artist. One instead examines how a particular canvas situates itself with respect to the historical nexus of practices that make it possible. Such an approach, extrapolating from the domains described by Foucault, allows one to analyze a canvas in terms of the ways of seeing that it makes possible or denies, the positions it assigns to the viewer, the historical position required on the part of the artist, the theoretical reflections it gives rise to, and the transformations the work inaugurates in the visible field.

As is always the case with Foucault, one begins with what is most immediate, the painting construed as a statement-event. One attempts to decipher the relationships that make it possible and that it in turn makes possible. One avoids introducing categories that would blind one to the actual functioning of a given painting. Instead one describes the material properties of a given work, specifying, as closely as possible, how these positivities function within a historical field. The archaeologist attempts to detail the challenges certain works portend for existing artistic practices by investigating and comparing, for example, the positions they assign to a painter as the subject of a discourse and viewer as addressee. From here one can attempt to determine whether the 'knowledge' inherent in these arrangements is also present in the theories, aesthetic canons, modes of instruction, techniques, and gestures of the painter (*AK*, 193–194).

If, for Foucault, commentary is theoretically specious, formalism is equally suspect, for it too fails to treat discourse at the level of its existence. While Foucault does not specifically mention the aesthetic formalisms of art criticism, his remarks about linguistic formalism make it clear that such methodologies are limited in scope. This is important, I suggest, for distinguishing Foucault's approach from critics like Clement Greenberg, with whom there is a superficial resemblance. Instead of treating discourse, or in our case painting, as an event that has, for good or for ill, actually occurred, formal analysis remains caught in an exploration of possible combinations. It describes the relationship between its elements, usually with the intention of passing judgment upon their combination, much in the way one examines a proposition's construction. Formalism, be it linguistic or aesthetic, never explains why a statement occupies a place of historical necessity or how it relates to other statements within a given discursive formation. Rather than working in the realm of possibility, archaeology wishes to show 'why [a discourse] could not be other than it was, in what respect it is exclusive of any other, how it assumes, in the midst of others and in relation to them, a place that no other could occupy' (*AK*, 28). While Foucault's immediate emphasis on painting's material properties seemingly brings his approach into contact with 'formal analysis,' he insists upon treating painting at the level of its historical existence. Archaeology is thus fashioned to allow us to watch as select tableaux actively displace the pictorial conventions of those that have preceded them. This, then, is how

I understand Foucault's overall approach to painting and what he means when he writes this:

> In this sense, the painting is not a pure vision that must then be transcribed into the materiality of space; nor is it a naked gesture whose silent and eternally empty meanings must be free from subsequent interpretations. It is shot through . . . with the positivity of knowledge (*savoir*). (*AK*, 194)

Just as the rules of scientific statements can be discerned by sticking closely to the surface of their discourses, archaeology can explain how, in a given period, painting functions with the regularity of a practice. It is appropriate to say that archaeology conceives of individual paintings as moves within a game, provided that we attend to how certain events displace received conventions by positing new ones. Rupture is the term reserved for these transformations at the level of the rules for the formation of statements (*AK*, 175–177). It is one such 'profound rupture' (*rupture profonde*) that Foucault locates in the work of Manet, contending that his paintings are events that fundamentally alter the practice of representation in Western art (*PM*, 22; All translations of this text are my own).

2.4 MANET: THE ARTIST OF THE ARCHIVE

Manet is, for Foucault, the first visual artist to compose his work explicitly in an exchange with the general system of painted-statements known as the archive. In his 1964 essay on Gustave Flaubert's *The Temptation of Saint Anthony*, Foucault explored the new imaginary space of the nineteenth century, first mined by Flaubert and Manet. In setting up their work within the archive, both artists included within the space of the imagination books and paintings. No longer, Foucault explains, is vision born in a flash of genius or through raw desire:

> Henceforth, the visionary experience arises from the black and white surface of printed signs, from the closed and dusty volume that opens with a flight of forgotten words; fantasies (*fantasmes*) are carefully deployed in the hushed library, with its columns of books, with its titles aligned on the shelves to form a tight enclosure, but within confines that also liberate impossible worlds. The imaginary now resides between the book and the lamp.[14]

It can be said that throughout his archival research, Foucault sought to detranscendentalize philosophy's most cherished notions. In this essay he subjects the imagination to ruthless scrutiny, arguing that the modern imagination must be understood in terms of the system of references that compose it. He demonstrates how Flaubert weaves a new space where archival elements (religious texts, commentaries, histories, painted and printed images) merge to form a network that, while dependent upon the past, is wholly original. 'The imaginary is not formed in opposition to reality as its denial or compensation; it grows among signs, from book to book . . . . It is a phenomenon of the library' (*FLib*, 91). As erudition replaces inspiration, the imagination arises through the patient reordering of what has been said. Foucault is quick to clarify that his is not a sour comment on the loss of originality or the nostalgia for a golden age of art that never was. It is a question of understanding an essential characteristic of the modern, cultural moment: the nineteenth century opened up a space in which 'each tableau henceforth belongs to the grand, squared surface of painting; each literary work belongs to the indefinite murmur of writing.' Flaubert and Manet are instrumental in this shift, making 'exist in art itself, books and canvases' (*FLib*, 92; *ST*, 327; The translation has been modified slightly).

For Foucault, Manet's *Déjeuner sur l'herbe* (1863) and *Olympia* (Figure 2) are the first canvases to be 'of the museum,' forming part of a rupture that inaugurates our modernity (*FLib*, 92; *ST*, 326; The translation has been modified slightly). In each canvas, painting establishes a substantially new relationship with itself. This is more than the recognition that art is composed with its own historicity in mind, but the insistence that paintings acquire new forms of interdependence in institutional settings. 'Flaubert is to the library what Manet is to the museum,' Foucault explains, highlighting the similarity in creative practice. 'They write, they paint in a fundamental rapport with what was painted and written—or rather with that in painting and writing which remains open indefinitely. Their art erects itself where the archive forms itself' (*FLib*, 92; *ST*, 327; The translation has been modified slightly). As we know, the archive is the inexhaustible system for the formation and transformation of statements. It contains those discursive practices through which a statement is transformed with the admixture of new discursive elements. Just as Flaubert's *The Temptation of Saint Anthony* derives its being from

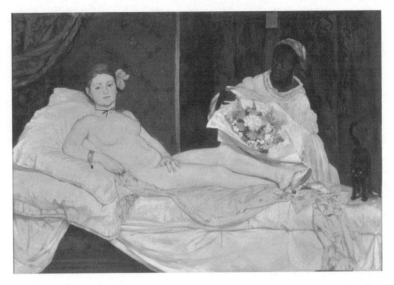

Figure 2 Édouard Manet, *Olympia*, 1863. Musée d'Orsay, Paris. Réunion des Musées Nationaux/Art Resource, New York.

the play of archival material, so too with the work of Manet. If this essay clarifies how Flaubert transforms multiple sources into a coherent whole, the comments about Manet are enigmatic at best. How should one understand Foucault's suggestion that Manet paints by means of a relationship with what has been painted? What does it mean to say that in modernity art erects itself in the space delineated by the archive? What does it mean to make canvases appear within art itself?

The historical precedents for each composition are well known. *Déjeuner sur l'herbe* borrowed its tri-figural arrangement from a detail in Marcatonio Raimondi's engraving *The Judgment of Paris* (*c.*1525), itself a copy of a lost cartoon by Raphael. Manet merged it with Giorgione's *Fête champêtre* (*c.*1510–1511), which he copied as an art student.[15] Scenes of pastoral repose, such as this one, have a long history in Western art, and were quite popular with the nineteenth-century French bourgeoisie. Manet's *Olympia* also has a venerable pedigree, taking its point of departure from Titian's *Venus of Urbino* (*c.*1538), a work he copied during a stay in Florence in 1853. The outrage that this tableau provoked at the 1865 Salon is legion, spurred by Manet's use of a racial stereotype and substitution of a stumpy prostitute for Titian's idealized female form. The identification of the desacralized goddess of love was made easy by the title, a common name for sex workers in nineteenth-century Paris (*19CA*, 283).

The significance of these operations, by which Manet invokes traditional arrangements in order to displace them, forms the focus of much of the scholarship on these canvases. For Robert Rosenblum, both works 'parody' their Renaissance prototypes in order to create a 'curious sense of decomposition' (*19CA*, 283). Examining *Déjeuner sur l'herbe*, Rosenblum explains that a final synthesis never seems to be struck, with each of the painting's elements—the three central figures, the bathing woman, the landscape, the still life in the foreground—remaining oddly disjointed. This is a scene 'only momentarily held together by the borrowed semblance of Renaissance order,' through which we witness the breakdown of compositional unity (*19CA*, 282). For Bataille, Manet ventures into a sacrificial economy where painting actively destroys its capacity for signification. Bataille: 'it is the negation of painting which expresses, as does language, sentiment.'[16] Easily recognized elements are introduced with a profound indifference to their historical precedents or real-world relations. This is the silence in which modern painting resides, a silence that, for Bataille, enables painting to be painting for its own sake.[17] For others, Manet's reliance on the art of the past is more practical, indicative of an inability to harmoniously combine figures in a compositional space. Gilles Néret maintains: 'Composition drove Manet to distraction. Only when the structures of an earlier master underpinned his work was he successful.'[18]

It is clear, however, that Foucault has in mind more complex operations than citation when he characterizes Manet's work as archival. For him, Manet is a pivotal figure because his works fundamentally transform the ways in which paintings are composed and received. This shift consists of allowing the material properties of painting to appear within the painting itself, such that painting's capacity for representation is itself critiqued. Undertaking to represent itself as something that represents, Manet's work ultimately makes it possible to surpass representation. While it is undoubtedly the case that Manet was a figurative painter, the transformations carried out upon painting's rules of formation render possible the twentieth century's explorations of abstraction.

2.5 DISPLACING *QUATTROCENTO* PICTORIAL CONVENTIONS

Traditional chronologies accord Manet the honor of having initiated the Impressionist movement in painting. Foucault undercuts this interpretation by demonstrating how Manet fundamentally alters the tradition of representation in the West. Indeed, his lecture is partially devoted to extricating Manet from such chronologies, and expounding the claim that his real legacy resides in twentieth-century abstraction. It is from the vantage point secured in this lecture that Foucault, in a 1975 interview, claims, 'Manet did in painting a certain number of things by comparison with which the Impressionists are absolutely regressive.'[19] In undertaking to represent that painting is some*thing* that represents, Manet challenges a pictorial tradition that had long sought to mask its own materiality. With Manet, painting's materiality—the fact that it is flat, struck by light, hangs in a physical space—is represented within the painting itself. No longer is painting content to represent things, but now acquires a self-referentiality about its ability to represent, a process that ultimately 'throws off' (*se débarrasse*) representation itself. What is at stake in Manet's art is the construction of the '*tableau-objet*,' the idea that the materiality supporting representation forms an inescapable part of the viewing experience. Said differently, Manet's work is the event by which Western painting discovers its destiny beyond representation.

In order to better situate these transformations, Foucault reminds his audience of the conventions that characterize Western painting from the fifteenth until the nineteenth century. This review of *quattrocento* pictorial conventions enables Foucault to bring into greater relief the innovations found in Manet's work, along with the momentum that propels art into modernity. Given the rapidity with which Foucault moves through these characteristics, one can assume that they are familiar territory for a Tunisian audience who had the opportunity to attend his 1968 course. For Foucault, the tradition inaugurated by fifteenth-century Florentine art should be understood as a game of evasion (*jeu d'esquive*): *quattrocento* painting conspires to make the viewer forget the materiality of the painting in favor of the representation it opens up. As such, painting masks the surface on which it rests (plaster, wood, canvas, or paper), along with its shape and dimensionality. The internal dynamics of the composition are almost entirely given over to the challenge of pulling three dimensions out of two. Orthogonal lines, spirals, right angles and tonal shadings configure a geometrical space that replaces the two-dimensional surface from which the representation springs.

Histories of Renaissance art situate this discovery of linear perspective in the highly politicized world of the Italian city-states. With the constant painting and repainting of family chapels, an abundance of public commissions and new forms of patronage, stylistic experimentations were encouraged and innovations rewarded. It is claimed that the architect Filippo Brunelleschi (1377–1446) discovered linear perspective during the first quarter of the fifteenth century, although dates for the technique's demonstration vary. Through the use of diagonal lines converging at a central point, the painted surface is given the illusion of depth; the scene is thereafter given over to a mathematically quantifiable regularity, whereby objects are accorded greater or lesser proportional space, depending upon their supposed distance from the viewer. This technique was employed, perhaps with Brunelleschi's help, in the construction of Masaccio's (1401–1428) fresco, *The Trinity with the Virgin Mary, Saint John, and Two Donors* (*c.*1425–1428), for the left wall of Santa Maria Novella in Florence. Masaccio's fresco opens up a fictive chapel in a physically prohibitive space, substituting the representation of depth for the flatness of the wall. We know from Rachida Triki that Masaccio was one of the *quattrocento* artists discussed in Foucault's 1968 course where he treated the depiction of Adam and Eve being expelled from the garden (*c.*1425–1428), a fresco from the Brancacci Chapel.[20] Jacqueline Verdeaux, the psychologist and family friend with whom Foucault traveled during the early 1950s, also attests to the importance of Masaccio for Foucault: 'He is the one who made me understand Masaccio's frescos in Florence.'[21] Masaccio's frescos are a prime example of the distributions that would, in the judgment of Renaissance historians, 'dominate European visual language until the nineteenth century.'[22] While Foucault's interest in these paintings extended beyond their formal structures, his analysis of the *quattrocento*, for comparison with Manet, would have focused on how they exploited geometrical techniques in order to mask the materiality of the surface on which they were painted.

The *quattrocento's* game of illusion is also facilitated by the substitution of represented light internal to the composition for the real, material light of the room. Whether from an artificial source such as a candle or a natural source like a window inside the tableau, interior light directs the way a painting opens itself up for inspection. Lighting thus represented serves to distance the viewer from customary expectations, allowing his or her vision to proceed according to the optical logic of representation. On this point it is worth recalling the place occupied by the analysis of light in Foucault's discussion of *Las Meninas*. Velázquez's composition exploits representational light to usher the viewer into the scene, and create the illusion that we are there posing before the painter.

At the extreme right, the picture is lit by a window represented in very sharp perspective; so sharp that we can see scarcely more than the embrasure; so that the flood of light streaming through it bathes at the same time, and with equal generosity, two neighbouring spaces, overlapping but irreducible: the surface of the painting, together with the volume it represents (which is to say, the painter's studio, or the salon in which his easel is now set up), and, in front of that surface, the real volume occupied by the spectator (or again, the unreal site of the model). (*OT*, 5)

In *Las Meninas*, the represented light provides the scene with its general visibility, establishing the illusionistic space in which the figures repose. Light moves in from the extreme right of the canvas and washes over the figures in the foreground, composing them in a fragile unity. As it does this, it provides an illusion of depth for the painter's studio, while extending out into the space occupied by the viewer. This operation suggests that one could traverse this distance and wander freely amongst the figures in the foreground. It is indeed, as Foucault suggests, that by means of the interior light, a common ground has been established between the spectator and those represented on the canvas.[23]

The third *quattrocento* characteristic Foucault describes is to some extent a product of the first two, namely, it assigns to the viewer a single, ideal place from which to behold the tableau. Dependent as it is upon the subtle play of line and light, the representation thus supplies the vantage point from which the game of evasion is best viewed. As historians explain, 'The perspective system not only creates a space inside the picture, but positions the viewer in the space before the painting as well, dictating a position out from the painting on a center line' (*ARI*, 205). Again, Foucault's analysis of *Las Meninas* is instructive.

From the eyes of the painter to what he is observing there runs a compelling line that we, the onlookers, have no power of evading: it runs through the real picture and emerges from its surface to join the place from which we see the painter observing us; this dotted line reaches out to us ineluctably, and links us to the representation of the picture. (*OT*, 4)

And, if the painter's gaze ultimately proves to be a bit unstable, incapable of holding the viewer completely motionless in this ideal spot, it is because of the light which, sweeping in from the right, solicits our movement through the canvas. *Las Meninas* proves to be so effective, for Foucault, because it holds these three elements of the *quattrocento* in a somewhat uneasy tension, playing one off against the other to give the viewer an uncanny sense of movement precisely where it has been forbidden by the painter's gaze.

These, then, are the received distributions of the *quattrocento* transformed in Manet's work. As we saw, archaeology's central task is to describe ruptures at the level of the discursive formation. Manet is, for Foucault, the place where such a 'profound rupture' occurs in that his canvases fundamentally alter the practices by which a painting's formal elements are distributed. This takes place by means of a reversal of the game of evasion, whose principles we have been reconstructing. Instead of hiding the material conditions of painting, Manet's canvases instantiate a new game, one that subtly invokes this materiality, indeed the preconditions of representation, within the representation itself. It is here that we begin to understand Foucault's contention that Manet painted in a rapport with that in painting which remained open, for what his work does is seize upon these principles and reverse them. And what Foucault attempts to show is how these regularities that had tacitly informed the practice of painting are, in Manet's work, subjected to reappropriation, redistribution and redeployment.

The outcome of this modern transformation is the '*tableau-objet.*' The tableau-object has three features that, for Foucault, distinguish it from Renaissance-inspired compositions. In place of the game of evasion through which representational space masks the materiality of the tableau, Manet's work invokes its own constitutive limitations, making explicit its status as representation. Foucault's analyses focus on the oblique ways Manet incorporates the conventions of the past in order to surpass them. Secondly, rather than representing a light internal to the scene, Manet relies upon the real light from the space in which the painting rests. The analysis of the modification carried out upon the lighting techniques of the Renaissance tradition is an essential aspect of Foucault's conceptualization of the tableau-object and, as we will see, crucial for his accounts of the scandals around *Déjeuner sur l'herbe* and *Olympia*. Finally, rather than assigning the viewer a single position, the tableau-object operates a work of decentering, putting in play the relationship between the viewer and the canvas. Foucault discusses this final operation in terms of Manet's *Un bar aux Folies-Bergère* (1881–1882), arguing that the uncanny impression the work leaves us with is the result of our inability to find our place before it. The tableau-object is therefore the result of operations carried out upon *quattrocento* conventions. Seizing upon the rules that structured the experience of painting for approximately 500 years, Manet's canvases stage their reversal. The visual experience that follows is an important piece of our modernity, one that continues to inform how we relate to works of art. No longer is the painted scene governed by the imperative of evasion, but instead insists upon itself as two-dimensional, struck by real light, and something which must be negotiated by a viewer. Foucault develops these three facets of the tableau-object separately, in a canvas-by-canvas analysis of 13 of Manet's major works. This approach is marked by the methodological preference for beginning with what is most immediate, the positivity of the painted-statement. It can be understood as an effort to overturn the philosophical penchant for neglecting the work at hand, and here we see the fruition of archaeology's commitments.

2.6 MARKING THE MATERIAL CONDITIONS OF REPRESENTATION WITHIN REPRESENTATION

Manet's insistence upon the materiality of the representation holds tremendous consequences for the trajectory of modern art. Foucault explains:

> This invention of the tableau-object, this reinsertion of the materiality of the canvas in what is represented, it is that . . . which is at the heart of the grand modification introduced by Manet into painting and it is in this sense that one can say that Manet

disrupted . . . all that was fundamental in Western painting since the *quattrocento*. (*PM*, 24)

The primary way Manet introduced painting's materiality into representation was by flattening out pictorial space. More, however, than insisting upon the flatness of modern painting, Foucault describes the ways in which Manet's work contains a quasi-discursive element, one serving to indicate that the regularities of painting's practice are being surpassed. Manet's work can be read, in large part, as an effort to find a visual language in which to carry out the critique of representation. Not only does Manet deflate the illusionistic space of classical painting, he marks this transformation within the composition itself, frequently deploying ironic references to *quattrocento* conventions.

Le bal masqué à l'Opéra (1873–1874) is a good example of this exchange, for it is a highly representational depiction of revelers dressed in the latest fashions, which at the same time exploits these costumes as 'packets of volume and surfaces.' The figures that crowd the foreground deny the viewer access to the depth of the room. The line of top hats calls attention to this impediment, repeating the white, horizontal wall at the back of the composition. This wall itself redoubles the grand horizontal axis and frames the scene. Compounded by the vertical barriers on either side, the entire frame is reduplicated inside the image. Because of the painting's subject matter, however, one nevertheless anticipates a depth denied by these elements. The viewer, armed with the visual expectations of classical painting, experiences frustration as he or she tries to pass these obstacles. Relief is granted by the opening at the very bottom corner of the left side of the canvas. By means of repeated blockages, vision has been forced to take refuge in this space: a temporary clearing accompanied by a 'sort of irony,' opening onto only the feet of those present in this area. Again, what is interesting for Foucault is the way in which this canvas depicts the displacement of painting's old rules by representing the material properties of painting within the painting itself. After being confronted with the brutal insistence of the medium's formal properties, we are given a glimpse of depth, just enough to let us know that the rules of the game have been changed.

A similar procedure is at work in *L'exécution de Maximilien* (1868), a subject Manet rendered several times.[24] This canvas documents, on a large scale, the execution of the Austrian Archduke

Maximilian in 1867. Napoleon III had placed Maximilian, the figure flanked on both sides by compatriots receiving the fire of the execution squad, on the throne of Mexico in 1864. French support was short-lived, and upon departure of the French forces the local opposition captured Maximilian, sentencing him to death. The event outraged most Europeans, at once horrified by the form of execution, the culpability of Napoleon III, and the impotence of Western diplomacy. Upon learning of the event, Manet set to work recording the scene on a grand scale. Large canvases such as this were generally reserved for historical or mythological subjects, and Manet's use of this format could be construed as a provocation, one that literally elevated a current event to mythic proportions. At the same time as it does this, however, the painting refuses to indulge in moral indignation. The indifference is palpable, with, in the words of one art historian, 'Manet remaining as poker-faced as the contemporary newscaster who recounts world disasters on a television screen' (*19CA*, 287). There is little emotion on display here, with the executioner at the right not even troubling to face the prisoners. Is he reloading? Has he arrived late? It is indeed difficult to tell whose indifference we witness here, given that the soldiers' uniforms combine both French and Mexican fashions, and that Manet posed Parisian soldiers for the painting (*19CA*, 286). Needless to say, the work was deemed politically explosive, with its public exhibition forbidden in France. Its casualness is all the more striking when compared with its prototype, Goya's *The Third of May 1808* (1814). Goya's work also presents a contemporary event—the execution of the leaders of the Spanish insurrection by Napoleonic forces—as a historical subject, but in a way that conforms to emotional expectations. A dramatic flash of light carries the viewer from the tips of the soldiers' bayonets to the kneeling victim, whose cry is nearly audible in his tortured expression. The soldiers themselves are intent upon exacting vengeance. Their muscles are taut, their alignment uniform, and the outcome is certain. Goya's soldiers function as a highly efficient killing machine; Manet's have the air of recent conscripts.

Foucault does not speculate about the nature of Manet's reference to Goya or reasons for the painting's impassivity. He first calls attention to the large wall that violently closes the space of the scene. This wall represents, within the representation itself, the material flatness of the painted support. As it did in *Le bal masqué à l'Opéra*, the wall thrusts the figures forward to meet viewer's gaze, itself barred from the depths. This operation creates an unreal space, leaving only a small piece of land for the execution. The firing squad crowds its victims, implanting its rifles directly in their chests. Indeed, even the distance implied by the rifles' length appears greater than the characters' positions on the ground. Even with very little depth offered to our view, we are still inclined to believe that a conventional distance separates these two figural groups. In Foucault's analysis, the viewer is caught between what is *perceived*—the flatness of the space—and what is *understood* as the distance required for the act. The effect is heightened by the diminution of the prisoners, a variation on a technique for creating the illusion of distance prior to the *quattrocento*. Manet redeploys it 'to signify or symbolize a distance which is not really represented' (*PM*, 28). Because we know things farther away appear smaller, the size differential between the figure groups forces the judgment that they are at a greater distance. In Manet's arrangement 'distance is not given to perception' but instead recorded as 'purely intellectual' (*PM*, 28). We see again Foucault's effort to navigate the disjuncture of seeing and saying. As he explains, 'depth is no longer the object of perception,' but instead supplied by 'signs that only have meaning (*sens*) . . . on the interior of the painting' (*PM*, 29). In this operation, Manet reverses the spatial practices that have governed painting since the Renaissance, and indicates that this transformation is underway. The 'purely symbolic' spatial relation thus marks Manet's challenge to painting's traditional distributions. It is a gesture that, on Foucault's reading, tests and critiques the limits of representation.

In *Le port de Bordeaux* (1871) Foucault highlights the way certain painterly flourishes incorporate the woven tissue of the canvas to bring another of representation's preconditions into the scene itself. The cluster of vertical and horizontal lines formed by the masts belonging to the boats in the upper left corner reproduce the web of intertwining fibers which compose the canvas. Foucault explains, 'it is as if the tissue of the canvas has started to appear and to manifest its internal geometry' (*PM*, 30). No longer seeking to hide the material upon which representation depends, Manet incorporates it into his image. The materiality of the canvas is not just allowed to manifest itself, but forms part of the representation itself. Here the warp and weft of the canvas function both as the support and, according to Foucault's rather idiosyncratic reading, the subject of this scene.

If the representative function of painting has been modified to comment upon both the flat space of the pictorial plane and the web of fibers that compose it, a way must be found to speak, however obliquely, about the fact that the canvas has two sides, i.e., a *recto* and a *verso*. Manet's solution is 'depraved' (*vicieuse*) and even 'nasty' (*méchante*) because for the first time representation will be forced to indicate that there is something that, by the nature of the medium, remains invisible. Foucault's analysis of the game of visibility and invisibility focuses on *Le chemin de fer* (1872–1873), a rather charming depiction of a woman and child in a train station. In his analysis, however, Foucault argues that the viewer is hard-pressed to say precisely what is represented in this canvas. In general, it is rare for more than one of Manet's figures to look in the same direction. In this canvas, however, there is something even more obdurate, with the figures' respective points of view confronting one another in opposition. The child takes up the viewer's gaze and projects it into the depths of the canvas; the woman meets it, contradicts it, and turns it back upon the spectator. The intensity of opposing gazes indicates that there is something absent from the scene itself, but the viewer is hard-pressed to say what that would be. Looking in the same direction as the child, steam and smoke cloud the scene and stop the advance of our inspection. The woman looks past the viewer to a location outside the pictorial plane. In neither case can one see what holds the character's attention. This strife, for Foucault, 'forces . . . the spectator to want to turn the canvas around, to change position in order to finally see what one feels one should see but which is not given in the tableau' (*PM*, 35). This game through which what is not present—which cannot be present because of the nature of the medium—is included in the representation introduces into the painting a discourse on the limitations of representation. It is a play on the material properties of the canvas such that the fact that it is something with two sides is no longer masked, but the subject of a discourse about the inability of the spectator to behold both simultaneously. Its status as a representation is shattered, for as Foucault explains, this is 'the first time that painting gives itself as that which shows us something invisible' (*PM*, 35).

These, then, are the ways in which the material properties of the canvas are brought into the representation itself. Through a subtle representation of the flatness, texture, and two-sided nature of the tableau, Manet's compositions invert the rules of *quattrocento* painting. Foucault thus describes the first property of the tableau-object by way of contrast with the *quattrocento*: Manet's work replaces the illusionistic space of representation with the material place of the real canvas. In place of the game of evasion, constitutive of painting as representation, Manet represents the conditions of possibility for painting's representative function. At the same time as this operation takes place, Manet marks this transformation within the image by including a reflection on that which sustains and grounds representation, in much the way that modern thought began to outstrip the Classical age through a consideration of that which underlies representation.

2.7 REPLACING THE *QUATTROCENTO'S* LIGHTING SCHEMA

In an analysis of a second group of canvases, Foucault calls attention to the ways in which Manet replaces the fictional lighting of the *quattrocento* with real light issuing from the exterior of the canvas. If the former system helped to hide the fact that the painting rested upon a rectangular surface struck by a real light, the latter exploits this light to draw attention to the space in which the tableau rests. This gesture, Foucault contends, is essential for understanding the scandals that accompanied two of Manet's major Salon contributions, *Déjeuner sur l'herbe* and *Olympia*. In addition to demonstrating how modern painting fashions a place for itself by replacing the *quattrocento's* regularities, his lecture also has the ambitious goal of demonstrating how these controversies were badly formulated, neglecting the ways in which this aesthetic change was replete with ethical implications for the practice of representation. His account of these canvases is schematic, touching briefly upon the controversies generated by them. This reflects the methodological direction inherent in constru-ing a painting as an event. While such information is indeed impor-tant, the archaeological point of view endeavors first to describe the rupture of vision carried out in a given work, before asking to what extent one can understand other historical details in terms of the displacement of painting's rules of formation. While such an analysis may neglect many interesting anecdotes—the correspondence between Manet and Baudelaire, for example—it has the benefit of allowing us to see a work in a new light. In his discussions of *Déjeuner sur l'herbe* and *Olympia*, Foucault thus attempts to show how 'the moral scandal was only a maladroit way of formulating something which was an aesthetic scandal' (*PM*, 39). By this, Foucault does not mean simply that these tableaux did not conform to expectations about what constitutes an appropriate subject for art; he argues they were experienced as disruptive precisely because of their radically new interplay of compositional elements. In describing the lighting changes carried by these works, Foucault wants to show how this transformation of painting's rules of formation compounded the perceived affront contained in the subject matter. Accordingly, *Déjeuner sur l'herbe* should be appreciated on the basis of two heterogeneous lighting systems, while *Olympia* should be understood for the way lighting implicates the viewer in its subject's nudity.

It has already been explained that Foucault is not interested in references to other works contained in *Déjeuner sur l'herbe*, and that his characterization of it as 'of the museum' should be understood in terms of the way it refers to and alters received pictorial conventions. *Déjeuner* is, for Foucault, characterized by a 'discordance' or 'heterogeneity' of two lighting systems, one classical and the other modern, whose copresence indicates the passage to a new threshold of visibility. The classical scheme illuminates the woman bathing in the river at the top of the canvas. Light is *represented* as entering from the top right of the scene, descending to illuminate the woman before passing into the shrubbery. For Foucault, there is a 'luminous triangle which sweeps across the body of the woman and models her face' (*PM*, 37). Indeed, when compared with the figural group in the foreground, this system supplies a great deal of vividness for a figure in the distance. The group of figures in the foreground, on the other hand, is outfitted with a different regime of visibility. Rather than being illuminated by an internal source, these figures attain visibility with a light that strikes the canvas at a perpendicular angle. This luminosity distributes their physical properties differently, with the overall effect being one of flatness. One could compare, for example, the simple features of the man in profile with the woman modeled in the background. This direct light underscores the personages' respective stages of dress, with the woman's white nakedness aggressively contrasted by the dark garments of her male companions.

The coexistence of these two incompatible motifs is, according to Foucault, signaled by the ambiguous gesture of the young man in profile. The outstretched pose of the hand is far from natural, and its central position is virtually inexplicable in terms of the painting's subject matter. For Foucault, this body language is used by Manet to mark the two rival systems of lighting that comprise the canvas. The thumb indicates the direction of the interior lighting source, while the folded index finger points out toward the origin of the exterior light. This detail underscores the transformation of the conventions of representation, marking the distance opened up with respect to the conventions of the *quattrocento*.

Traditional lighting is also displaced by Manet's *Olympia*, which, as Foucault contends, is partially responsible for the scandal that greeted her debut at the Salon of 1865. We know from contemporary accounts that guards were stationed around the canvas to prevent it from being attacked by outraged visitors. For Foucault, the shock of seeing a scene from the life of a courtesan, stripped of all pretenses to opulence, is intensified by a lighting that renders explicit what is at stake in the representation of the female body. The comparison with Titian's *Venus* is instructive in this sense. The Renaissance prototype is coy about the act of representing the female form, softening voyeuristic pleasure with a lighting schema that allows for a certain amount of discretion. Light enters from what we suspect is a window at the upper right of the room, sweeps from the left to the right, and gently envelops the woman's body. This 'principle of visibility' structures the canvas, discloses the Venus' nakedness, but refrains from directly involving the viewer. Foucault explains this interplay:

> If the body of Titian's *Venus* . . . is visible, if she gives herself to the regard, it is because there is this luminous source, discreet, lateral and golden which surprises her, which surprises her despite her and despite us. There is this naked woman there, . . . there is this light which, indiscreetly, comes to strike her or to caress her; and us, the spectators, who surprise the game between this light and this nudity. (*PM*, 40)

The game between body and light takes place independently of the viewer's position before the canvas. As the lateral-moving light renders nudity visible, the spectator remains largely incidental. Here we witness a scene that appears as though it were an accident, something not intended for our gaze, and from which it is still possible to withdraw.

Olympia, on the other hand, does not shrink from what is obvious: this scene has been shaped and this girl undressed for the viewer's pleasure. Even more strongly, Foucault claims we are 'necessarily implicated in this nudity and we are, up to a certain point, responsible for it' (*PM*, 40). This results from the use of real, exterior lighting. Instead of cascading softly across the woman's body in a lateral direction, Manet's 'violent light' strikes the canvas directly, hailing from the same position as the spectator's gaze. For Foucault, Manet thus equates this perpendicular light with the viewer.

We are the ones who render her visible; our regard on *Olympia* is light-bearing (*lampadophore*), it brings light; we are responsible for the visibility and nudity of *Olympia*. She is only naked for us because it is we who render her nude and we render her nude because, in looking at her, we light her up, we illuminate her, because, in any case, our gaze and the lighting do one and the same thing. (*PM*, 40)

Whereas in Titian's composition there was a distinction between the principle of visibility and the place of the spectator, Manet collapses the two. The upshot, for Foucault, is that painting is no longer coy about what is at stake in painting: these are representations created for a viewer. By calling attention to the way Manet's manipulation of lighting changes the viewer's relationship with the painting, Foucault gives us the resources for critiquing the ethical and political assumptions of representation. It is important to note, however, that this takes place not in a general discourse about the role male pleasure plays in the history of painting, but through the archaeological description of that which is most immediate, the painted-event.

2.8 THE USE OF UGLINESS: MANET'S *LE BALCON*

Foucault's examination of *Le balcon* (Figure 3) presents in summary form many of the aesthetic changes Manet's work operated on *quattrocento* formulae, since nearly every one of its compositional elements serves as a transition to a new threshold of visibility. One senses this was an important canvas for Foucault, given that it occupies a crucial position in his lecture and that he mentions it at several different points during the years 1966–1975. A discussion of this canvas formed part of his correspondence with René Magritte, when Foucault inquired about the variations that Magritte made in his version of it, *Perspective: le balcon de Manet* (1950). He cites it again in a 1975 interview when he explains that there is an aggressive form of 'ugliness' (*laideur*) at work in *Le balcon*. When asked to clarify

Figure 3 Édouard Manet, *Le balcon*, 1868. Musée d'Orsay, Paris. Erich Lessing/Art Resource, New York.

what is meant by '*laideur*,' Foucault explains that he does not have in mind the conventional associations with lowness or meanness, but the total disregard for aesthetic conventions.

Manet was indifferent to the aesthetic canons which are so rooted in our sensibility that even now one does not understand why he did that, and how he did that. There is a profound ugliness which today continues to howl, to grate. (*QRP*, 1574)

It is important to note that the destruction Foucault describes is not merely the valorization of the unsightly for its ability to shock. Rather, Manet staged the destructuring of the rules governing artistic production. The harmonious arrangement of *Le balcon* is anything but ugly, conventionally understood, and Foucault's claim about its aggressiveness should be understood in terms of the operations that it carries out with respect to the conventions, the aesthetic canons, governing painting.

Upon examining the painting, we immediately see that the composition is structured by a great number of strong vertical and horizontal lines, which, given their position within the scene, redouble the rectangle of the tableau itself. The metal grillwork in the foreground emphasizes the material flatness of the canvas, barring direct access to the scene. The dramatic horizontal of the railing cuts the image in two, with the vertical lines reproducing miniature rectangles within the larger rectangle of the canvas. Metal shutters, rendered in what Foucault judges a 'strident' shade of green, frame the scene. Each shutter marks off the sides of the canvas, highlighting the existence of the window, another reduplication of the canvas's rectangularity and perhaps a comment about its space of visibility. If there is anything that can be construed as ugly, it is this ironwork. The 'garish green' (*le vert criard*) suggests decay, as this is the appearance black metalwork takes through oxidation. The archaeologist does not hypostatize this color, but instead explores how it belongs to a color schema, and how that schema belongs to or contests a discursive formation. This is exactly what Foucault does, describing how this use of color alters a prior system of aesthetic conventions. In the style of painting inaugurated by the *quattrocento*, coloring was reserved for personages and their garments, while the structuring elements of the composition were rendered in black and white. *Le balcon* inverts this arrangement: the figures are cloaked in somber whites and blacks, with sharp hues reserved for the shutters and railing. More than just a displeasing color, this reversal challenges the aesthetic proprieties inherited from the *quattrocento*. Ugliness, therefore, in Manet's work, is the defiance of aesthetic expectations, one that unfolds through the elaboration of a form, a composition, a use of color, without precedent. Ugliness is always what confounds the viewer, precisely because he or she is unable to see the new regularity governing the work. And, if the ugliness of Manet's work still 'howls' today, that is because it still defies our lines of sight.

Foucault's analysis of the type of visibility imported by *Le balcon* also recalls another important theme, one familiar from his analysis of the breakdown of representation in *OT*, namely, the canvas inaugurates a strife between the visible and the invisible. Indeed, *Le balcon* is for Foucault 'the explosion of invisibility itself,' such that the composition is a pretext for commenting upon the broader exchanges between the visual and the obscure forces underpinning it (*PM*, 43). The window, which in classical painting provides visibility, here opens onto darkness. Visual expectations are frustrated, for only with strain can we discern the traces of light striking a metallic object, perhaps a coffee pot, carried by a small boy. The window frame thus marks a threshold where 'three personages are suspended between obscurity and light, between the interior and the exterior, between the room and broad daylight' (*PM*, 42). This explains, for Foucault, why Magritte replaces these figures with coffins. Positioned in a type of limbo, these figures straddle the line between life and death. Magritte renders explicit what Manet hinted at: 'It is really the limit between life and death, of light and darkness, which is there, shown by these three personages' (*PM*, 43).

To indicate this surge of invisibility opening up within the representation, Manet's characters each point the viewer in a different direction, suggesting that there is something taking place outside of the representative space. This game by which the direction of each character's glance annuls those of the others leaves the viewer in an uncertain position. What are these figures looking at? How should one approach this scene? As we saw in Foucault's analysis of *Olympia* and *Las Meninas*, a composition's lighting assigns the viewer a position, directing his or her gaze as it unpacks a scene. *Le balcon* provides no such line of sight, as the different orientations supplied by its personages confound the viewer. This operation by which the viewer experiences his or her mobility before the canvas is the third feature of the tableau-object. It is developed most completely through Foucault's analysis of Manet's *Un bar aux Folies-Bergère* (1881–1882).

2.9 THE PLACE OF THE VIEWER

Whereas *quattrocento* compositions conspired to fix for the viewer a certain ideal space from which the tableau functioned as a representation, Manet's canvases undo this relationship, making it ambiguous and mobile. Uncertain of where exactly to position him or herself,

RUPTURE

the modern spectator encounters the canvas as a real, material object that may be inspected from many perspectives. Foucault explains, 'Manet makes play this property of the canvas so that the space is in no way normative . . . . The canvas appears like a space in front of which and in relation to which one can move' (*PM*, 47). With the onset of modernity, the tableau is a real object inhabiting a space that the viewer, in his or her freedom, must negotiate. Vision itself assumes a more tactile, mobile, and bodily form as the viewer becomes increasingly aware of his or her role in the construction of the visual experience.

Un bar aux Folies-Bergère was exhibited in the Salon of 1882 and is undoubtedly Manet's last great work. Critics immediately recognized it as a complex masterpiece, one in which the composition captures the energy natural to its subject matter.[25] Its dynamism results from the freedom of mobility the viewer experiences in attempting to locate a position before it. For Foucault, this fluidity does not just spring from the avoidance of the *quattrocento's* system of perspective and use of lighting; it is the result of three complex systems of incompatibility, which complicate the viewer's relationship to this image. If, as Daniel Defert explains, this canvas fascinated Foucault as the 'inverse' of *Las Meninas*, it is because these incompatibilities systematically dismantle the place of the king.[26] Like *Las Meninas*, *Un bar aux Folies-Bergère* relies upon a mirror for putting in play the viewer's position; however, rather than constituting it as a representation, Manet's mirror destabilizes the scene, forcing a confrontation with the materiality of the tableau itself.

The mirror that occupies the entire background of the scene serves not only to flatten the space of the canvas, but, somewhat paradoxically, depicts what is in front of the barmaid as taking place behind her. This, for Foucault, is a double negation: the illusion of depth is denied, at the same time as the foreground is substituted for the background (*PM*, 44). The transposition is not exactly seamless, indicated by the ensuing distortion. Foucault points out, for example, that it is practically impossible to account for the same elements in the two viewing spaces. The greatest misrepresentation occurs between the server and her reflection, which is placed to the right of the space she occupies when facing out from the canvas. For Foucault, this unusual placement accounts for the 'malaise' felt before this canvas. In order for this reflection to be brought to the extreme right of the canvas like this, it would be necessary for painter and spectator both to move

83

toward the right. The face of the woman, which we view at a perpendicular angle, contradicts this movement. The mirror's reflection thus opposes the painting/viewing position required by the woman's face. Foucault summarizes the outcome of this incompatibility: 'The painter thus occupies—and the spectator is thus invited after him to occupy—successively or rather simultaneously two incompatible places' (*PM*, 45). The mirror here bifurcates the single position supplied by the *quattrocento*'s orthogonal lines. Rather than designating a space directly in front of the canvas, Manet, through this first form of incompatibility, presents us with two rival positions.

Added to this central inconsistency is 'the incompatibility of presence and absence.' This is the visual to nonvisual clash created by the gentleman with the top hat at the extreme right of the canvas. The mirror's reflection includes him most emphatically, organizing the server's solicitude around him. The frontal depiction of the woman, however, carries no trace of his presence, with her gaze unencumbered as it encounters the viewer. While clearly present in conversation with the woman as she appears in the reflection, Foucault finds no traces of his presence—shadows, for example—in the center of the composition. Light arriving at a perpendicular angle illuminates the rosy hue of the woman's face. Technically, such an arrangement would be impossible, if the gentleman were directly in front of her. He is thus both present and absent. A third incompatibility exploits the instability of the gazes between these two figures. While the server, as she faces outward, appears to lock eyes with the would-be spectator, the reflection at the right depicts a fundamental dissymmetry in the height of the two figures. This disparity is at odds with the look of the server as she faces outward, for in the reflection, her line of sight must be directed upwards. In the frontal view, the server's gaze hails from slightly above the spectator and traces a descending path. The discrepancy between these two lines of sight again opens two different positions for the viewer (*PM*, 45–46).

In contrast to representative space, *Un bar aux Folies-Bergère* contains a system of mobile positions viewers can negotiate at will. Not only does this account for the strange fascination prompted by the composition, it underscores the work's reliance upon its material properties. Whereas the *quattrocento* positioning of the spectator complements a game of evasion whereby the painting's formal properties are disguised, Manet makes it inescapable that one stands before a real surface. The large mirror thus inaugurates the movement through which the painting's formal properties are incorporated into the representation. This forces this canvas to be viewed outside the constrictions imposed by representation. In enables the viewer to discover beneath the regimented space of representation the material forces working to undermine it.

2.10 THE TABLEAU-OBJECT

While Manet's work is certainly representative, the play of the formal elements instantiated by the construction of the tableau-object makes it possible for painting to ultimately bypass representation. Indeed, throughout Foucault's lecture what we witness is the event by which painting, through its increased reflexivity and attention to what sustains representation, gathers the momentum to surpass representation.

> Manet certainly did not invent non-representative painting since everything in Manet is representative, but he made play in representation the fundamental material elements of the canvas. He was thus in the midst of inventing . . . the tableau-object, the painting-object, and that was without a doubt the fundamental condition so that finally one day one might throw off (*se débarrasse de*) representation itself and let space play with its pure and simple properties, its material properties themselves. (*PM*, 47)

Manet's work is thus, for Foucault, a pivotal moment in the emergence of modern painting. It is the rupture that allows painting to function outside of representation, becoming instead the organization of colors, forms, and forces. In Manet, painting takes itself as its own object and begins to operate through a consideration of its regularities and values. This self-reflexive property is the hallmark of the tableau-object, a painting that calls attention to itself as some*thing* painted. By incorporating the material elements of the tableau into the representation, Manet opens up a discourse upon painting within painting. This practice renders possible the pure play of formal elements characteristic of abstract painting, for instead of referring these elements to something exterior, Manet forces them into relation with one another. Foucault's comparison with the Impressionists is significant in this sense, for their work remains wedded to the principle that painting must affirm something external to itself—even if it takes liberties with the optics of presentation. The real legacy of Manet's work is the annulment of the obligation to represent the external world. Painting's indifference to its capacity for external reference is a central aspect of modernity, and will be considered in greater detail in Chapter 3.

Through a contestation of the aesthetic regularities of classical painting, Manet's work forms the rupture so central to our modernity. No longer does painting set itself up as the mirror of the world, but undertakes to represent itself as something capable of representation. It is this transformation within the practice of a knowledge that archaeology is designed to capture. The application of archaeological thought to painting describes how certain works function as events that transform the rules of artistic production. The tableau-object is thus Foucault's way of encapsulating the fact that in modern painting, the work's conditions of possibility are inescapably present in the viewing experience. In place of a representation that masks its preconditions, viewers henceforth encounter the forces residing underneath representation.

2.11 PAINTING AS A PLAY OF FORCES: THE WORK OF PAUL REBEYROLLE

One can argue that Foucault tracks Manet's rupture through the work of the French artist Paul Rebeyrolle (1926–2005). Foucault's essay 'The Force of Flight' was published in March of 1973 for an exhibition of Rebeyrolle's work at the Maeght Gallery in Paris. The show consisted of ten mixed-media compositions depicting a small dog's confinement and eventual movement to freedom. The subject of this series undoubtedly appealed to Foucault, as his research and activism during this period were occupied with incarceration and the struggles between power and freedom. Rebeyrolle's canvases are not, however, simply representations of power, but presented by Foucault as a play of forces, ones which pass between and eventually beyond this series of paintings. The violent application of pigment, the introduction of foreign objects, and movements of body and brush transfer into these images forces surpassing representation. The materiality of these forces are present in a way that mere representation never could be, and Foucault thus finds in these events the legacy of a movement inaugurated by Manet. Thus, even though forms, figures, and serial narratives characterize this period of Rebeyrolle's work, it nevertheless employs the pictorial conventions inaugurated by the tableau-object. Indeed, it is this oscillation between representation and abstraction, between form and force, which, for Foucault, gives this work its political import.

This essay comes at the close of the epistemological phase of Foucault's work, and corresponds with the intense period of political involvement between the publication of *AK* and *Discipline and Punish* (1975). For David Macey, it is 'perhaps the most dramatic piece of writing produced in this period' (*LMF*, 323). Likewise, James Bernauer, whose landmark study takes its title from this essay, contends Foucault's reflections read like an 'unanticipated portrait that captures both his spirit and his experience of thought.'[27] While his courses from the early- to mid-1970s attest to the continuing significance of the archaeological method, the analysis of power will occupy a progressively larger place in his thought. This essay is one of the first places where power is explicitly thematized, and the essay's close pairing of power and freedom is a motif that comes to the fore in years ahead. Reading this essay, one gets the sense that much is taking place offstage and that we are viewing the theoretical formulation of lessons learned on the ground.

Even though his inaugural address at the *Collège* proposed to question the functioning of the Penal Code in terms of its reliance upon a discourse of truth, nothing could have prepared his colleagues for the controversies he was to take part in—only a few months after his appointment.[28] G.I.P. (*Groupe d'information sur les prisons*) was formed to support the struggle against the intolerable French penal system.[29] Numerous groups had already taken an interest in the conditions under which prisoners were held, and sought to institute reforms. When hunger strikes and street protests in January of 1971 failed to bring change, new tactics were needed. G.I.P. was a truly innovative organization, at once masterful in its navigation of the media, while spontaneous, self-organized, and devoid of doctrinal trappings. These qualities allowed G.I.P. to be a meeting point for groups of different persuasions: Christians, Maoists, and liberals converged upon Foucault's home, set aside theoretical differences, and worked together to combat a common enemy.

The aims of G.I.P. were modest, seeking only to empower those without resources to improve their situation. Foucault once explained the group's objective: 'We would literally like to give speech to prisoners.'[30] This is essential for understanding G.I.P. and Foucault's activism during this period. Rather than seeking to create a discourse of reform, exploit the prison for a larger struggle, or even formulate a theory of penality, it served as a locus for the transmission of knowledge. Deleuze once commended Foucault for G.I.P.'s innovations, tying its political practice to the theoretical critique of representation: 'In my opinion, you were the first—in your books and in the practical sphere—to teach us something absolutely fundamental: the indignity of speaking for others.'[31] Convinced official information was inaccurate, G.I.P. gathered first-hand accounts of prison life. Because of the group's ideological fluidity, many forward-thinking prison officials felt comfortable sharing information. Because they were convinced the group did not seek to exploit them for further gains, many prisoners, ex-convicts, and their families became involved. This participation was essential, for as Foucault explains, prisoners 'possessed an individual theory of prisons, the penal system, and justice' that served as a necessary corrective to academic and official accounts. 'It is this form of discourse which ultimately matters, a discourse against power, the counter-discourse of prisoners and those we call delinquents—and not a theory about delinquency' (*IP*, 76).

Foucault, Daniel Defert, Jean-Marie Domenach, then editor of *Esprit*, and the historian of ancient Greece, Pierre Vidal-Naquet, coordinated G.I.P.'s collective voice. David Macey reports the group took up much of Foucault's time, with the philosopher assuming many of its operational tasks (*LMF*, 257). Foucault made several trips to the provincial town of Toul when riots broke out at its prison in December of 1971. He traveled there again in January of 1972 when its chief psychiatrist Dr. Edith Rose denounced the institution's practices—the use of restraints as punishment, heavy work quotas, and policies that encouraged recidivism—in an open letter to the President of the Republic and the Minister of Justice. Her statement was quoted extensively, and the French media circulated images of rebellious prisoners on the prison's roof. These images soon served as a subject for the French hyperrealist painter Gérard Fromanger. Two paintings in his 1975 exhibition, *Le désir est partout*, for which Foucault composed a catalogue essay, adopt these images as a point of departure and are considered in Chapter 4.

The prison is a good example of how a local struggle holds the potential to impact many lives. The very existence of such mechanisms changes the nature of the social fabric such that everyone's liberty is at stake. In Foucault's mind, this accounted for the wide-ranging support their opposition received: anti-penal movements are struggles against forms of power touching everyone's life. Foucault's writings call attention to the ubiquity of the penal apparatus, particularly the *communiqués* from this period that were designed to reach a mass audience. The Rebeyrolle essay bears the hallmarks of this G.I.P. ephemera. The opening lines of 'Force of Flight' and 'Manifeste du G.I.P.' present the addressee with the possibility of his or her incarceration. The latter begins, 'None of us can be sure of escaping prison. Today less than ever.'[32] 'Force of Flight' likewise draws out the similarities between the gallery's enclosed space and the confinement depicted in Rebeyrolle's canvases.

> You have entered. Here you are surrounded by ten tableaux that wrap a room in which all the windows have been carefully closed. Is it your turn to be in prison, like the dogs that you see rising up and bumping against the wire netting? (*FF*, 1269)

Rebeyrolle's animals are also an echo of a G.I.P. questionnaire's chief assertion: 'The situation in the prisons is intolerable. Prisoners are being treated like dogs' (Quoted in *LMF*, 261–62). But, as with Rebeyrolle's dogs, those confined generate forces that ultimately pass to the outside. As Foucault recounts the genesis of his involvement: 'This movement started in the prisons and expanded to the exterior of them. It is from that moment there that I began to take an interest.'[33] A contagious movement also animates Rebeyrolle's series, where Foucault tracks forces passing from the painter, through the canvas, to the outside.

It is often said, not incorrectly, that Foucault set his sights upon the forms of imprisonment unique to modern men and women. As his analysis of Rebeyrolle's work reveals, however, his thought is equally, and perhaps primarily, concerned with possibilities of movement, exchange, and resistance. Considering the place of this essay in a chronology of Foucault's works, particularly those concerned with power, we should not be surprised to find him later insisting upon the primacy of resistance. And, in addition to all that it holds for understanding Foucault's genealogy of modernity, it is perhaps the place to begin to rethink questions of power and resistance. This is indeed the most explicitly political of all of Foucault's writings on art, and not simply because of the circumstances surrounding its completion.

In this essay, he analyzes the forces at work in Rebeyrolle's painting. He views these works as part of the continued repudiation of representation, and here gauges the ethical and political import of an art predicated on its refusal. The period of Rebeyrolle's work that most interested Foucault is the culmination of a classical training in figurative painting, explorations in abstraction, and the use of collage. Rebeyrolle was part of the post-World War II generation of French painters deeply influenced by Picasso. His work from the late 1950s to the early 1960s is almost exclusively abstract, while canvases from 1965 onward are distinguished by the use of collage. In the late 1960s and early 1970s, the figurative concerns of his youth made a resurgence. These compositions are arguably Rebeyrolle's most innovative. As Foucault reads them, they dig into painting's representative capacity to unearth a play of forces. Merging abstraction with figuration, these canvases are composed of the energy generated by the breakdown of representation. If we are to appreciate some of their appeal for Foucault, we should note Manet's legacy in this interaction between form and force. All are highly physical works that exploit the medium's materiality, placing it on display as that which underpins, overwhelms, and surpasses representation. Elements of collage—a wooden board and wire netting—are fused to canvas such that they cannot be removed. Instead of a depth hinted at through an evasion of the canvases' properties, a real texture is created with the addition of these objects. The wire netting also serves as a figurative element, imprisoning and physically torturing the dog brushing against it. The board dominating the tableaux is, for Foucault, a rigid power that organizes the series and directs the dog's confinement. Its power is contrasted with the window in the background—for Foucault, a symbol of impotence. It is significant that when the dog escapes, it is not through this 'futile window' (*fenêtre vaine*), but through a crack worked in the wall. The philosopher remarks upon this truism: 'In the struggle of men, nothing important ever passes through windows but always through the triumphant collapse of walls' (*FF*, 1270). In the analysis of this window, we hear Foucault's suspicion of reformist discourses—the window is already implied by the space of the prison—and the lesson that illusory escapes are often delineated in advance of struggle.

The inclusion of these elements—wire netting, board, and window—is, by Foucault's reading, the gesture that ultimately collapses the wall. 'By means of these three elements . . . the splendor of this painting is willingly pulled down from aesthetics and from the powers of enchantment onto politics—the struggle of forces and of power' (*FF*, 1270). In this series, Rebeyrolle's technique passes the forces generated by the activity of painting into the internal workings of the compositions. He moves force through representation to shatter the representation. 'Rebeyrolle has found the means to make pass in a single gesture the force of painting in the vibration of the painting' (*FF*, 1272). This consists of giving over the composition to the force itself, rather than condemning it to remain aloof as a representation. In suppressing representation, Rebeyrolle creates a movement by which the 'act of painting swoops down onto the canvas where it struggles for a long time' (*FF*, 1272). The ensuing conflict ultimately levels the wall represented in the composition. Deleuze made a similar remark about the G.I.P's strategies: 'No theory can develop without eventually encountering a wall, and practice is necessary for piercing this wall' (*IP*, 74). Rebeyrolle's collage is a practice that ruptures painting's representative capacity. This movement engenders the instability that undermines the place of confinement. Upon the discovery of this force, Foucault claims, 'Painting has at least this in common with discourse: when it makes a force pass which creates history, it is political' (*FF*, 1269).

The force of these works comes from being low. Foucault remarks several times about the forces generated by changes of altitude. Painting, when detached from a purely representative function, gains added power. Likewise, the dog, an animal from below, is a creature whose terrestrial proximity gives his being a force not to be mastered by the rigid powers of the board. This is a recurrent theme in Foucault's writings, one encountered again in Chapter 5 when we consider the forces of truth generated by the dogs of the Hellenistic world, the Cynics. Here, however, it is important to attend to the forces moving from the painter, across the tableaux, and then beyond. Force is 'not represented on a canvas, but inexpressibly produced *between* two canvases, in the flash of their proximity' (*FF*, 1271; The italics reflect those in Foucault's text). Energy moves from the action of painting, down to the dogs, across the canvases, ruptures the wall, and passes from the scene. Rebeyrolle's technique does not attempt to capture in a single representation this movement's intensity. 'The form is no longer charged . . . with representing force' (*FF*, 1272). It is instead painting as a play of forces.

The invocation and then avoidance of representation creates within these canvases the conditions for their power. In constructing these events, Rebeyrolle allows a force to pass from the exterior to the interior and then out again. As with Manet, the use of the medium's material properties alters the way in which we relate to what is before us. With Manet, the *quattrocento's* vantage point was undercut to present the viewer with his or her freedom. In Rebeyrolle's hands, however, the viewer's position is turned into one of confinement. As power passes swiftly to the exterior of the compositions, the bewildered spectator is left to turn in the space of the gallery/prison.

CONCLUSION

Both the lecture on Manet and the Rebeyrolle essay testify to the power of the archaeological method, which provides philosophy with a means of looking beyond an image's content to the operations it carries out. The former allowed us to explore how painting eclipsed the dictates of representation in becoming modern. The latter provided an indication of how philosophical analysis might proceed by considering the forces transmitted between technique, object, and audience. In construing painting as an event, Foucault attempts to free thought from the interpretive questions that often obscure the work. Whether through the analysis of the ways in which Manet's canvases question the rules of a previous aesthetic formation, or the description of the interplay between form and force in Rebeyrolle's compositions, Foucault continually transforms the question, 'What does this work mean?' into 'What does this work do?' In doing so, he distances himself from forms of criticism that attempt to capture a work's essence through speculation about the meaning of its content. This orientation is necessary, as we soon see, because, for Foucault, modern art functions according to an anti-Platonic logic of simulacrum. This means, in a rather technical sense, post-representational art is without meaning.

CHAPTER 3

NONAFFIRMATIVE PAINTING

INTRODUCTION

If there is a consensus in the secondary literature devoted to Foucault's essay on the Belgian painter René Magritte, we arrive at it indirectly: no one can say definitively what this essay is about.[1] Since its publication in 1968 and expansion into book form in 1973, this essay has baffled its readers, producing a number of divergent readings. Foucault's essay is much like the art discussed therein: it holds many traps, first among them the illusion that words might adequately describe what we see before us. The essay, '*un petit truc*,' was, in Foucault's mind, minor, intended simply to memorialize the work of a fellow traveler.[2] This does not mean it is not an important essay. It has achieved canonical status within philosophical discussions of art, and functions as an essential reference point in conversations about the relationship between word and image in twentieth-century art.

What I propose in this chapter is to move the discussion away from the puzzles that arise when confronted with Magritte's well-known images of pipes paired with negative statements—*La trahison des images* (*Ceci n'est pas une pipe*) (Figure 4) and *Les deux mystères* (1966)—toward a consideration of this essay's evaluation of modern painting. I hope to show how this essay fits the direction we have witnessed thus far in Foucault's writings on art: it endeavors to think the status of artistic products with respect to their historical uniqueness. As is often overlooked, Foucault's essay is more concerned with diagnosing the deeper 'process whose formulation is in some sense given by *Ceci n'est pas une pipe*' than cracking the particular riddles posed by Magritte's art (*TNP*, 54). Reading this essay for its archaeological contributions, it becomes clear Foucault's interest extends

93

Figure 4 René Magritte, *La trahison des images* (*Ceci n'est pas une pipe*), 1929. Los Angeles County Museum of Art, Los Angeles. Banque d'Images, ADAGP/Art Resource, New York. © 2008 C. Herscovici, London/Artists Rights Society (ARS), New York.

beyond the canvas from which his essay takes its name, into the more general visual rearrangements it bespeaks. Rather than probing the deep meaning supposedly contained within these canvases—something Magritte himself was reluctant to do—we should understand these compositions as events that undermine the assumptions of classical painting. Taking an archaeological look at Magritte's work, we see that it is a very deliberate response to the received conventions of painting. It takes as its goal the silencing of painting's referential function, i.e., painting's ability to point to something outside of itself. We thus gain a better understanding of the voyage undertaken by modern painting as it sheds its representational vocation, becoming what Foucault calls 'nonaffirmative.'

This chapter serves as further illustration of archaeology's application to art. In this sense, Foucault's essay can be viewed as complementing his discussions of Manet: both treat an art designed to flaunt the patterns of seeing established by representation. As we see, new distinctions enable us to further characterize the shape of post-representational art. The essay on Magritte was composed during the height of Foucault's interest in Manet, and completed during the month he proposed *Le Noir et la couleur* to *Éditions de Minuit*.[3]

Even though at the level of visual appearance, Manet's tendencies toward abstraction and Magritte's highly refined depictions of everyday objects are seemingly at odds, the archaeological point of view unites them in the endeavor of escaping representation. Both fashion events that refuse painting's traditional goal of capturing the visual world. We see in Chapters 4 and 5, however, that painting's new condition does not mean modernity's images are ineffectual. Despite their independent and somewhat unreal status, these products retain the ability to shape subjectivity, occasion pleasure, stir emotion, and present critical forms of truth.

In Foucault's analyses of Manet and Magritte, what we witness is a method that takes a selection of major cultural products, construes them as events, and endeavors an understanding of the rules, regularities, and practices occasioning their appearance. This method isolates moments of rupture, points at which painted-statements cease to follow the rules of a previous order, themselves generating new ones. The terminology is here slightly different, with 'classical painting' (*la peinture classique*) replacing the analysis of *quattrocento* conventions. The chronology Foucault offers is roughly similar with classical painting including, as did the *quattrocento*, both the Renaissance and Classical age. Foucault in this essay, however, dates the assault on the principles of classical painting with the start of the twentieth century, and not, as with Manet, the latter half of the nineteenth (*TNP*, 32). This shift need not overly concern us. Foucault, while still performing an analysis of the distance separating modernity from the preceding period, has altered slightly the target of analysis. Rather than examining painting's formal properties—the handling of space, source of light, and positioning of the viewer— Foucault provides a more general account of its relationship with the external world. Throughout this chapter it should be apparent that Magritte's 'nonaffirmative' art is one of the ways painting overcame the destiny of representation in becoming modern. It achieved this by acting upon a previous system of conventions, here termed classical painting, whose epistemological status also defined the *quattrocento*. As we have seen, archaeology first describes the regularities of a previous period to provide a comparison with what follows. We find this in *Ceci n'est pas une pipe*; however, instead of preceding the analysis of Magritte's art, it occurs within the middle of it. For clarity of presentation, that is where we start.

3.1 TWO PRINCIPLES OF CLASSICAL PAINTING

According to Foucault, two principles have dominated Western painting since the fifteenth century. That is, its tableaux have been governed by two general rules regulating their being before paint is put to canvas. Employing the language of *OT*, we can say these historical *a prioris* structure a painting's formal elements, distribute its field of visibility, and determine its relationship with the external world. The interplay of these two rules, slightly in tension with one another, shape Western painting until the start of the twentieth century. Classical painting is constituted such that it 'speaks.' Foucault supplies the words lurking behind its images: 'What you see, it is that' (*TNP*, 34; *CP*, 43; The translation has been modified slightly). From modernity's vantage point, classical painting tends toward that moment where it moves beyond itself, fixing its meaning in something outside of itself. Classical painting is, therefore, the arrangement by which painting, however obliquely, points to, affirms, names, or references something external. Modern painting, as we have already seen with Manet, works to silence this representative dimension in painting. It does this in order to constitute a silent, 'nonaffirmative' space. To witness Magritte overcome painting's traditional occupation, we need to explore these principles his art overturns.

The first principle is seemingly at odds with Foucault's assertion that classical painting speaks. It calls for the rigorous separation of linguistic and visual signs within the tableau. This is not to say that words never enter into the space of the canvas, but that, as we have seen, the grammars of seeing and saying are essentially different. Images move across differences upon the basis of resemblance. Words function through differences, bringing with them the possibility of reference. This is important because it means the task of naming is generally restricted to language, while images remain mute. Painting's visual experience is thus, for Foucault, essentially different from language, linking things according to similarities. This echoes his claim in *OT* that 'what we see never resides in what we say.' It points to the gulf separating images from words, even where they are joined in a single space. 'The two systems can neither merge nor intersect' (*TNP*, 32). Reading moves in a different direction and, essential for Foucault, brings a referential element into play. Words are charged with saying *that*, of pointing to something beyond themselves. The separation principle does not mean language never exists within the framework of classical painting. When present in an image, linguistic elements remove the viewer from the movement and spatiality of the form itself. Their copresence in a given arrangement favors either the visual or linguistic sign.

> In one way or another, subordination is required. Either the text is ruled by the image (as in those paintings where a book, an inscription, a letter, or the name of a person are represented); or else the image is ruled by the text (as in books where a drawing completes, as if it were merely taking a short cut, the message that words are charged to represent). (*TNP*, 32)

One can follow the flow of the image or the direction of language, but not both at the same time, and their arrangement follows from this principle, privileging one over the other.

Were classical painting shaped exclusively by this principle, its images would remain mute. Classical painting, however, speaks incessantly, despite this separation that constitutes visual resemblance. This is because its second principle reintroduces something like speech. Quite simply: resemblance implies affirmation. Through it, painting's ability to point to the world outside of itself—whether it accurately reflects it or not—is restored.

> Let a figure resemble an object . . . and that alone is enough for there to slip into the pure play of the painting a statement (*énoncé*) . . . (It is like an infinite murmur that torments and encloses the silence of figures. It invests that silence, mastering it, making it exit from itself, and finally reverses it into the domain of things that one can name). (*TNP*, 34; *CP*, 42–43; The translation has been modified slightly)

Thus, in spite of the separation between linguistic reference and plastic forms, reference creeps into the image. Resemblance inevitably carries the association of resemblance *to* something, thereby forcing painting into contact with something external. Despite the exclusion of language, resemblance contains a quasi-linguistic dimension that undermines the purity of visual play. Importing a discursivity that silently builds, it forces the viewer beyond the canvas into a mimetic economy. The 'pure play of the painting' is thus ultimately subordinated to the tasks of referring, naming, or affirming.

In the final section of his essay, Foucault characterizes classical painting as oscillating between these two principles.

> Separation between linguistic signs and plastic elements; equivalence of resemblance and affirmation. These two principles constituted the tension of classical painting, because the second reintroduced discourse (there is only affirmation where one speaks) into a painting from which the linguistic element was carefully excluded. Hence the fact that classical painting spoke—and spoke constantly—while constituting itself entirely outside language; hence the fact that it rested silently on a discursive space; hence the fact it provided, beneath itself, a kind of common place (*lieu commun*) where it could restore the links (*les rapports*) between the image and signs.[4]

Resemblance weaves, as the French indicates, a *lieu commun*, where images assimilate to a linguistic model. Despite its best efforts, classical painting remains mimetic, with its images thereby judged according to the dictates of a reality they are supposed to imitate. These images, as Foucault's pun suggests, remain 'commonplace,' weighed down by the constraints of reference and comparison with an external world.

Throughout the twentieth century, visual artists seek ways to displace these principles, and thereby painting's referential function. Magritte is best understood in these terms, for his operations abolish this common place where painting transmuted into language. Foucault's analysis shows how Magritte systematically unhooks modern painting from these measures, carving out a nonreferential space where everyday mysteries occur. He demonstrates how with Magritte, painting becomes nonaffirmative. Magritte's art is indicative of a certain status of word and image on the far side of modernity. The phrase '*Ceci n'est pas une pipe*' stands in for larger processes at work behind the paintings on which it is inscribed, and thereby confirms painting's new status. Foucault nevertheless follows the concrete operations by which this transition takes place. The essay's canvas-by-canvas analysis should be thus understood as a demonstration of how, in one artist, emblematic of the tendencies shaping modernity, the affirmative dimension of painting is silenced.

To bring clarity to this dense essay, we follow the general orientation of the archaeology therein, parsing Foucault's discussions according to the two principles Magritte attacks. We treat the second principle first, showing how Magritte disassociates resemblance from affirmation. Next, we examine how Magritte unites linguistic and plastic elements on an unstable terrain to uproot the separation principle. Handling these principles in reverse is not arbitrary. It takes us to the heart of Magritte's idiosyncratic conception of Surrealism. Moreover, the distinction between resemblance and similitude that Foucault draws will provide a better sense of what is at stake in Magritte's introduction of linguistic elements. Finally, given that Foucault's discussion of resemblance in *OT* initially compelled Magritte to contact the philosopher, it returns us to the beginning of the relationship that prompted Foucault to compose this essay.

3.2 SILENCING REFERENCE: DISTINGUISHING SIMILITUDE FROM RESEMBLANCE

It should come as no surprise that Magritte was interested in philosophy. His canvases are themselves designed to provoke such questions, some even containing explicit references: *The Human Condition* (1935), *The Pleasure Principle* (1937), *Praise of Dialectic* (1937), and *Hegel's Holiday* (1958). More strongly, one might say his work is itself philosophical, posing in a visual idiom some of modern thought's abiding questions: How, in an increasingly banal world, is transcendence possible? What is meaning? What are the limits of representation? Magritte strongly rejected the conception of the artist as a craftsperson slavishly imitating the world. He maintained that the artist is a thinker who works to solve visual problems. In correspondence with Foucault, he traces this orientation back to Velázquez. 'There is a thought that sees and can be visually described. *Las Meninas* is the visible image of Velázquez's invisible thought.'[5]

This strong intellectual component distinguishes Magritte's art from the aesthetics of mainstream Surrealism. Magritte was active in the main group between 1927 and 1930 while he resided in Perreux-sur-Marne, a Paris suburb. He helped shape the organization's approach to visuality, contributing to the movement's publications images synonymous with Surrealism itself. Nevertheless, his conception of creativity differed greatly from the methods propounded by its literary wing. Magritte explicitly rejected the explosive conception of beauty championed by André Breton (1896–1966), and viewed creation not as the violent struggle of the unconscious to express itself, but the extension of thought's rational powers. He distrusted

the group's emphasis on chance and accident, speaking of his canvases as deliberate efforts to pose a question, illustrate thought, or
evoke mystery. He poetically reworked everyday objects, deploying
an exacting realism designed to pass through representation and
reach the point where enigma overwhelms vision. His is a *sur-realism*,
a form of painting that carried representation to its breaking point,
whereupon reality was discredited. In a calculated approach to the
visual world, Magritte's canvases surpassed appearances, revealing
the mystery lurking beyond the limits of representation. Magritte is
thus primarily a visual thinker who occupied himself with modernity's chief question: What lies beyond representation?

In the spring of 1966, Magritte sent a letter to Foucault inquiring
about the use of 'resemblance' and 'similitude' in the opening pages
of *OT*. We saw in Chapter 1 that Foucault employed the two terms as
virtual synonyms in describing Renaissance knowledge as structured
around discovering instances of the Same across apparent differences. Magritte, for his part, was less interested in the historical reso-
nances of these terms. Admitting dictionaries offer little help, the
painter queried: Is there not a meaningful difference between resemblance and similitude?[6] He provides this distinction:

> It seems to me that, for example, green peas have between them rela-
> tions of similitude, at once visible (their color, form, size) and invisi-
> ble (their nature, taste, weight) . . . . Things do not have among
> themselves resemblances, they have or do not have similitudes.[7]

Magritte continues, asserting: 'Only thought resembles. It resembles
by being what it sees, hears or knows (*connaît*), it becomes what the
world offers it' (See *TNP*, 57). Resemblance is thus, for Magritte, a
property of thought, designating the mind's capacity to contact
external reality. One commentator has shown that this should not be
construed simply as a passive mirroring, but the movement by which
thought acts to transform what is given.[8] Similitude, on the other
hand, refers to the properties of objects, instances of the same
existing among beings. Relations of similitude thus exist between
beings, independent of apprehension by thought, and resemblance
refers to the mind's ability to receive and reconfigure what the world
provides.

If the painter offers this simple distinction, the philosopher either
misinterprets it, finds it insufficient, or forgets it when composing

his homage. Offering a different account, Foucault nevertheless contends that the distinction holds the key to Magritte's work. Foucault:

> It appears to me that Magritte dissociated similitude from resemblance, and brought to play the former against the latter. Resemblance has a 'pattern,' an original element that orders and hierarchizes the increasingly weaker copies that can be struck from it. To resemble presupposes a first reference which prescribes and classifies.[9]

Foucault's definition places resemblance squarely within the mimetic framework of classical painting. To resemble is to imitate a model. Resemblance references an original element, then used to order copies approximating it to a greater or lesser degree. Classical painting inspires such a reading when it leads viewers to assess the fidelity between painted images and the known world, and resemblance brings affirmation. Like linguistic reference, resemblance points, and points to a superior element thought to decide the image's meaning. It thereby encourages viewers to look beyond the picture toward what, it is thought, provides its justification.

Similitude, on the other hand, silences this voice of external affirmation growing within resemblance. Within the art of Magritte, similitude is an aggression. It works against reference by confusing the distinction between copy and pattern. Similitude is, by Foucault's definition, the creation of a copy so faithful that it substitutes itself for the original. As such, it disrupts all attempts to situate images within a hierarchy based on fidelity to a model.[10] 'The similar (Le similaire) develops in series that have neither beginning nor end, that can be followed in one direction as easily as in another, that obey no hierarchy, but propagate themselves from small differences among small differences' (TNP, 44). Similitude and resemblance are thus closely related: both are relations of the Same that expose commonalities of visual form. Similitude, however, usurps the model's priority by simulating its pattern and confusing all sense of origin. Similitude thereby undermines the reference resemblance smuggled into vision. Foucault continues:

> Resemblance serves representation, which rules over it; similitude serves repetition, which ranges across it. Resemblance predicates itself upon a model it must return to and reveal; similitude

circulates the simulacrum as an indefinite and reversible relation of the similar to the similar. (*TNP*, 44)

Whereas resemblance is a genuine imitation, a relation that returns to the model to better copy it, similitude is parodic. It is an empty form of resemblance or, more precisely, resemblance freed from adhering to a pattern, approximating a model, or affirming something external. For Foucault, Magritte's similitudes indicate that modern painting has come into its own. It now inhabits a self-referential space where problems of vision can be posed without undue concern over whether they correspond to something real. Keeping in mind this historical-diagnostic perspective, we should note that Foucault finds precedent for this assault on resemblance's affirmative dimension in the work of Vasily Kandinsky (1866–1944). Although their compositions differ dramatically, with Kandinsky escaping representation by means of abstraction, the archaeologist locates the received conventions they seek to disrupt, thus showing how, at the archeological level, both artists are engaged in a shared endeavor. It is precisely this principle—that resemblance implies affirmation—that Foucault credits Kandinsky with having ruptured through nonfigurative abstraction.

3.3 FROM THE ABOLITION OF RESEMBLANCE TO ITS SIMULATION

By many accounts, Kandinsky was the first modernist to create tableaux composed solely of shape and color, when in late 1913 and early 1914 he created completely abstract 'improvisations.'[11] He thereby overcame the representational orientation of painting by directing the medium away from the observed world into notions adopted from music—harmony, order, and balance. In Foucault's terms, Kandinsky dissociated resemblance from reference, creating compositions of pure affirmation, that is, arrangements whose aesthetic worthiness, it is thought, rests solely on the combination of painting's formal properties. Henceforth, painting refers only to itself.

Kandinsky's is a naked affirmation clutching at no resemblance, and which, when asked 'what it is,' can reply by referring itself to the gesture that formed it; an 'improvisation,' a 'composition'; or to what is found there: 'a red shape,' 'triangles,' 'purple orange'; or to tensions or internal relations: 'a determining rose,' 'towards the top,' 'a yellow *milieu*,' 'a rosy compensation.' (*TNP*, 34–35; *CP*, 43; The translation has been modified)

Kandinsky, deepening Manet's rupture, throws off once and for all the representational orientation of painting. His abstractions silence the reference inherent to classical painting by refusing to direct its elements toward anything except internal relationships. In short, what we see is what we get: lines are lines, forms are forms, and colors are colors. In accomplishing this silence, however, Kandinsky does more than simply unhook resemblance from representation; he destroys resemblance, the result being that his paintings no longer appear like anything.

On one level, Magritte is obviously far removed from this project of abstraction. His images are clinically precise evocations of objects and figures. If they referred to anything real, it would be tempting to classify them as a form of realism.[12] His tableaux, however, preserve only the *appearance* of resemblance, creating, in Foucault's words, 'the ruse of a convincing resemblance' (*TNP*, 43). This means that resemblance is never simply destroyed, as it was by Kandinsky, but created by the movement of similitude. Similitude simulates resemblance to create a space where reference is drowned in the proliferation of voices circulating *within* the canvas. 'Similitude multiplies different affirmations, which dance together, tilting and tumbling over one another' (*TNP*, 46). Like Kandinsky, Magritte's work outstrips the mimetic imperative, and thus presupposes the same archaeological shift in painting. It achieves this, however, not through resemblance's destruction, but with a dizzying display of affirmation. Magritte does not aggressively exploit painting's materiality, but its ability to conjure visions liberated from reality.

With Magritte's *Représentation* (1962) this escape unfolds by placing in series two images, identical depictions of a soccer match. For Foucault, this procedure undermines our ability to identify which is the game and which the representation. 'In the same painting, two images bound thus laterally by a rapport of similitude are enough for exterior reference to a model—through resemblance—to be disturbed, rendered uncertain and floating. What "represents" what?' (*TNP*, 44; *CP*, 62; The translation has been modified slightly). The serial operation abolishes the old space of painting where the 'monarchy' of an external model ruled over the canvas (*TNP*, 44–45). It ushers in a completely reversible space, one without beginning or end, since no anchor halts the canvas's movement. The miniature match wedged between two columns at the left *could* be the original to which the larger scene on the right refers. The inverse could just as easily be true. Or, as Foucault suggests, upon zooming in on the smaller of the two images, we might discover the same scene again. A different device was employed to the same end in *Les liaisons dangereuses* (1936). There, a nude poses awkwardly, using a mirror to shield her nakedness from the viewer's gaze. It covers the physical space of her torso, but in a dramatic twist reveals her backside. This is doubly implausible: the mirror faces out toward the viewer, while a blank wall protects the woman's flank. This operation renders it impossible to determine where, if anywhere, the painting's 'model' resides. Even though the mirrored surface faces the viewer, in an astounding gesture it comes to reflect the one who holds it. For Foucault, this is a clever way of indicating that painting no longer looks outside itself for its subjects. 'Through all these scenes glide similitudes that no reference point can situate: translations with neither point of departure nor support' (*TNP*, 52). That is, modern painting must be thought, like this canvas, according to the series of contortions by which it takes itself as its own model.

3.4 INCURSIONS OF WORD AND IMAGE: EFFACING THE SEPARATION PRINCIPLE

As we have seen, classical painting was predicated upon the separation of linguistic and plastic elements. Even when coexisting within the same pictorial space, one is subordinated to the other. Paradigmatic are the arrangements found in educational texts or in paintings depicting a book or letter. In the former, the text is charged with explaining the meaning found in the image (*TNP*, 32). It dominates the image's reception, moving in as visual information is processed to explain a detail, divulge its context, or state the intention behind its placement. Within a painting, on the other hand, an open letter, for example, assumes its place according to the scene surrounding it (*TNP*, 32). Its language is, strictly speaking, not written, but represented. Words serve the visual panoply of which they form a part. Rarely, Foucault concedes, is either deployment completely stable. One can shift focus from linguistic to plastic elements, thereby overturning an established hierarchy. Nevertheless, the point stands: Western culture has established spaces in which words and images remain foreign to one another. Foucault: 'What is essential is that verbal signs and visual representations are never given at once' (*TNP*, 32–33). They can be joined together in a single space, it is true, but never in such a way as to efface their fundamental differences. Designation and design do not overlap, for the simple reason that each is maintained in its place by conventions of image and language placement.

The order of classical painting is obviously different than, for example, a textbook. It is, nevertheless, this experience of order, prior to the pairing of words and images, that Foucault invites us to observe.

On the page of an illustrated book, one does not usually pay attention to the small space running above the words and below the drawings, forever serving them as a common frontier. It is there, on these few millimeters of whiteness, on the calm sand of the page, that all the relations—of designation, of nomination, of description and of classification—between words and forms are established. (*TNP*, 28; *CP*, 33–34; The translation has been modified slightly)

In this sense, the essay on Magritte should be viewed as an extension of Foucault's archaeology of the mobile relationship between seeing and saying. His paintings are test cases, experiments designed to efface the age-old separation of linguistic from visual signs. They erase this principle, inventing a new mode of the image and new forms of vision. Magritte's images belong to the far side of our modernity, that space where the rules governing painting's practices are once again in play. For Foucault, it is precisely the rupture of this principle separating words from images in an artistic context that Magritte carries out. He accomplishes this in many ways: by making conspicuous the relationship between a painting and its title, by including linguistic elements in a highly ambiguous manner, and in some cases, by having linguistic signs assume the place of visual forms. These experiments with language attack that neutral space, that 'calm sand,' where images and words agreed upon a truce. Stripping them of that common place where they peacefully coexisted, Magritte revives the conflict between plastic and discursive signs. With the demilitarized zone rendered volatile, they launch incursions into one another, covert operations that subtly undermine the principle by which these elements maintained their separation. Even if he is one of the most inventive, Magritte is not the only visual artist who destabilizes this principle. His work is part of the larger shift bringing modern painting into being through an assault on classical painting's rules of formation.

3.5 KLEE AND THE SEPARATION PRINCIPLE: READING OR VIEWING?

The Swiss artist Paul Klee (1879–1940) was one of the first painters to confront the separation principle. Klee was associated with Kandinsky, first through *Der Blaue Reiter* in Munich, and then as a faculty member at the Bauhaus School in Weimar. Despite these affiliations, however, Klee never accepted abstraction as the fulfillment of modern art, and even his most abstract compositions retain figurative elements that grope at a world exterior to painting. Moreover, from what is known about his working methods and conception of creativity, one would be hard-pressed to argue that Klee abandoned painting's traditional task of responding to the world: his tableaux were planned compositions, worked through in a series of preparatory sketches, or immediate responses to the world's self-presentation (*HMA*, 329–331). The overall result is that his work retains an organic sensibility foreign to the enterprise of pure abstraction (*HMA*, 331). In Foucault's idiom, we might say that Klee's art bears enough resemblance to the external world that it remains referential—even as it undercuts the priority of representation by presenting the world in nonrepresentational terms. Klee's painting remains wedded to the task of contacting something external to itself; however, in the process, it becomes analytical, placing both painting and representation in question. It presses on viewers an awareness of painting's representative dimension, thereby forcing thought outside the categories of representation.

This challenge is easily witnessed in those compositions where linguistic elements function as visual forms and in which plastic designs are given as signs to be read. As Foucault rightly points out, Klee undermines classical painting's separation of reading from seeing by placing these elements together in an equivocal manner. He assigns linguistic signs a peculiarly visual role, and visual elements a referential function. Both thus assume an uncertain status, vacillating between linguistic representation and plastic resemblance.

Boats, houses, persons are at the same time recognizable forms and elements of writing. They are placed and travel upon roads or canals that are also lines to be read . . . . And the gaze meets, as if they had strayed to the heart of things, words which indicate the road to follow, which name the landscape that it is in the process of traveling. And at the nexus of these figures and signs, the arrow that crops up so often (the arrow, sign which carries with it a resemblance of origin as if it were a graphic onomatopoeia, and figure that formulates an order), the arrow indicates the direction in which the boat moves, it shows that the sun is setting, it prescribes the direction that the gaze must follow, or rather the line according to which it must imaginatively move the figure that had been placed provisionally and a bit arbitrarily. (*TNP*, 33; *CP*, 41–42; The translation has been modified slightly)

Foucault's language is at times difficult, but the analysis is straightforward. Klee's inclusion of linguistic signs, or signs that carry the type of reference found in language—for example, an arrow—disturbs a purely visual experience of the tableau.[13] These ambiguous signs force the viewer into the position of a reader. In order for the boat to move, the sun to set, and the painting to come alive, one must follow the arrow's direction, like the narration of a book. Giving his scenes added vivacity, suggestive of the world's energy, Klee breaks with vision, supplying directions like a literary text: 'you, viewing-reader, move this over there.' At the same time, however, these linguistic elements retain their status as visual figures. Arrows, letters, and hieroglyphics are deployed because they evoke forms in the natural world, and harmonize with the painting's formal elements. Does the red exclamation point in *Contemplation at Breakfast* (1925) indicate that this scene should be read with excitement? Is it included because it complements the shape and color of the rooster?

Klee's work thus links visual form with linguistic reference at the same time as it places linguistic signs according to their value as formal elements. For Foucault, this assault on classical painting's principle of separation is indicative of the rearrangements shaping modernity itself. In interviews given after the publication of *OT*, Foucault was asked to provide examples from the domain of art to encapsulate modernity in the way that *Las Meninas* captured the Classical age's experience of representation. In both cases, he cited the work of Paul Klee. In the first instance, he presented Klee's art in many of the terms used to describe the modern *episteme* and the art of Manet. In tandem with the general movements of modernity, Klee's art is the becoming-self-reflexive of painting. It constitutes itself through a 'knowledge of painting' (*savoir de la peinture*), much like Manet's critique of representation and the analytic of finitude. Painting reflects upon its most basic conditions when 'Klee makes appear in visible form all the gestures, acts, graphics, traces, lineaments, surfaces that can constitute painting.'[14] This is the movement we have seen throughout our survey of modernity: painting investigates its fundamental properties in order to rediscover new possibilities for itself. Foucault's use of the word *knowledge* in this context is important because it means that Klee's art cannot be understood as brutal, expressionistic gesture, but the controlled reflection upon gesture itself. 'His painting is not *l'art brut*, but a painting recaptured by the knowledge (*savoir*) of its most fundamental elements' (*HEM*, 572).

This analysis fits with Foucault's comments about modernity in general, but not the presentation of Klee in *Ceci n'est pas une pipe*. Klee's painting is described as self-reflexive in much the same way as knowledge within modernity: it constitutes itself through a type of doubling where it investigates representation's conditions of possibility. Foucault: 'Klee's painting composes and decomposes painting in its elements which, even though they are simple, are not any less supported, haunted, and inhabited by the knowledge of painting' (*HEM*, 572). These comments from mid-1966 are heavily inflected by the characterization of the modern *episteme* in *OT* and could equally apply to many other modernists. About a year later, when asked again for a modern equivalent to *Las Meninas*, Foucault once more pointed to the work of Klee. This time, however, his reasons are more precise, and obviously informed by the analysis in *Ceci*. Foucault himself acknowledges the reconsideration, offering this summary:

> Klee is the one who brought to the surface of the world a whole series of figures which had value as signs, and who orchestrated them within the interior of the pictorial space, leaving intact their form and structure as signs, in short, in maintaining their mode of being as signs and at the same time making them function in a manner that is no longer that of signification. And the

non-structuralist, the non-linguist in me is ecstatic with such a utilization of the sign: that is to say, of the sign in its mode of being as sign, and not in its capacity to make meaning appear. (*QV*, 642)

One should not make too much of these different understandings of Klee's work. What transpired between these two interviews, of course, is that Foucault devoted more time to considering the different facets of artistic modernity. He had begun the Magritte essay, and, as he explains, studied more closely the relationship between Klee and Kandinsky.[15] This work was decisive. It allowed him to disentangle different strands within modern art, and to chart the moves that each made with respect to the regularities of classical painting. Most significantly, it enabled him to introduce important distinctions within modernism itself and to separate the types of vision found in Manet, Kandinsky, Klee, and Magritte.

3.6 RADICALIZING THE ATTACK

Klee's subversion of the separation principle means that the inclusion of language within the pictorial plane no longer obeys the rules of subordination that classical painting forced upon it. Henceforth, linguistic and plastic elements assume new modes of being. They become thoroughly unstable, and, in the case of Magritte, attempt to usurp each other's place. Even though words and images are defined by a fundamental heterogeneity, Magritte creates spaces where they crash into one another. These confrontations are designed, according to Foucault, to infuse his canvases with a calculated ambiguity: is one reading, viewing, or both? Foucault understands Magritte's strategies as moves to exacerbate Klee's rupture. They weave new relationships between words and images that strip both of their once-supposed purity. Magritte does not, however, announce his intentions as directly as Klee, who overtly fused the functions of plastic resemblance and linguistic reference. Magritte seemingly preserves the old, didactic arrangement whereby images show and words speak. For Foucault, he only feigns this traditional arrangement, while launching subterranean attacks on their separation. Words, which conventionally anchor the image through commentary, here undermine it, converting it from resemblance into similitude. The comparison between Klee and Magritte on this point is important for grasping the stakes of Foucault's analysis.

Patiently, Klee constructed a space without name or geometry, intertwining the chain of signs with the weft of figures. Magritte secretly mines a space that he *seems* to maintain in the traditional arrangement. But he hollows it out with words: and the old pyramid of perspective is nothing more than a molehill about to collapse. (*TNP*, 36; *CP*, 48; The translation has been modified; The italics are my own)

With Magritte, separation is simulated to such a degree that viewers cannot help but view these images and read these words according to the conventions of classical painting. This, of course, is the trap that prevents the viewer from realizing that the image has been invaded by the surrounding words. Again, Foucault's comparison with Klee is instructive.

In order to arrange his plastic signs, Klee wove a new space. Magritte lets the old space of representation reign, but only on the surface, because it is nothing but a polished stone, bearing figures and words: beneath, there is nothing. (*TNP*, 41; *CP*, 56–57; The translation has been modified)

The words accompanying Magritte's tableaux invade his images, assuming privileges traditionally reserved for the painted form. Because they are similitudes, and essentially empty, Magritte's images are easily penetrated by words appearing to respect the proprieties of classical painting. In fact, 'They have made the object take flight, revealing its filmy thinness' (*TNP*, 41; *CP*, 56; The translation has been modified).

This interplay between word and image is more than the instability Foucault located at the heart of the separation principle, whereby the hierarchy between the two elements could be reversed. Those operations preserve the heterogeneity defining plastic resemblance and linguistic reference, even when shifting priority from one to the other. Klee's art challenged this separation by creating hybrid elements that alternatively put themselves forward as signs to be read and images viewed. Magritte's events are more insidious, masking the operations by which they displace the principle of separation with a simulation of the proprieties of word and image. That is, Magritte first under-cuts the space of classical painting, and then covers over his treach-ery with a similitude of traditional order. His canvases are in fact sites of confrontation, places where words and images affirm them-selves and, moreover, their right to the place of the other. Words do not directly contradict the accompanying images as much as they put themselves forward in visual form, saying, 'I can show you more.' Images do not negate the adjoined words as much as usurp language's referential capacity with the statement, 'What you see is that.' We are dealing here with an indirect negation, one created by the prolifera-tion of affirmations joined together within the same space. All of these affirmations, as we will see, in fact hide the essential void over which these compositions hang.

3.7 TRANSFIGURATION OF WORD AND IMAGE

For most viewers, this game between seeing and saying is announced by the titles assigned to Magritte's images. Many of these enigmatic names, for which his works are famous, were chosen after the paint-ing's completion, according to a logic intended to stimulate, strain, and surpass rational explanation. Picture a cloud set against a moun-tain range, supported by a delicate drinking glass, entitled *La corde sensible* (1960). Often, these titles were selected in a kind of parlor game in which studio visitors would offer possible names, which might be retained by Magritte, who, despite the apparent random-ness of the process, conducted the proceedings in a semi-orderly fashion, and ultimately remained responsible for the final decision. Jacques Meuris recounts that Magritte was looking for 'a title which accorded with the mental process which had led the artist to paint the picture,' one that required participants to 'proceed along the same mental path' initiated by the painting (*RM*, 120). Accordingly, the title finally selected was a partial reconstruction of the thought behind the painting's visible form, one linking words and image to compound the sense of wonder. Magritte was clear about his inten-tions and the relationship between these elements: 'The titles are not descriptions of the pictures and the pictures are not illustrations of the titles' (René Magritte, quoted in *RM*, 121). The result was more explosive than explicative, with language, image, and thought each altered by the crossing. The aim was, as Magritte states, 'to prevent anyone from assigning my paintings to the familiar region that the automatism of thought appeals to in order to escape from anxiety' (René Magritte, quoted in *TNP*, 36; *CP*, 47–48; The translation has been modified).

For Foucault, the results are even more multifaceted than Magritte's statements would lead one to believe. Not only do these titles occasion unfamiliar mental states, they confuse, complicate, and enhance visual experience itself. 'This title must bear some sort of relationship with the painted scene,' it is thought, 'let us discover this connection.' Despite Magritte's avoidance of the traditional rapport between painting and title, the latter structures the expectations viewers bring to these scenes, and the interpretations they generate from them. This convention, however, is put to unconventional ends, with the visual experience being complicated, rather than clarified, by the anticipations Magritte nurtured in the surrounding words. For Foucault, these operations do more than pose questions about the relationships between titles and paintings.

Magritte names his tableaux . . . in order to call attention to the naming. And yet in his split and drifting space, strange relationships form, intrusions take place, brusque and destructive invasions, avalanches (*chutes*) of images into the milieu of words, and verbal lighting flashes that streak and shatter the drawings. (*TNP*, 36; *CP*, 47–48; The translation has been modified)

Magritte's titles cling to the painted scenes in a highly ambiguous fashion. They suggest a visual presence where there is none, 'contradict' the image, and form tentative connections that are quickly undone. But above all, they 'insert themselves into the figures,' acting both as 'supporting pegs and termites that gnaw into it and cause it to fall' (*TNP*, 38; *CP*, 50–51; The translation has been modified). That is, Magritte's titles slowly insinuate language into the cracks of visual evidence. As words seep in, vision is altered and the image rendered fragile. Magritte often indicates this rapport in humorous ways, leaving viewers to ponder, does the scene's title stem from its appearance, or does it appear this way because of its title?

This penetration of word into image is perhaps most pronounced in the canvas *Le soir qui tombe* (1964), a new twist on the canonical theme of nightfall. The viewer is presented with an iridescent horizon, glimpsed through a window frame flanked by two curtains. The sun shines brightly in the distance and does not appear to be in the process of setting. Closer inspection reveals that the window is broken, shards of glass on the floor, and a second sun detectable on the pane's remnants. Things cannot fall without breaking something, language tells us. This notion, evoked by the painting's title, works its way into the image, causing glass to fall with the sun. Words, those notoriously insubstantial entities haunting the borders of ontology (the 'non-place of language,' as Foucault termed it in *OT*) assume substantive form and produce physical results.

In other canvases, words take on a more explicitly material form, rivaling the painted forms themselves. In *L'art de la conversation* (1950), words are the very building blocks of the human world. For Foucault, the two figures in the foreground speak an 'inaudible discourse,' one reabsorbed by the stones overshadowing their conversation. Depending upon how one looks upon these massive rocks, they spell '*Rêve*' (dream), '*Trêve*' (truce), or '*Crève*,' (death). This painting presents Foucault with a philosophical point about the coagulation of language: '*L'art de la conversation* is the anonymous gravitation of things which form their own words in the midst of the indifference of men, imposing themselves there, without anyone even knowing it, in their daily chatter' (*TNP*, 37–38; *CP*, 50; The translation has been modified). Likewise, in *Personnage marchant vers l'horizon* (1928–1929), language assumes a material form capable of standing in for visual experience. 'Word-bearers' (*porte-mots*) provide the scenery through which Magritte's ubiquitous man with the bowler hat marches. The painting's figurative objects have been replaced by colored blobs carrying the inscriptions 'gun,' 'armchair,' 'horse,' 'cloud,' and 'horizon.' These words are not, as in Klee, linguistic-visual hybrids; they affirm the reality of language and its vision-inducing powers. Their occurrence within the space of the tableau eliminates the need for the object's representation, placing the name *there*, where an image is normally supplied. Foucault quotes Magritte: 'Sometimes the name of an object can take the place of an object in reality' (René Magritte, quoted in *TNP*, 38). Within the painting, these words are not approximations of the objects they replace; they have a life of their own. Foucault: 'These "word-bearers" are thicker, more substantial than the objects themselves' (*TNP*, 39). Objects can therefore be dispensed with, for words shape vision, and within the painted surface assume a visual form. As Magritte explains of their transfiguration, 'In a tableau, words are of the same substance as images. One sees images and words differently in a tableau' (René Magritte, quoted in *TNP*, 39; *CP*, 52; The translation has been modified).

3.8 WHEN CALLIGRAMS COME UNDONE[16]

With this examination of classical painting, and the subsequent challenges to its reign, we are in a position to understand Foucault's analysis of Magritte's images of pipes. As we have seen, classical painting was constituted by a tension between two principles: the first excluded linguistic reference by containing and subordinating language within the painted scene; the second, on the other hand, surreptitiously reintroduced resemblance's referential voice: 'what you see is that.' The canvases to which the words '*Ceci n'est pas une pipe*' have been affixed respond to these two principles, signaling that their rupture has been definitively accomplished. First, they bring together linguistic signs and visual forms in a fashion that destabilizes their respective boundaries. This results in a calligram, a picture formed by the arrangement of words on a page, made famous by Guillaume Apollinaire (1880–1918).[17] After these incursions between word and image have been accomplished, Magritte distributes these elements according to the traditional arrangement of classical painting, separating the pipe's image from the words accompanying it. This space, however, is completely fictive, revealed by Foucault's analysis to be merely the simulation of the separation. What lies underneath, he contends, is an 'unraveled calligram' (*calligramme défait*), a textual-image whose elements have been broken apart, dispersed, and placed within the sanctioned space of the object lesson. This similitude spreads a fog across the canvas, one that makes it difficult to determine how extensive these incursions between word and image have been, and impossible to restore elements to their rightful places.

Magritte's operations erase any vantage point from which one might sort linguistic from plastic elements. Without this position, viewers remain within the surface of the canvas as different similitudes rush forward, demanding attention. This combination, within a single space of multiple affirmative discourses, overwhelms the ability of painting to affirm something external to itself. Of their combination, Foucault explains: 'It inaugurates a play of transferences that run, proliferate, propagate, and correspond within the layout of the painting, affirming and representing nothing. Thus in Magritte's art we find infinite games of purified similitude that never overflow the painting' (*TNP*, 49). Within Foucault's analysis, pipes proliferate at a dizzying pace, and it becomes increasingly urgent to remind ourselves that nowhere in these phantasms is there a pipe. This series of simulated affirmations is the movement by which resemblance is finally detached from affirmation. In creating a space where affirmations compete endlessly for the viewer's attention, the picture plane remains intact and reference is thwarted. The affirmative dimension of painting, the murmur that built and overwhelmed resemblance, is silenced not through simple destruction, but the solicitation of greater and greater affirmations. To see more precisely how this unfolds, we must follow the steps of Foucault's analysis, watching as text and image are brought together, taken apart, and placed together within the simulacrum of classical space.

Magritte's images, Foucault points out, are not, strictly speaking, contradictory. Contradictions exist only at the level of the statement. There is only one statement here—'*Ceci n'est pas une pipe*'—and 'this' of course is *not* 'a pipe.' Misleading the viewer is the ineluctable force by which the painting conflates the visual and linguistic registers. Foucault:

> What disconcerts us is the inevitability of connecting the text to the drawing (as the demonstrative pronoun, the meaning [*sens*] of the word *pipe*, and the resemblance of the image invite us to do here), and that it is impossible to draw a map which would permit us to say that the assertion is true, false, or contradictory. (*TNP*, 20; *CP*, 19; The translation has been modified)

As a result of their placement, we bring the image into contact with the words, reading it too as a statement. At the same time, we become tripped up by linguistic conventions: when asked, 'What is this?,' one ineluctably replies, 'a pipe,' sensing the error. The arrangement of the canvas deliberately multiplies these slippages. The '*ceci*,' the 'this,' is the central ambiguity that engenders this destabilizing play. Foucault contends that it, the *ceci*, has at least three possible references, whose multiplication denies the viewer a stable position from which to permanently separate statement from image. Moreover, the painting's pedagogical space imports the conventions of an object lesson: please name that which you see here. Viewers, spurred by the academic arrangement—one that for Foucault mimics the simplicity of a page torn from a botanical manual—connect image to text (*TNP*, 19).

The apparent self-evidence of Magritte's drawing exacerbates our tendency to shout, 'It's a pipe! It's a pipe!' These traps are only the beginning, masking even more insidious mergers of word and image taking place below this space. The text, '*Ceci n'est pas une pipe*,' Foucault observes, is painstakingly rendered in a highly 'artificial' script. This meticulous handwriting conjures up so many different impressions that one is hard-pressed to classify it as a written element. In fact, it so closely resembles what one might find in a convent or a child's school notebook, as Foucault imagines it, that it might be more precise to term it the 'image of a text' (*TNP*, 23). Thus, what we are looking at, according to Foucault, is a visual form simulating the legends found in textbooks. Moreover, Foucault observes, the pipe's image, rather than providing an accompanying illustration, appears to extend the writing below it. The drawn pipe is, from a certain vantage point, a 'figure in the shape of writing' (*TNP*, 23). This means that the shape of the pipe replicates the canvas's graphic elements. The drawn pipe above resembles the '*ceci*' below to such a degree that it could be interpreted as a written element. This is exactly what the pedagogical space entreats the viewer to do: treat the drawn pipe as a statement. The '*p*'s in '*pas*' and '*pipe*' could easily be replaced by the drawn pipe above, were it turned sideways. In fact, the longer we stare at this scene, the more it appears as though the pipe's image could replace any of the linguistic elements in the phrase below. But might we not equally say these written elements simulate the shape of the pipe? The '*n*'s of that convent script approximate its curves, just as the combination of the '*u*' and the '*n*' in '*une*' suggests the pipe's bowl and neck. Hence the central ambiguity, as Foucault presents it: do the textual figures simulate the shape of the pipe or does the pipe simulate the image of the written text below?

For Foucault, these incursions have all the hallmarks of a calligram, but one whose elements have been unraveled and dispersed. Traditionally, the calligram is a device that plays creatively with the respective limits of seeing and saying. It joins together in a single figure-text the image of the thing described in words. It deploys words spatially as plastic elements, repeating in visual form that which its language evoked. In so doing, the calligram sets a double trap for its object, conjuring it by means of both language and vision. The calligram thereby strains at the limits of both, attempting to overcome their heterogeneity by uniting what we see and say together in a single space. Foucault explains: 'Thus the calligram aspires to playfully efface the oldest oppositions of our alphabetical civilization: to show and name; to shape and to say; to reproduce and to articulate; to imitate and to signify; to look and to read' (*TNP*, 21). The calligram does not, however, completely do away with these boundaries. This is important: it exploits the tensions between the two directions, but can never erase the opposition between viewing and reading. Foucault: 'By ruse or impotence, small matter, the calligram never speaks and represents at the same moment; this same thing that is seen and read is hushed up in the vision, masked in the reading' (*TNP*, 24–25; *CP*, 28; The translation has been modified slightly). For all of its playfulness, therefore, the best the calligram can do is join together the two functions in a single figure-text. It cannot, however, efface their differences. The text says nothing to the viewer gazing upon its shape, just as reading its words blinds one to the vision contained therein (*TNP*, 24). Thus, despite all its complexity, the calligram nevertheless retains a clearly defined vantage point, a 'common place,' from upon which one can recognize, define, and separate linguistic from plastic elements. And, depending upon whether one is reading or viewing, one can thus assess its visual resemblance or linguistic reference.

In contrast with the traditional calligram, Magritte's 'unmade calligram' (*calligramme défait*) erases all reference points. Circulating in his scenes are thus ambiguous elements, no longer easily defined. Foucault explains Magritte's design:

It seems to be made from the pieces of an unraveled calligram. Under the guise of returning to a previous arrangement, it recovers the three functions of the calligram—but in order to pervert them and thereby disturb the traditional rapport between language and the image. (*TNP*, 22; *CP*, 23; The translation has been modified slightly)

Magritte confronts the viewer with compositions that retain all the evasiveness and ambiguity of the familiar calligram, but compounds their mystery by denying the viewer/reader the means of defining the separateness of its functions. 'Magritte knits together verbal signs and plastic elements, but without referring them to a prior isotopism' (*TNP*, 53). Taking apart the calligram, Magritte deprives the viewer of that 'common place' where image and text meet, are separated, and stabilized. This means that it is impossible, in these scenes, to determine what should be read and what viewed. With Foucault's analysis of Manet in mind, one might suggest that this is another means by which the viewer was liberated from the *quattrocento's* central vantage point. Not only does this canvas not provide the spectator with a stable line of sight, it forces the question, is the person before it still a viewer?

For Foucault, the calligram's unraveling springs from this tableau's absence of external reference. Foucault: 'Magritte reopened the trap the calligram had sprung on the thing it described. But in the act, the object itself escaped' (*TNP*, 28). This void generates a movement that spreads throughout the canvas, leaving in its wake the simulation of a traditional rapport between text and image. The calligram, once undone, cannot capture its referent with either of its usual means, by describing it with words or designing it in visual form. Magritte's calligram instead disguises the fact that this painting, strictly speaking, means nothing. All its energy, all the interweaving of text and image, conceals the fact that nowhere is there a pipe. In being founded upon this fundamental silence, the linguistic and plastic elements take on a conspiratorial air: painting no longer refers to anything external to itself, and it conceals this by conjuring false presences. All is similitude—the represented pipe, the words below it, and the pedagogical arrangement between the two. There is no model, and representation is thus impossible.

> The trap shattered on the emptiness: image and text fall each to its own side, of their own weight. No longer do they have a common space, nor a place where they can meet, where words are capable of taking shape and images of entering into the lexical order. The slender, colorless, neutral strip, which in Magritte's drawing separates the text and the figure, must be seen as a hollow space (*creux*), an uncertain and foggy region that now separates the pipe, floating in its imagistic heaven, from the mundane tramp of words marching in their successive line . . . . No longer can anything pass between them save the decree of a divorce, the statement at once contesting the name of the drawing and the reference of the text. (*TNP*, 28–29; *CP*, 34–35; The translation has been modified slightly)

Foucault's comment about the space separating the pipe from text should not be taken to mean that their traditional separation was restored after the games of the calligram have been played out: the old hierarchy does not reign in this arrangement. A deep and abiding uncertainty creeps into these elements, erasing the stable ground upon which they could be sorted. It is impossible to decide how extensive their intermingling has been, and to determine where word and image act as themselves. Magritte's similitude mocks the traditional arrangements of word and image, such as those found in a classroom. In doing this, he hides the interweaving of text and image accomplished by the calligram. The process thereby denies the viewer a position from which to untangle them, to treat them alternatively as written or plastic elements. This is the emptiness Foucault locates at the center of this calligram: unlike the traditional calligram which represents its object twice, Magritte's undone calligram presents the viewer only with its absence: nowhere is there a pipe. The fact that this calligram resembles nothing, and moreover, does so twice, generates a disorder that sweeps through the entire canvas. We begin to see pipes everywhere: in the writing lurking below, and the simulacrum of a pipe looming overhead in the 1966 version. At the same time, we confront the simulacrum of imagistic writing below and the written pipe overhead. Both text-images are, as we have seen, infinitely reversible one into the other, and it is impossible to determine where the image of writing stops and the real writing begins; just as it is forever ambiguous how deeply the image has been inflected by linguistic elements. How, in the final analysis, are we to determine where written elements begin and end? How do we know, Foucault questions, which pipe is the genuine copy? Without resolution to these questions, it is impossible to break the ambiguity, to say, this *is* a pipe. The clamor of these images, therefore, silences the affirmation inherent in resemblance. Under the empty weight of similitude, painting finally stops speaking.

    In spite of their aspirations, traditional calligrams tacitly maintained a separation between the functions of reading and viewing. They respected the proprieties of each, never speaking and representing in the same moment. They were read or viewed, but not both simultaneously. These calligrams, therefore, maintained in spite of themselves a common ground, that white space upon which the stability of plastic and linguistic elements depends. They never succeeded thus in completing the task with which they had been charged: effacing the opposition between showing and naming. Magritte's unmade calligrams, however, triumph precisely where those that remained intact failed. They eliminate the grounds for separation by merging word and image into a single figure, and then dispersing its particles. Their placement within the simulated space of pedagogy renders it impossible to determine how extensive their intertwining has been. The white space between text and image has been undermined by the rivalry between the two elements, at the same time as the absence of any external referent denies us the possibility of defining a perspective from which to say what is written and what drawn. Without either, it is impossible to introduce into this rush of similitudes any order not forced and artificial. In this sense, Magritte's 'defeated calligram' (*calligramme défait*) is the first one to be truly victorious. It achieves what others only aspired to: the erasure of the difference between plastic resemblance and linguistic reference.

CONCLUSION

All of this, as we have seen throughout this chapter, is an indication that painting has stopped affirming. Within modernity, the canvas can no longer be measured by the dictates of an external model, which would explain its meaning and guide its interpretation. In Magritte's art, we witness one of the events by which painting comes to silence its referential function, assuming the right to speak, quite literally, only for and about itself. For Magritte, it was not simply a question of affirming painting's nonaffirmative status, but an exacting process by which the discursivity lurking in resemblance could be contained within the painting plane. As we saw in Chapter 2 with Foucault's analysis of Manet and Paul Rebeyrolle, one of the directions the breakdown of representation opened up for painting was abstraction. As representation was forced to give way, painting pursued that which resided outside of and sustained representation— its own formal conditions—in a variation on modern thought's analytic of finitude. The work of Magritte is not foreign to the modern *episteme*, but it belongs to the far side of modernity, that place where these questions have begun to relinquish some of their hold on thought and sight. It belongs to that nebulous region that for Foucault was coming into view: that place where language was being rediscovered in all its density and where the image was beginning to assert its independence. At the archaeological level, one can say Magritte's canvases are events designed to overcome one of the implicit and guiding principles of representational painting, namely, that there is something external to painting, whose task it is to represent it. As painting ceases to be ruled by the dictates of representation, it also gives up its ambitions of capturing an external object. Postrepresentational art operates in a completely fictive space where the vision supplied by the art object is no longer subordinated to questions about its relationships with the world. If anything, we might say art images now wield power over reality itself. For modernity, there is a tendency on the part of art to overtake its model, offering itself in its stead. This simulacral element of modern culture is not, for Foucault, something to be decried: who cares that there is no pipe? The last lines of *Ceci*, added to the expanded 1973 edition after Foucault's important essay on the simulacrum in the thought of Gilles Deleuze, offer us a glimpse of what is to come. They invoke the work of Andy Warhol and astutely place pop art within the trajectory opened up by Magritte's similitudes. 'A day will come when the image itself, along with the name it bears, will lose its identity by means of the similitude transferred indefinitely along the length of a series. Campbell, Campbell, Campbell, Campbell.'[18] As we see in Chapters 4 and 5, the fact that art operates in increasingly unreal ways does not mean it is without consequence or that we must give up on many of the things we have come to expect from it— edification, pleasure, ethical-political significance, the capacity to convey critical forms of truth. While it is difficult for traditional forms of thought to say anything about these products operating outside of meaning and interpretation, the viewpoints supplied by archaeology and genealogy place us in a position to analyze them. Treating cultural products as statement-events asks how they fit within a historical-visual field, how they alter the regularities of cultural practice, and how they carry new ways of seeing. It also reminds us to be attentive to how we ourselves, in our ways of relating to ourselves, are formed and informed by these images. As we saw in Foucault's analysis of *quattrocento* painting, and its subsequent displacement by Manet, the position painting assigned to its viewers formed a rich field for archaeological investigation. In this chapter, it was suggested that Magritte's works also operate on this relationship. Not only do they force the viewer to find a place before the canvas, but they exploit the different demands made by reading and viewing, to pose, even more radically, the question of what type of relationship one has with these objects. When confronted with these similitudes, it is legitimate to wonder if one is reading or viewing. And, even more strongly, one might wonder about the identity of that being, surrounded by Magritte's simulacra, standing where the king and queen once held sway. Is he or she still a viewer? What becomes of thought, emotion, passion, and the body in this new, post-representational space where images can be conjured up from nothing? To think through the implications of modern visual art is to examine the type of subjectivity entailed in its reception and production. It is to this undertaking that we now turn.

CHAPTER 4

ANTI-PLATONISM

INTRODUCTION

Foucault announces the anti-Platonism of modern art in his 1970 essay 'Theatrum Philosophicum,' a review of Gilles Deleuze's *Difference and Repetition* (1968) and *The Logic of Sense* (1969). Anti-Platonic art is, for Foucault, characterized by two refusals: first, it refuses to engage in the search for essences; and, secondly, to remain self-identical. These are highly duplicitous artistic products deliberately transgressing boundaries through the assumption of false identities. As such, these images foster sentiments and thoughts not governed by economies of identity, truth, and signification. These products enable subjectivity to escape from itself and be reformed upon the differences occasioning it. Foucault's review can be understood as a continuation of his effort to develop a philosophical thought that is, as it were, up to date, capable of considering modern images as events replete with ethical reverberations. Reading Deleuze, Foucault provides a more visual account of the notion of the event, deploying it in analyses of Andy Warhol, Gérard Fromanger, and Duane Michals. The event—understood as that which continues to circulate in images precisely because they are images—forms the starting point for Foucault's discussions of visual art throughout the 1970s. The critical attention paid to subjectivity, the defining characteristic of his late investigations, also emerges in this context. For Foucault, the hybrid images of artists such as Fromanger and Michals are one of the more powerful ways in which identity can be contested. Both men's creative practice involves acts of transgression, the perversion of their mediums to unexpected ends. The images Foucault thus champions refuse to identify unambiguously with a single artistic form. The experience of these events ultimately challenges the identities that representational thought constructs through the containment of differences. As I hope to show throughout this chapter, the 'acategorical thinking' developed across the exchange between Foucault and Deleuze helps us to take account of the ways in which modern images, those not bound by representation, conduct the forces forming the self.

4.1 OVERCOMING PLATONISM'S ETHICAL ORIENTATION

In his review, Foucault develops Deleuze's notions to remind us that, at bottom, the reduction of the teeming mass of existence to thought's categories depends upon an ethical orientation. This form of self-relation relies upon a pact of goodwill, which promises to think in communion with others. 'But what if,' Foucault wonders, 'we gave free rein to ill will? What if thought freed itself from common sense and decided to function only in its extreme singularity?' (*TP*, 182). For Foucault, Platonism is the product of the will to contain the phantasm-event (*d'evénément-fantasmes*). Behind its doctrines, Foucault contends,

> we encounter the tyranny of goodwill, the obligation to think 'in common' with others, the domination of a pedagogical model, and most importantly, the exclusion of stupidity (*bêtise*)—the disreputable morality of thought whose function in our society is easy to decipher. (*TP*, 181)

In this mention of stupidity, Foucault is not suggesting that society at large is stupid, but rather that philosophy in its haste to avoid grappling with stupidity removes itself to the security of categories in which one is not stupid but simply wrong. As Deleuze explained, representational thought avoids stupidity (*bêtise*) through the dogmatic limitation of the field of its application. This is the significance of error: it constrains thought to respond according to predetermined principles. 'Error acquires a sense only once the play of thought ceases to be speculative and becomes a kind of radio quiz.'[1] This concept thus blocks thought's 'misadventures,' ones which, for Deleuze, can be creative, immersing philosophy within a richer field of differences. This leads to a paucity of thought-action in that society, and its products—artistic, literary, imaginative—are off limits, or at least must be treated with a fair amount of disdain, if one wants to remain within the province of philosophy. The philosophical apparatus, as Foucault and Deleuze characterize it, orders differences around the figure of the Same. Operating within the space inaugurated by Platonism, it is incapable of thinking differences as differences but conceives of them conceptually, as relationships between identities. For the image, this means that one never thinks it on its own terms, for the philosophy of representation removes itself to categories, hastily sorting it according to a perceived resemblance with the world.

Foucault reminds, however, that since this division is historical and dependent upon a certain will to truth, it is capable of being redirected. 'We must liberate ourselves from these constraints; and in perverting this morality, philosophy itself is disoriented' (*TP*, 181). To reverse Platonism, as Foucault credits Deleuze with having done, is to turn our wills in the opposite direction: instead of seeking to contain the phantasm, it is to cultivate the paradoxical, to risk stupidity, and to think outside of the categories that prevent us from seeing images as events. It is, perhaps, like dropping acid.

> We can easily see how LSD inverts the relationships of ill humor, stupidity, and thought: it no sooner eliminates the supremacy of categories than it tears away the ground of its indifference and disintegrates the gloomy dumbshow of stupidity; and it presents this univocal and acategorical mass not only as variegated, mobile, asymmetrical, decentered, spiraloid, and reverberating, but causes it to rise, at each instant, as a swarming of phantasm-events (*d'évenément-fantasmes*). (*TP*, 190)

These endeavors bend the self back upon itself in much the way that Foucault describes ethical formation. Both drugs and the deliberate perversion of philosophical ethics upset the distinction between seriousness and stupidity upon which the sorting operation of representational thought depends. To pervert good sense is to indulge our fascination with the phantasm and its surface effects. It is to engage in a practice of 'affirmative thought whose instrument is disjunction,' even at the expense of apparent contradiction (*TP*, 185). Repetition, the repeated affirmation by thought of differences, is, for Foucault, productive; it enables thought to slip outside of concepts and reform itself upon the differences from which it springs. These practices force thought into a confrontation with itself and the reality sustaining it. In short, they make it possible to think once again. If thought is to consider modern images on their own terms, rather than assimilate them to concepts, it must continually displace itself in an effort to think a constantly shifting center. It is this which the blank repetition of differences by thought accomplishes: it affirms the contradictory and thus opens the figure of the Same to its outside.

4.2 THINKING THE MODERN IMAGE

Despite the obvious pleasure Foucault took in composing this essay, these exercises are not so much 'games with oneself' as the effort to accord philosophical credibility to the image. This piece can be understood as the attempt to do justice to a key aspect of modernity: through production, reproduction, and proliferation, the image has been liquidated, at the same time as it has been imbued with an even greater causality. Deleuze: ' [M]odern thought is born of the failure of representation, of the loss of identities, and of the discovery of all the forces that act under the representation of the identical. The modern world is one of simulacra' (*DR*, xix). Are the phantasm and simulacrum really devoid of being as Platonism leads us to think? Are images less real than the concepts with which they have been traditionally paired? The problem with Platonism and the space of representation it sustains is that it leaves thought in a poor position from which to think the image. In place of a thought passing from image to the Idea, Foucault proposes a form of analysis capable of tracing and tracking the effects generated by images and simulacra alike. Rather than simply treating them as instances of lesser or non-being, thought must analyze the ruptures created by certain images, along with the relationships to which they give rise. If the archeological method attempted to formulate a thought capable of treating discourse at the level of its existence, Foucault, in his reading of Deleuze, seeks to extend that project further into the visible realm by developing a thought of the image as an event, i.e., that which continues to happen in an image by virtue of the fact that it is an image. 'After all, what most urgently needs thought in this century, if not the event and the phantasm' (*TP*, 180).

This involves attending to the image's unique causality, what Foucault calls its 'incorporeal materiality' (*matérialité incorporelle*).[2]

These are the ways in which the phantasm forms the body, shapes thought, and constructs identity, and these effects are the primary reason one can characterize Foucault's analysis as 'ethical.' It is this causality, this level of existence that comes into view when we conceive of works of art, images, and discourses as events. Such a point of view is predicated, as we have seen, upon overcoming philosophy's historical prejudices. Here, Foucault continues his assault, placing it within the Deleuzian problematic, inherited of course from Nietzsche, of reversing Platonism. 'To reverse Platonism with Deleuze is to displace oneself insidiously within it, to descend a notch, to descend to its smallest gestures—discrete, but *moral*—which serve to exclude the simulacrum' (*TP*, 168; The italics reflect Foucault's own). In Foucault's hands, Deleuze's project assumes a more ethical, bodily form. It becomes, for him, a question of freeing thought from its tendency to sort images according to truth and falsity, to allow it to measure the effects they hold for subjectivity.

4.3 DELEUZE, FOUCAULT, AND THE REVERSAL OF PLATONISM

Rejecting the Heideggerian denunciation so common today, Foucault credits Deleuze with giving new life to the discipline of metaphysics. Deleuze's breakthrough came not through a sanctimonious discourse on the unfolding of thought in the West, but a genealogy of its tacit, moral assumptions. It is thus, Foucault explains, not with a refutation of its doctrines, but a systematic perversion of its ethics that Platonism can be reversed. The impetus behind the Platonic project, as Deleuze explains it, is the construction of an apparatus for the sorting of images. Focusing on three dialogues, *Statesman*, *Phaedrus*, and *Sophist*, Deleuze notes that what is at stake is not the distinction between real being and appearance, but the creation of a lineage permitting one to distinguish true imitation from false. In the hierarchy passing from, for example, the Idea of justice, to the quality of being just, to individual examples of just men, the final term in such a series is the just man's simulacrum, his parodic double. This final position provokes the greatest anxiety: how does one distinguish the true pretender, who genuinely participates in the model, from the false pretender, merely aping the copy? This trepidation over the image leads Platonism to construct a model upon which the distinction can be made. Deleuze:

We are now in a better position to define the totality of the Platonic motivation: it has to do with selecting among the pretenders, distinguishing good and bad copies or, rather, copies (always well-founded) and simulacra (always engulfed in dissimilarity). It is a question of assuring the triumph of the copies over simulacra, of repressing simulacra, keeping them completely submerged, preventing them from climbing to the surface, and 'insinuating themselves' everywhere.[3]

From the Platonic perspective, the simulacrum is a carcinogenic power, one capable of spreading throughout the philosophical body. Indeed, whereas the copy resembles the Idea, the simulacrum is an aggression, threatening to subvert not only the image, but also the model. As Foucault explains, in Deleuze's theater, 'The sophist springs up, and challenges Socrates to prove that he is not the illegitimate usurper' (*TP*, 168).

Deleuze thus reads Platonism as an essentially aesthetic philosophy. It deploys its onto-epistemological resources to separate one type of image from the other, and is, he contends, concerned primarily with containing the phantasm-simulacrum. Deleuze again: 'The great manifest duality of Idea and image is present only in this goal: to assure the latent distinction between two sorts of images' (*SAP*, 257). The two types of images are: copies, 'well-founded pretenders' that adhere to the laws of resemblance, and simulacra, 'false pretenders' whose appearances hide a 'deviation' from the model. Internal resemblance, at once volitional and 'spiritual,' thus defines Platonism's distinction between icons (good copies) and idols (malicious simulacra).[4] Both images are pretenders, but the copy truly resembles the thing in question, while the simulacrum's pretension is a subversion concealing a fundamental dissimilarity. With recourse to the Idea, Platonism selects amongst pretenders in a test of purity, thus avoiding the image itself. Where resemblance to the Idea can be detected, one is dealing with a true copy (icon); where resemblance is absent, a simulacrum (idol). In this system, then, where participation in the Idea guarantees being, simulacra are thus discarded. They are repressed on the basis of a higher identity from which it is possible to think the copy as similar. The simulacrum is not, as is sometimes thought, the copy of a copy. It is an image thought as difference, not in terms of fidelity to an originary element.

Aesthetics itself suffers under the sway of Identity, making it difficult to consider images in and of themselves, while remaining within the province of philosophy. Deleuze explains Platonism's legacy for the theory of art, 'It always pursues the same task, Iconology . . .' (*SAP*, 260). Whether in classical metaphysics or phenomenology, Deleuze detects the same attempt to corral differences under the figure of the Same, and to adjudicate amongst true and false resemblances. 'Always the selection among pretenders, the exclusion of the eccentric and the divergent, in the name of a superior finality, an essential reality, or even a meaning of history' (*SAP*, 260). This is evident in the Marxist tradition, which simply cannot function without decrying the alienating influence of images as post-auratic or spectacle.[5]

If, as Foucault and Deleuze argue, the image's degradation is predicated upon the will to contain the phantasm, then a different orientation may permit us to follow its course. This new direction should place thought in a position to analyze the phantasm's happening. What is needed is a thought that moves with the same seriality and rhythm as the modern image. The acategorical thought they call for does not seek to arrest the image's supposed alienating power, but attends to how images are produced, deployed, and take effect. Foucault and Deleuze thus lift the privilege of Identity by developing a language sensitive to the image's 'incorporeal materiality.' Phantasms are not purely imaginary creatures. They have clearly definable functions, describable in ethical terms: they touch bodies, prescribe relationships, mark out paths, and create blockages. Foucault:

Phantasms must be allowed to function at the limits of bodies; against bodies, because they stick to bodies and protrude from them, but also because they touch them, cut them, break them into sections, regionalize them, and multiply their surfaces; and equally, outside of bodies, because they function between bodies according to laws of proximity, torsion, and variable distance— laws of which they remain ignorant. Phantasms do not extend organisms into an imaginary domain; they topologize the materiality of the body. They should consequently be freed from the restrictions we impose upon them, freed from the dilemmas of truth and falsehood and of being and non-being. (*TP*, 169–170)

It is also possible, as we will see, to consider these events in terms of the relationships between self and self or self and other that they give rise to.

For Foucault, this point of view is predicated upon the refusal of the ready-made boxes of categories. He explains, 'They suppress the anarchy of difference, divide differences into zones, delimit their rights, and prescribe their task of specification with respect to individual beings' (*TP*, 186). Exiting from categorical thought is, following Deleuze's usage, stupid, an ontological leveling that treats everything as equivalent, while at the same time hoping to detect difference. Within categories we make mistakes; outside of them we are stupid.[6] Simultaneous with the suppression of categories, thinking requires the affirmation of the univocity of being. Such affirmations were articulated in the philosophies of Duns Scotus and Spinoza, yet both held being was expressed in the same way for different things. For Foucault, such ontologies reintroduce the ordering of differences around the figure of the Same. He imagines instead an 'ontology where being would be expressed in the same fashion for every difference, but could only express differences' (*TP*, 186–187). That is, one where identity is thought indirectly in that beings are alike only as differences. Being would thus no longer be thought of as a grounding unity, but as the repetition of differences.[7] Wading into the river of differences, one renounces categorical thought's certainty of avoiding stupidity. This is necessary, for as Foucault explains, 'Thought must consider the process that forms it and form itself from these considerations' (*TP*, 178). To think through stupidity, rather than avoiding it in advance, compels thought to produce itself spontaneously in the repetition of differences. Allowed to play outside the confines of truth and error, thought hopes not to be completely dissipated, and to recognize its own difference as thought. It disavows its identity in the effort to think difference as difference, waiting for the 'shock' which allows it to break from stupidity and become active upon the detection of its own difference. In short, thought risks losing itself in the confrontation with stupidity so that it might revitalize itself upon the play of differences that, as Deleuze puts it, 'engender "thinking" in thought' (*DR*, 147).

For Deleuze, such conceptions of difference are to found by mining the history of philosophy. In Epicurus, and especially Lucretius, Deleuze locates the thought of the diverse as diverse. He credits both with composing a naturalism of intensities, analogies, and gradations that avoid the dialectic of identity and difference.[8] Foucault, given his decidedly more visual orientation, finds the hero of this form of thought in the practice of Andy Warhol.[9] Thinking stupidly treats the phony and genuine copy in the same fashion or, more to the point, refrains from questioning an image in terms of its relationship with reality. Such steps are necessary, Foucault contends, if we are to think the modern image outside of the dialectic of truth and falsity, with a view to its incorporeal effects. Notice how Foucault reformulates the Deleuzian problematic from one of thought to vision.

To think within the context of categories is to know the truth so that it can be distinguished from the false; to think a thought 'acategorically' is to confront a black stupidity and, in a flash, to distinguish oneself from it. Stupidity is contemplated: the look (*le regard*) penetrates its domain and lets itself become fascinated; carrying one along gently, its action is mimed in the abandonment of oneself; on its fluidity without form, one rests; one watches for the first jolt of an imperceptible difference, and with an empty look (*le regard vide*), one watches attentively, without fever, the return of the light.[10]

The thought of difference is thus, for Foucault, a type of visual practice, one that surrenders its identity as thought in favor of an empty but attentive observation.

4.4 ANDY WARHOL AND THE THINKING OF DIFFERENCE

As we saw, Foucault's landmark essay on Magritte ended cryptically with an affirmation of painting's nonaffirmation: Campbell, Campbell, Campbell, Campbell. In Chapter 3 it was explained that modernity uncoupled painting's traditional pairing of affirmation and resemblance. While Magritte was the primary focus of that essay, the reference to Warhol's serial presentation of soup cans opened the essay to a consideration of the course of modernity in general. To paint is no longer to affirm the necessity of an identification, but to circulate an image that undermines the pretensions of the original. For Foucault, Warhol's painted sign is, paradoxically, no longer a sign inasmuch as his repetition frees it from the obligation to signify. Here, the thesis is sustained in the language of Deleuzian metaphysics, with the anti-Platonic orientation of Warhol's thought occupying center stage. The passage is worth quoting at length, as it provides Foucault with a concrete example of how this thought functions within the realm of art.

This is the greatness of Warhol with his canned foods, senseless accidents, and his series of advertising smiles: the oral and nutritional equivalence of those half-open lips, teeth, tomato sauce, that hygiene based on detergents; the equivalence of death in the cavity of an eviscerated car, at the top of a telephone pole and at the end of a wire, and between the glistening, steel blue arms of the electric chair. 'It's the same either way,' stupidity says, while sinking into itself and infinitely extending its nature with the things it says of itself; 'Here or there, it's always the same thing; what difference if the colors vary, if they're darker or lighter. It's all so senseless—life, women, death! How ridiculous this stupidity!' But in concentrating on this boundless monotony, we find the sudden illumination of multiplicity itself—with nothing at its center, at its highest point, or beyond it—a flickering of light that travels even faster than the eyes and successively lights up the moving labels and the captive snapshots that refer to each other to eternity, without ever saying anything: suddenly, arising from the background of the old inertia of equivalences, the striped form of the event tears through the darkness, and the eternal phantasm informs that soup can, that singular and depthless face. (*TP*, 189)

Foucault's reading of Warhol, admittedly schematic, should be understood against the general misunderstanding of Pop Art on the part of European commentators. Instead of seeing it as a countervailing tendency within modernism itself, one with a different logic and politics, critics tended to construe it in terms of earlier movements that grounded claims to arthood in opposition to popular culture, that is, they viewed Pop Art as an art of negation.[11] In the case of Warhol, this is to miss the universally affirmative nature of his work. Foucault, on the other hand, understood that Warhol was perhaps the twentieth century's most stupid artist. Warhol: 'When I have to think about it, I know the picture is wrong . . . . As soon as you have to decide and choose, it's wrong. And the more you decide about, the more wrong it gets.'[12]

Warhol's art is the place of an ontological leveling where Mao and Mick Jagger coexist without rivalry, where images of the electric chair have no more charge than cans of soup, and where everyone is famous. Warhol is the great fan of everything mundane at the same time as his incessant celebration of the fantastic reduces it to banality. It's the same either way. Warhol: 'The reason I'm painting this way is that I want to be a machine, and I feel that whatever I do and do machine-like is what I want to do.'[13] It is, however, by moving into this stupidity of equivalencies, with blind affirmation, that differences are freed. By embracing and repeating the boundless monotony of commercial imagery, Warhol's work aestheticizes it rather than criticizes it. That is, his work does not denounce the images of late capitalism as instances of unreality, but erects itself in their unfolding. In doing so, it opens itself to the experience of difference, 'the sudden illumination of multiplicity itself.'

This shock of difference, whereby thought gathers itself in the recognition of its own difference, is a rather obscure point in Deleuze and Foucault precisely because it is paradoxical: How is it possible to think in terms of pure differences? The example of Warhol perhaps clarifies the process, and locates a precursor for its practice. The event Foucault points to is best witnessed in Warhol's films, exercises in affirmation, monotony, and the illumination of minor differences. These works do not attempt to capture essences, but continually overstep their references in attempting to repeat them completely. Formally, Warhol's films unfold in real time, use a single camera, and eschew zooming, panning, and tracking shots. The absence of cinematographic techniques minimizes the distance between objects, actions, and their celluloid impressions. In terms of content, these films redouble commonplace activities: *Sleep* (1963), *Eat* (1964), *Blow Job* (1964). They thereby turn the viewer's attention to the banal fabric of the modern world, while themselves attempting to disappear. The effacement of the artist by stupidity is nearly total: 'All my films are artificial, but then everything is sort of artificial. I don't know where the artificial stops and the real starts.'[14] Try as they might to record such activities with minimal thought and artistry, these films always contain moments of divergence, that is, points where it becomes impossible to remain enmeshed in the stupid. From monotony of repetition, differences emerge. Whether through technical flaws, happy accidents, or slight actions, banality is undermined by the small differences that engender thinking. In seeking to repeat their objects so closely, Warhol's films stage the differences set in motion by the initial affirmation. As Foucault explains, the repetition is a double affirmation, a kind of stutter that undoes the power of the Same (*TP*, 184). In Warhol, this takes place either through a break in the film's formal properties, which reinforce the necessary difference between the object and its double, or through the incorporation of insubstantial actions to disrupt the film's monotonous content.

Dave Hickey describes such instances of difference in Warhol's *Haircut* (1963), likening them to the accidents integral to good rock-and-roll.[15] According to Hickey, whereas jazz and abstract art function by bringing participants up against the limits of freedom—music never materializes if all insist upon improvising simultaneously—Warhol's films and rock music work through their failure to eliminate differences completely. Just as abstract art and jazz attempt to stretch the boundaries of expression, ultimately recoiling before the abyss of non-music, pop and rock give themselves over completely to the unfreedom inherent in the repetition of the same, only to be thrust outside of it by distortion, feedback, and other accidents. In *Haircut* the moment arrives when, in the monotony of the cutting, the man receiving the trim reaches into his pocket, pulls out a pack of cigarettes and lights one. Given the surrounding frames, this gesture amounts to major action. As Hickey recounts, 'Warhol's film . . . told us what we needed to know, that, no matter how hard we tried, . . . we probably *were* free, in some small degree, whether we liked it or not.'[16]

Warhol's films, with all their faux primitivism and universal affirmation, erupt on the exterior of the Same, making it possible to see and think differently. As Warhol once described it, 'Once you "got" Pop, you could never see a sign the same way again. And once you thought Pop, you could never see America the same way again . . . . The mystery was gone, but the amazement was just starting.'[17] Pop art, as Foucault presents it, functions as an exercise in altered perception. It immerses viewers in the signs cluttering their perceptual world in order to facilitate the development of a better vantage point. To philosophy, the obsession with everyday minutiae is tantamount to stupidity; the sudden illumination of difference that unfolds within, however, is, for the thought of difference, pure inspiration. This is the experience Foucault points to with his invocation of Warhol, an event that enables him to present in concrete form the new thought emerging in modernity's serial reproduction of imagery. If we are to understand the functioning of these images, which as we have seen maintain ambiguous relationships with reality, then we must rid ourselves of thought's Platonic biases. Reversing Platonism restores to thought the possibility of thinking the phantasms that form the self. While David Macey's assessment that Foucault's review does not explicate Deleuze's thought as much as join a dance of celebration, we must, nevertheless, attend to the differences between the two thinkers (*LMF*, 253). The point of divergence, as I have articulated it, amounts to the isolation of an ethical plane for analyzing the image. This should be taken in two senses: first, Platonism and the philosophy of representation rely upon a historically conditioned form of self-relation, itself determined by the will to contain the phantasm; and, secondly, phantasms have functions which themselves prescribe relationships between self and others. Foucault protests the denigration of simulacra-phantasms by pointing to their effects, and in short order we have the occasion to chart some of their functions. While they are indeed incorporeal, this does not mean they are unreal. Images, like statements, are events and can be described as such.

4.5 STYLIZATIONS OF FREEDOM: GÉRARD FROMANGER

Foucault's essay on the French hyperrealist painter Gérard Fromanger, 'Photogenic Painting,' opens up a broader historical perspective buoyed by further theoretical refinements, in order to attend to these image-events.[18] Foucault composed this essay for an exhibition at Galerie Jeanne-Bucher in February of 1975, '*Le désir est partout*' ('Desire is Everywhere'). According to Macey, the essay 'was a gesture of friendship' that did Fromanger's career 'a lot of good' (*LMF*, 337). We must not let the friendship between the two overshadow the genuine enthusiasm, easily detectable in this essay, which Foucault felt for Fromanger's work. Indeed, Fromanger's practice was deeply interesting to Foucault for ethico-historical reasons, and his images can be viewed as an extension of Foucault's interest in Pop Art. By the time Foucault composed this essay, luminaries such as Jacques Prévert and Gilles Deleuze had already championed Fromanger's work, and it is therefore doubtful that Foucault thought of this endeavor as a favor. It is best read, I contend, as a celebration of the practices of the image inherent in Fromanger's work, and the occasion to consider a central aspect of modernity, the rise of photography.

Fromanger was an attractive subject for many of the same reasons as Warhol. His work is a rigorous investigation of modern culture, in particular the culture of images born with photography's invention. The Hungarian artist László Maholy-Nagy (1895–1946) once proclaimed that in the modern world 'knowledge of photography is just as important as a knowledge of the alphabet,' famously predicting the 'illiterates of the future will be ignorant of the use of camera and pen alike.'[19] The ontogenesis of photography not only changes how images are produced, but the relationships we have with them as well as ourselves. For Foucault, Fromanger's work responds to this challenge, teaching something essential: how to love these images. Foucault sidesteps much of twentieth-century aesthetics' attempt to distinguish between photography and painting. He champions instead the practices that emerged on the frontiers of both media, where practitioners, unconcerned with identities, found pleasure in displacing themselves. 'Perhaps they were less in love with paintings or photographic plates than with the images themselves, with their migration and perversion, their transvestism, their disguised difference.'[20] For Foucault, Fromanger must be understood as the culmination of this 'shared practice of the image' developed on the borders of photography and painting between 1860 and 1900. And his incorporation of photographs into his paintings should be viewed as a reactivation of the image's transvestism (*PP*, 88).

Adrian Rifkin suggests that Foucault's essay explores contemporary art in the light of a ' "photogenic" *dispositif*.'[21] This formulation is potentially misleading. To understand this point, we should keep in mind the strategic nature of this term for Foucault, and note that it is conspicuously absent from this essay. Frequently translated into English as 'deployment' or 'apparatus,' its use began in 1975 as an effort to describe the multifarious relationships between knowledge and power in a given historical period. It effectively replaced the *episteme*, which Foucault began to broaden after the publication of *OT*. Whereas the *episteme* is primarily discursive in nature, a *dispositif* is more heterogenous, designed to capture the links between the discursive and nondiscursive. In a 1977 roundtable, Foucault enumerated a partial list of its elements: discourses, institutions, architectural developments, regulatory decisions, laws, administrative measures, scientific statements, along with philosophical, moral and philanthropic propositions.[22] As we have seen, the nondiscursive was never absent from Foucault's formulation of archeology. Indeed, the archeological description of painting was precisely one of the 'other archaeologies,' not directed toward the *episteme*, specified as a field of possible application. There, nondiscursive elements formed part of the consideration, even if described in terms borrowed from the analysis of discursive practice (*AK*, 193–194). The notion of the *dispositif* is therefore not a repudiation of the *episteme* but its expansion into a more strategic analysis. In Foucault's thought, it is used to analyze tactical uses of knowledge/power within a specified historical terrain. 'That is the *dispositif*: strategies of relations of forces supporting types of knowledge, and likewise supported by them' (*LJF*, 300). The *dispositif* offers a way to read texts, institutions, laws, architectural arrangements, etc., as moves within a field of force relations. 'For the logic of the unconscious, one must thus substitute a logic of strategy. For the privilege accorded . . . to the signifier and its chains, it is necessary to substitute tactics with their deployments (*dispositifs*).'[23] As has been noted, Foucault's own thought functions strategically in framing this notion. It is his effort to map the positions of opposition supplied in advance by a constellation of knowledge/ power, so they may be avoided.[24]

The *dispositif's* essentially strategic nature means any application to art must proceed cautiously. While its structure is present in the analysis of Fromanger—Foucault here considers the relationships between discursive and nondiscursive elements, in particular between technology, artistic practice, and theoretical reflection—it would be difficult to argue that he is mapping or making strategic moves. We should recall Foucault's comment from an interview, given just prior to the publication of this essay: 'What pleases me precisely in painting is that one is really forced to look. It is my rest.' He continues, 'It is one of the rare things on which I write with pleasure and without battling with anybody. I believe I have no tactical or strategic relationship with painting' (*QRP*, 1574). Given the content of this essay, it is more precise to say that Foucault performs the archaeology of a space of liberty. What interested Foucault in the *AK* was the regularity and transformation of painting's practices from one period to the next. The orientation here is the same: Foucault analyzes a period in which the rules of image production are called into question, and uses its description to understand our present.

What fascinates Foucault about the period between 1860 and 1900 is the ease with which images migrate, the relative absence of force relations, and the informality with which art professionals and amateur practitioners develop new means for sharing images. This is not to say Foucault is unaware of the contentious salon reviews, political squabbles, and court cases dealing with whether photography deserved the same artistic-political status as traditional forms of art. His essay begins by citing Neo-Classical painter Jean-August-Dominique Ingrès (1780–1867) vociferously denying that photography is art. The petition was submitted in the famous Mayer and Pierson case of 1862, where, despite protests from prominent artists, it was declared that photographs deserved the same copyright protection as paintings.[25] Nor does Foucault suggest Fromanger's art is without political relevance. Fromanger's work is widely recognized as having a political dimension, and Foucault contends his practice teaches an essential, political lesson: how to actively reappropriate the images with which we are bombarded. Foucault's primary argument, however, is that Fromanger's paintings should be understood as reactivating this bygone space of liberty where practitioners, freed from the constrictions of identity, took little notice of power struggles. The liberties described take place after photography's public demonstration in 1839, and last until the beginning of the twentieth century. For Foucault, these games traffic in false identities, willfully appropriate the work of others, and circulate forgeries—all minor offenses when measured against the love of images these practices inspire.

With recourse to the techniques of art professionals and the manuals of amateur photography, Foucault describes the practices by which this freedom was stylized. He cites the many means of transforming images developed by nameless practitioners as evidence of the great liberty at their disposal during the period of 1860 to 1900. Foucault fixes this date because by the end of the 1850s it was possible for artists to project and fix the camera's image upon the canvas itself. The practice was first embraced by portrait painters eager to spare their sitters time and money, but was eventually used for group portraits, genre paintings, and landscapes. By the mid-1860s it was common for painters to project photographic enlargements upon canvases and incorporate their outlines into their compositions.[26] Photographers themselves enhanced images with touches of paint, and many of the miniature painters displaced by photo portraiture found work as colorists (*AP*, 21–22).

The boundaries between the two media were further blurred by techniques whose intentions were more ambiguous. Elaborately painted scenes served as backdrops for indoor photographs so that when printed they would appear to have been taken outdoors. Other image-makers staged scenes from the history of painting that, upon being photographed, resembled photographs of real paintings. Foucault mentions Oscar Gustave Rejlander (1813–1875) and Julia Margaret Cameron (1815–1879), both of whom composed photographs as references to Renaissance paintings: Raphael in the case of Rejlander and Perugino for Cameron. Such moves are frequently interpreted as attempts by a nascent medium to ground claims to art-hood in a historical trajectory. For Foucault, however, these practices are less a strategy designed to secure status than an affirmation of the pleasures involved in perverting painting by photography and photography by painting. Within the medium of photography itself, Foucault describes the practices by which images were recombined to form new compositions. After the discovery of the gum-bichromate process, one could work on the negative to add or remove details, and many exploited this process to add painterly flourishes. Lastly, because of innovations made by amateur practitioners, the image was transported and fixed upon many different surfaces—eggshells, lampshades, porcelain, and glass—indicating a desire to free the image from the grasp of experts.

One might ask: were these practices 'no more than trifles, amateur bad taste, parlor games and family amusements?' Foucault's response is both yes and no. On the one hand, these techniques were developed by amateurs, whose productions might be viewed with mild amusement; however, they were also employed by professionals in the production of fine art. The essential thing is not to distinguish between the two; it is to grasp 'what a lot of fun was had with all these little techniques that made sport of Art,' and to see how, echoing the title of Fromanger's exhibition, 'Desire for the image was everywhere . . .' (*PP*, 88; The translation has been modified). It is important to note how Foucault described this vibrant culture in anti-Platonic terms, ones which highlight how, in contesting identity, these practices deepened the space of liberty. The resulting images provided pleasure because of their 'surreptitious differences.' Produced in games of deception, the point was to fabricate images to be 'mistaken for one another' or to appropriate and pass along another's image. Let us not dull this down: these are people who would, in a different cultural climate, face charges for theft of 'intellectual property.' Foucault does not skirt this issue. These practices are, on one level, 'theft' and 'unscrupulous,' with the best practitioners categorized as 'smugglers' (*contrebandiers*). And yet, in Foucault's mind, these transgressions are nothing when compared with the freedom they attest to and the communities to which they gave rise. He even asks, 'How might we recover this madness (*folie*), this insolent liberty that accompanied the birth of photography?' (*PP*, 84; The translation has been modified).

4.6 THE ANTI-PLATONISM OF TRANSVESTITE IMAGERY

Motivating these practices is the anti-Platonic love of the surreptitious that Foucault outlined in the excursus on Warhol. For the selfsame thought of the Idea, these practitioners substituted games of phantasms, simulacra, multiplicity, and transmigration to ridicule the idea that images could be possessed. 'To them nothing was more disgusting than to remain captive, self-identical (*identiques à soi*), in *one* painting, *one* photograph, *one* engraving, under the sign of *one* author' (*PP*, 84–85; The translation has been modified slightly; The italics reflect Foucault's own). From its inception, photography was decried as the triumph of the material over the Ideal. Not only does it replace idealized forms of art with base capture, it harbors the potential for deception. In Foucault's analysis of these games, we see again the importance of techniques in producing the tiny differences integral to freedom. Just as Rebeyrolle's practice created the freedom for forces to pass, new techniques for the image's transmission generate possibilities for its dispersion and fracture. For Foucault, the modern image must not be thought in terms of the figure of the Same, that is, one should not look to these images for what they supposedly represent. Rather one should attend to their existence, movements, and exchanges within a broader tapestry of image-events. The images that most interested him are those that draw viewers beyond themselves. It is this capacity for duplicity, confusion, and flight to which Foucault calls attention, terming these compositions 'beautiful hermaphrodite[s]' and a 'tranvestism' of the image (*PP*, 83–84).

Oscar Gustave Rejlander's *The Two Ways of Life* (1857) belongs intimately to these games of deception and identity contestation. While composite photographs, such as this, were common in England during the late 1850s, a composition this ambitious was unprecedented. At the time of its completion, Rejlander's photograph was the largest in the world. It was produced over six weeks, utilizing more than thirty different negatives (*AP*, 81). The subject of this complex image is at once reminiscent of Raphael's (1483–1520) *School of Athens* (1510–1511) and Thomas Couture's (1815–1879) *Romans of Decadence* (1847), and Rejlander's ambiguous pairing of the mind with figures of easy virtue proved intolerable in its day. For Foucault, the composite nature of this image is an indication of the artistic liberty created by the contamination of photography by painting, and, what is more, the possibilities opened by, as Foucault later describes it, 'refusing what we are.'[27]

While this place of liberty is quickly closed down by forces that Foucault only briefly alludes to—photography's professionalization, increasing abstraction in painting, and the partitioning of the two in twentieth-century aesthetics—the joy inherent in such games is nevertheless rediscovered in Fromanger's work. For Foucault, the simple pleasure of looking at these products should be stressed. In an interview, he describes his affection for hyperrealism and Pop art:

> It was without a doubt linked to their gambling upon the restoration of the rights of the image. And this after a long disqualification. For example, when, in Paris, where one is always very behind, one took out the canvases of some amateurish painters (*peintres pompiers*) like Clovis Trouille, I was all at once struck by my pleasure of looking and by the pleasure that people were having. It was a joy! A current passed, bodily, sexually. All of a sudden the incredible Jansenism that painting had imposed upon us for decades and decades became quite obvious (*sautait aux yeux*).[28]

Foucault's contrast between the joys of the image and painting's 'Jansenism' should not be taken as an indication that he deplored abstract painting. We have seen his affinity for nonrepresentational elements in Manet, and his sensitivity to the nonfigurative compositions of Paul Rebeyrolle. What Fromanger and the hypperrealists accomplish, however, is a lifting of the priority accorded to the 'destruction of the image,' in both practice and aesthetic discourse. Foucault characterizes this culture as follows:

> Gloomy discourses have taught us that one must prefer the slash of the sign to the round-dance of resemblances, the order of the syntagm to the race of simulacra, the grey regime of the symbolic to the wild flight of the imaginary. They have tried to convince us

that the image, the spectacle, resemblance and the false semblance, are all bad, both theoretically and aesthetically, and that it would be beneath us not to despise all these trifles. (*PP*, 88–89; The translation has been modified)

We see here not only Foucault's concern to challenge the favor granted to abstraction in the second half of the twentieth century, but also his evaluation of the affects, both pleasurable and pernicious, created by simulacra. The banishment of these images is not without consequences, for it results in the illiteracy against which Maholy-Nagy sounded the alarm. This neglect, by means of which we are 'deprived of the technical ability to produce images, subordinated to the aesthetics of an art without images, . . . forced to read them only like a language' leads to a situation in which 'we could be handed over, bound hand and foot, to the power of other images, political and commercial, over which we had no power' (*PP*, 89). Foucault instead envisions a thought adequate to the challenges posed by the accelerated proliferation of imagery, and a *savoir-faire* of image production that leaves us in a position to rearrange the signs that shape us. These are the lessons we might learn from an art that reimmerses us in the practices of the past. Fromanger restores credibility to all these amateur techniques, reactivates its space of liberty, and by dispelling these gloomy discourses, allows us to see the pleasures inherent in these games. Foucault: 'Pop art and hyperrealism have re-taught us the love of images. Not by a return to figuration, not by a rediscovery of the object and its real density, but by plugging us in to the undefined circulation of images' (*PP*, 90; The translation has been modified). Such a 'plugging in' encourages viewers not only to attend to images, but also to create their own. As such, these movements exhort us, 'To banish the boredom of Writing (*l'Écriture*), to suspend the privileges of the signifier, to dismiss the formalism of the non-image, to unfreeze content, and to play, scientifically and pleasurably, in, with and against the powers of the image' (*PP*, 89; The translation has been modified). Joining this game, participants invariably find themselves absorbed in the past.

4.7 LIBERATING THE IMAGE'S EVENT

Fromanger reactivates this bygone space of liberty through the very process of painting. His work, much like the thought of difference, follows the spectacle of consumer society—blankly, stupidly. The images forming the substratum of his paintings were chosen without much aesthetic consideration. Throughout the late 1960s and early 1970s, Fromanger exploited magazine and newspaper images, with little regard for their quality as photos. For *Boulevard des Italiens*, his 1971 solo exhibition at the *Musée d'Art Moderne de la Ville de Paris*, Fromanger and the press photographer Elie Kagan decamped to the second *arrondissement* of Paris. They took photos of this *quartier* on an ordinary February day.[29] These images, projected upon the canvas, formed the starting point for 25 of Fromanger's vibrantly colored paintings. This method was also used for the canvases in *Desire is Everywhere*, an exhibition which brought together Parisian street scenes, mass media images of the Toul prison revolt, and snapshots of Fromanger's tour of China. As Foucault insists, these are not photographs that naturally lend themselves to paintings but random photos culled from an amorphous flow of imagery. It is on this basis that Foucault draws a subtle but important distinction between Fromanger's art and American Photo-Realism. Whereas Richard Estes (b. 1932) and Robert Cottingham (b. 1935) select photos in anticipation of the painted form, Fromanger's are 'innocent of any complicity with the future painting' (*PP*, 92). This is significant, for what Fromanger's technique does is release the event (*événement*) circulating in these everyday scenes. Foucault attaches great importance to Fromanger's method—sitting in a dark room, staring at projected images—or, as we might say with Foucault's comments on Warhol in mind, his confrontation with stupidity. His is a thought that loses itself in the image to discover the lines of flight extending out from it. 'What is he looking for? Not so much what might have been happening at the moment the photo was taken; but the event which is taking place and which continues endlessly to take place in the image' (*PP*, 92). It is important that Fromanger does not use these photos to compose sketches, as many have done since the invention of the *camera obscura*; he paints directly upon the shadows cast by the photograph. Fromanger does not incorporate images through technique, but uses the techniques of painting to free up the image; his painting is not concerned with capturing images, but passing them along. Skipping the drawing stage, Fromanger speeds up the process to immerse viewers in the image's happenings. This, as Foucault explains, creates a tableau-event (*un événement-tableau*) on the photo-event (*l'événement-photo*). His process creates a 'short-circuit' that plugs the viewer into the image's multifarious possibilities. The process allows these images to be seen for the first time, that is, it enables viewers to see these images as events.

As we saw in Chapter 2, Foucault's involvement with Toul prison provided him with direct knowledge of practices of incarceration. Images of the December 1971 riot were disseminated by the news media, momentarily capturing the attention of the French nation. Of these images Foucault questions: 'Rebellious prisoners on a roof: a press photograph reproduced everywhere. But who has seen what is happening?' (*PP*, 94). When incorporated into Fromanger's web, however, both the tableau-event and photo-event are released. *Rebellion, Toul prison I* and *Rebellion, Toul prison II* (Figure 5) liberate the event that went undetected in the news photographs. Foucault: 'What commentary has ever articulated the unique and multiple event which circulates in it?' (*PP*, 94). In adding dashes of bright color to a drab background—itself a replication of the newsprint's tonal quality—Fromanger overcomes the seemingly static character of the media image. He brings the event to the fore, drawing 'countless celebrations from the photograph' (*PP*, 94). Through Fromanger's technique, these images are placed back in the flow of imagery and opened to multiple futures.

The distinction between Photo-Realism and Fromanger's method is again informative. Whereas the former investigates photography's optics, Fromanger's practice 'liberates a whole series of events'

Figure 5 Gérard Fromanger, *En révolte à la prison de Toul I* (left) and *En révolte à la prison de Toul II* (right), 1974, from the series *Le désir est partout*. Courtesy of Gérard Fromanger.

(*PP*, 98–99). Estes and Cottingham incorporate photographic viewpoints into their paintings, while Fromanger opens up a perspective on the photographic way of seeing itself. His canvases thereby enable us to see the events circulating in images—not only what might have been happening as the photo was taken, but the forces that continue to flow by virtue of the fact that they are images. Hyperrealists and Pop artists magnify or 'liberate' (*libère*) the multiplicity inherent in the image. As Foucault reiterates, this is not to insist upon the depth of imagery, or to resort to a form of commentary, but to move the image into future passageways: 'A painting peopled by a thousand present and future exteriors' (*PP*, 98–99). Simply put, Fromanger, like Warhol, teaches a way of looking/thinking that creatively confronts the photographic transformation of the world.

With Fromanger, post-representational art becomes an 'endless branching-out' (*buissonnement indéfini*). It accomplishes this by rejecting painting's identity as a place of capture. Its practice serves as a relay in the game of imagery. 'This is painting as a sling-shot of images,' Foucault exclaims, contrasting Fromanger's thoroughfare of images with the work of Eugène Delacroix (1798–1863), Edgar Degas (1834–1917), and Aimé Morot (1850–1913), all of whom used photographs to better capture reality in their paintings (*PP*, 90–95). Degas' canvases, for example, exploited the snapshot's instantaneous perception in order to capture positions and movements, most notably of ballet dancers, perceptible only to a photographic eye. Degas' compositions depict that which, prior to the advent of high-speed photography, would have been deemed unlikely by observers of the human form (*AP*, 139–143). Hyperrealists, on the other hand, do not capture reality in their use of photographs, but exploit the image as such: 'They do not incorporate images through their painting technique, they extend technique into the great sea of images. It is their painting which acts as a relay in this flow without end' (*PP*, 91; The translation has been modified). Hyperrealists are less concerned with an image's hold on reality than its possibilities for inaugurating new relations. They are content to drive along the image and assume their place next to all the other looters, past and present, in the game of images. These are less paintings than painting-events unfolding within a nexus of past and future relationships.

As we saw in his treatment of Paul Rebeyrolle, Foucault was tracking the passage of a force that moved from artist to canvas, and which was incorporated into the image, thus instantiating the movement necessary for the painting to escape representation. The spirit of the analysis is the same here: the work is thought as the product of forces that originate outside of it, pass through it, and have futures elsewhere. The figure of the artist is, at this point, of little interest to Foucault, as he attempts to understand these events in terms of the movements tying them together. The artwork is the momentary form that these forces are stabilized into, and, in the case of Fromanger, the site of their intensification. Deleuze's estimation that 'In all Foucault's work there's a certain relation between forms and forces that's . . . basic to his conception of politics, and of epistemology and aesthetics too' is correct, provided we do not strip Foucault's analyses of their content, as Deleuze's presentation of Foucault tends to do.[30] The insight, however, means that Foucault's approach is readily distinguishable from the varieties of formal analysis that tend to view visual arrangements in abstraction from the play of forces sustaining them. Thinking art in a post-representational fashion means that one attends to its dynamism, historical sources, and the play it inaugurates with its outside. As Foucault explains of the street scenes resulting from Fromanger's travels, 'The paintings no longer need to *represent* the street; they *are* streets, roads, and paths across continents, to the very heart of China or Africa' (*PP*, 98; The italics are my own). As we will now see in Foucault's reflections on the work of Duane Michals (b. 1932), photographs too contain this power of transport. They make things circulate: emotions, thoughts, dreams.

4.8 BETWEEN THOUGHT AND EMOTION: CREATING AND CONTESTING IDENTITY

In Duane Michals' carefully sculpted scenes, it is the intermingling of obscure thoughts and emotions that interests Foucault. These images, Foucault contends, cause thought-emotions (*pensées-émotions*) to arise in the viewer, though their provenance remains shrouded in mystery. They are the intensification of experience, and through a reversal of expectations, spaces that cause forces to pass. Further, we can say these movements of force are ethical, for they involve the construction and contestation of identity. As such, they are invitations to indiscretion, soliciting from the viewer, as Foucault himself attests, the desire to fix their movement within a narrative. This occurs even though, as Foucault insists, Michals' images do not capture appearances, but facilitate their escape. This flight results, as we will see, from Michals' turning the photographic medium against itself. His work exploits the expectation that photography is the medium most suited for capturing reality. Once again Foucault considers contemporary production in terms of the relationship between photography and painting. It is often wrongly assumed that only the latter provides access to 'spiritual' matters, while photography passively reflects reality. For Michals, this optical bias constitutes photography's decisive advantage as he sets to work exploiting viewers' predispositions. Foucault thus shows how in Michals' work the medium of photography is manipulated to create sentiments and thoughts otherwise off-limits. In annulling what Foucault terms the 'ocular function' of photography, Michals calls into question its very ethics, 'this heavy ethic of the regard,' exhibiting the invisible: dreams, emotions, movements of the mind, and phantasms.[31] In the process, he subverts the age-old prejudices upon which their capture was predicated, restoring to thought the possibility of thinking the obscure events of the soul (*l'âme*).

Foucault composed 'Thought, Emotion' for Duane Michals' 1982 retrospective at the *Musée d'Art Moderne de la Ville de Paris*. This essay is a startling distillation of the themes that have occupied Foucault's writings on visual art since *OT*. Not only does it extend his discussion of the rapport between painting and photography, it reaches back to his analysis of the techniques employed in Magritte's liquidation of the image. Foucault was invited to compose this essay by the novelist and photography critic, Hervé Guibert (1955–1991). Foucault accepted, despite his distaste for photo narratives, the genre in which Michals' work is traditionally placed, and devotes large portions of the essay to extricating Michals from this line of interpretation (*PE*, 1063). Foucault shows how Michals' work, on the one hand, invites narrative, while at the same time sets a series of snares designed to thwart such efforts. In the process, the viewer becomes trapped between the sensory and intellectual. As such, Michals' art should be viewed/understood as experiments that create ambiguous experiences.[32] Foucault thus places Michals among a group of artists whose works transmit experiences by rejecting the identity of a fixed *oeuvre* in favor of experiments opening beyond themselves. 'I like these forms of work which do not move forward like an *oeuvre*, but which open because they are themselves experiments (*des expériences*): Magritte, Bob Wilson, *Under the Volcano*, *The Death of Maria Malibran*, and, of course, H.G.' (*PE*, 1063).

The initials are, of course, those of Hervé Guibert, who later attained fame for his fictionalized accounts of the philosopher's life in '*Les Secrets d'un homme*' (1988) and *À l'Ami qui ne m'a pas sauvé la vie* (1990).[33] Foucault mentions his work in one other place, praising his *La Mort propagande* (1977) in an interview with Bernard-Henri Lévy as an example of the growing resistance to sexualization in literature. While *La Mort propagande* is ostensibly a piece of erotica, Foucault construes it as outstripping the injunction to put sex into words. Guibert's novel thus challenges modernity's monarchy of 'sexography.'

> [I]t seems to me that it is the opposite of sexographic writing which has been the law of pornography and sometimes of good literature: going progressively toward naming what is most unnameable of sex. Hervé Guibert begins the game with the worst and most extreme—'You want us to speak about sex, okay, let's go, you will hear more about sex than you have ever heard'—and with this unspeakable material he constructs bodies, mirages, castles, fusions, tendernesses, races, intoxications; the whole heavy coefficient of sex is vanished.[34]

Foucault likewise praises Malcolm Lowry (1909–1957), author of *Under the Volcano* (1947), in two other contexts. In a 1966 interview, he was placed in the literary tradition inaugurated by Mallarmé, according to which the novel is the place of the author's disappearance at the hands of language (*HEM*, 572). Lowry receives mention again in 1982 as an author who produces large emotions.[35] Given the emphasis on emotion in the Michals essay, it is most likely for this that he serves as a point of comparison, although the idea of disappearance is a Foucaultian mainstay and undoubtedly relevant to a discussion of Michals' images. Robert Wilson (b. 1941), the American visual artist, stage director, and famed collaborator of the composer Philip Glass (b. 1937), is mentioned just this once. Wilson's theater-installations emphasize images and movement over scripts and narrative. They are, one might say, worlds unto themselves, lasting upwards of 12 hours and involving large numbers of players. His visual environments have an affinity with Michals' work in that both use images whose connections are ambiguous and whose presence is fleeting. Likewise, in Chapter 3 we saw that Magritte was the painter of nonaffirmation. As Foucault explained, the artist's similitudes enabled painting to escape its moorings in an external referent. As such, Magritte's images belonged to their own realm, existing somewhere between sight and thought. The relationship between Michals and Magritte will be considered more closely in what follows. It will be explained how Magritte was an important source for Michals, and how certain of his works unfold according to processes termed 'Magrittean.'

Of these works that Foucault sets in orbit around Michals, the most significant is the film *The Death of Maria Malibran* (1971) by German director Werner Schroeter (b. 1945).[36] Foucault had a profound admiration for Schroeter's work, in particular *The Death of Maria Malibran*, and, according to David Macey, regretted not having secured his participation for the film adaptation of *Moi, Pierre Rivière*.[37] Foucault first mentioned Schroeter in a 1975 interview with the film magazine *Cinématographe*. He repeatedly rejected an interviewer's attempt to interpret European cinema in terms of sadism. Indeed, Foucault's statements in this interview are quite telling about his distaste for forms of aesthetics claiming Sade as inspiration: meticulous, ordered, regulated, and hierarchical scenes are fantasies of the disciplinary society and thus boring.[38] In this overly programmatic erotics/aesthetics, bodies and their pleasures are held in place by an anatomical vision suppressing differences, divergences, and free play. In Sadean erotics there is 'No open fantasy (*fantasme*), but a carefully programmed regulation' (*SSS*, 1686). Such an orientation is cinematographically bankrupt, leaving 'No place for an image' (*SSS*, 1686).

Foucault instead focuses on the new ways of handling the body in contemporary cinema, with *The Death of Maria Malibran* as his guiding example. Whereas the aesthetics of sadism delimit the body, carving it up into isolated organs, Schroeter's film celebrates its refusal to be ordered.

What Schroeter does with a face, a cheekbone, the lips, an expression of the eyes has nothing to do with sadism. It is a question of a multiplication, of a burgeoning of the body, an exaltation, in some way autonomous, of its lesser parts, of the lesser possibilities of the fragments of the body. There is an anarchization of the body where the hierarchies, the localizations and designations, the organicity, if you like, is being undone. (*SSS*, 1686–1687)

For Foucault, these new ways of relating to the body are born of cinematographic techniques: 'What the camera does *chez* Schroeter is not to detail the body for desire, but to raise the body like a 'pastry' and have it give birth to images, which are images of pleasure and images for pleasure' (*SSS*, 1688). Foucault's interviewer, on the other hand, insists upon the essentially sadistic relationship between camera and human form, citing Marilyn Monroe's treatment in *Some Like it Hot* (1959). On this point, we should recall the parallel Walter Benjamin once drew between the movie camera and invasive medical surgery. Not only does the camera's penetration into reality mask its relationship with the real as something composed and edited, its operations are far from benign. Whereas the painter is comparable to the magician-healer, curing sickness by a laying-on of hands, film images are produced through invasion. Benjamin:

—Magician is to surgeon as painter is to cinematographer. The painter maintains in his work a natural distance from reality, whereas the cinematographer penetrates deeply into its tissue. The images obtained by each differ enormously. The painter's is a total image, whereas that of the cinematographer is piecemeal, its manifold parts being assembled according to a new law.[39]

For his part, Foucault shuns the injurious aspects of Benjamin's characterization, focusing instead on the possibilities for flight inherent in cinema's new laws of perception. This, as we have seen, is one of the returning themes in Foucault's writings on art: the best images are those which, rejecting the confines of identity, make things pass: forces, pleasures, and emotions. For Foucault, Schroeter's images are thus ethical, teaching new ways of relating to our bodies along with those of others.

In a 1981 conversation with Schroeter, Foucault again describes these movements of pleasure by reading these films in terms of the passions linking their various characters. Understood as the mobility of sense that gives rise to thought and subjectivity, the passion Foucault finds in Schroeter is similar to the movements of emotion solicited by Michals. As Foucault characterizes passion,

It is a state, it is something which falls on you from above, that seizes you, that grasps you by the shoulders; it knows no pause and has no origin. In fact, one doesn't know where it comes from . . . . It is always a mobile state, but one that does not move toward a given point.[40]

In Schroeter's films, this force, not narrative, decides the characters' interactions and relates their 'stories.' Something equally obscure and pre-cognitive—thought-emotions—move through Michals' photographs.

> These are mixed thoughts, confusedly shared, it is this obscure circulation that Duane Michals presents to those who look at his photos, inviting them to the indecisive role of reader-spectator, and proposing to them thought-emotions (since emotion is this movement which stirs the soul [*l'âme*] and spontaneously propagates from soul to soul). (*PE*, 1067–1068)

In both Schroeter and Michals, these forces do not just inhabit the work; they pass to the viewer. These movements are not without consequence for the identity of the viewing subject, and function as invitations to transformation. They mediate the self's relationship with itself, introducing unfamiliar elements to disrupt the self-sameness of thought.

There is, as Foucault explains, an elimination of psychological depth in both Schroeter's films and Michals' photographs that frees them to follow the movements of emotion. These are not commentaries upon the mind's inner reaches, but traces left by the shared experiences of curiosity, pleasure, anxiety, and loss. Foucault describes this approach to creativity as a rejection of Platonism's search for essences:

> One is lost in life, in what one writes, in the film that one makes precisely when one wants to wonder about the nature of the identity of something. This is 'failure,' because one enters into classifications. The problem is precisely to create something that happens between ideas and to which it would be impossible to give a name, and it is thus at each instant trying to give a coloration, a form and an intensity to something that never says what it is. That is the art of living.[41]

Not only do these statements provide insight into Foucault's conception of creativity, they link his reflections on modern art's anti-Platonism to his understanding of ethics as aesthetic creation. If our problem there is to create new experiences and forms of life, then we must reject ideas in favor of those nameless occurrences that undermine the security of identities. We must reconsider those long-disparaged counterparts to ideas—emotion, passion, and sensation—precisely because they lead away from where we have been. This is what these engagements with art accomplish in the space of Foucault's thought, and one of the reasons why he found Michals' work so compelling.

In Chapter 2 we discussed Foucault's objections to the use of *oeuvre* in archaeological analysis. It was explained how this seemingly harmless notion threatened to blind us to the divergent happenings within individual works by subordinating what is unique to the already established. For Michals and the artists that Foucault places in his company, the problem is different: the rejection of *oeuvre* is indispensable for creation. Foucault lauds these practitioners because they escape classification, refusing to create works as works. These artists reject the received identities of their respective media in favor of experimentation upon their limits. On this point, one should note something hesitant and uncertain in all of them, as if they did not quite know themselves, or how best to escape from themselves. These are practices that unfold beyond themselves because they creatively play with their own identities. In attempting to understand why these figures appealed to Foucault, Gary Shapiro has noted their affinities with Foucault's own methods and experimental conception of philosophy (*AV*, 375–376). The concern, however, as I see it, is more intimately bound up with the creative movement produced by the rejection of identity itself. Therefore, in this context, we should cite not only those passages where Foucault links his approach to a type of Nietzschean experimentalism, but also those that insist upon escaping identification.

'What, do you imagine that I would take so much trouble and so much pleasure in writing, do you think that I would keep so persistently to my task, if I were not preparing—with a rather shaky hand—a labyrinth into which I can venture, in which I can move my discourse, opening up underground passages, forcing it to go far from itself, finding overhangs that reduce and deform its itinerary, in which I can lose myself and appear at last to eyes that I will never have to meet again. I am no doubt not the only one who writes in order to have no face. Do not ask me who I am and do not ask me to remain the same: leave it to our bureaucrats and our police to see that our papers are in order. At least spare us their morality when we write.'[42]

Lest we miss the seriousness with which Foucault attempted to live out his labyrinth, we should remember that in 1980, Foucault proposed a game called the 'year without a name' in which books would appear without identifying their authors in the hope of producing genuine communication.[43] Further, such a strategy of rejecting the confines of identity is suited not only to artistic and literary productivity but informs the very substance of a living and breathing philosophy. 'The displacement and transformation of frameworks of thinking, that changing of received values and all the work that has been done to think otherwise, to do something else, to become other than what one is—that . . . is philosophy' (See *EST*, 327).

Despite Foucault's initial reservations about the invitations to narrative inherent in Michals' serials, it is this commitment to searching out new experiences of the self that ultimately fascinated him. Thus, in his presentation, Foucault focuses on the ways in which these photos escape—narrative, visibility, representation, and identification. He describes the maneuvers by which the medium was experimentally distorted, to supply the viewer with intimations of the forces of thought and emotion residing outside of representation's visibility. Nothing could be closer to Foucault's experience of philosophy. As we have seen, such escapes are made possible with recourse to the archive. For this reason, Michals is understood as a photographer who overturns the conventions of photography by reaching into its history to unearth alternative strategies.

4.9 STRATEGIES OF THE IMAGE: CREATING THE THOUGHT-EMOTION

Like Fromanger, Michals' images are invigorated by the interaction between painting and photography. Whereas one often expects that painting provides access to the more fleeting aspects of human existence, and photography unfettered access to the real, Michals reverses this relationship. His photos mock these expectations, at the same time as they are the events which annul photography's ocular ethic. As both Foucault and Michals point out, metaphors of vision have dominated photographic practice since its inception. Michals' work reverses this orientation, freeing photography from the obligation to fix reality so that his images might circulate as thoughts. Michals: 'Photographers are usually defined by their eyes but our real definition is our minds.'[44] This is not to say that Michals replaces photography's ocular ethic with something purely intellectual. His photographs are not a Platonic recolonization of the realm of images. They are the visible occasion for an obscure communication between Michals and his audience, or between the viewer and him- or herself. Foucault's employment of the hyphenated thought-emotions (*pensées-émotions*), underscores the bodily, visible, and mobile basis of thought, much as he articulated in his essay on Deleuze. Michals frees photographs from their identity as photos, so they will resonant between body and mind. No longer immobilized places of capture, these experiences overtake the viewer. They efface the boundaries between artist and viewer, as Foucault attests, remarking upon its inability to limit the effects of these images:

I am drawn to them as experiences. Experiences which were only made by him; but which, I don't know how, glide toward me—and, I think, toward anyone who looks at them—inciting pleasures, worries, ways of seeing, sensations that I have already had or that I anticipate having to undergo (*éprouver*) one day. And thus I always wonder whether these experiences are his or mine, knowing full well that I owe them to Duane Michals. (*PE*, 1063)

Such reflections are relatively commonplace in the theorizations of art that attempt to account for the power of photographic images. It is asked, for example, why certain images 'hold,' 'move,' and 'compel,' while others do not?[45] Given the thrust of Foucault's essay, along with its references to his ethical investigations, we should note not only how this analysis treats the image's properties, but also how Foucault charts its ability to enter into the subject's constitution. Michals' images take the viewer beyond him or herself, mingling the work's thought-experiences with the identity of the viewer. By means of Michals' experiments, we share experiences that are not our own in such a way that we are no longer self-possessed. The experiences that pass, like those in Schroeter's *The Death of Maria Malibran*, disrupt the viewer's habitual orientation and open up new possibilities of self-relation. This takes place when images, carefully constructed, stimulate the emotions to give rise to mixed and obscure thoughts. Again, Foucault rejects the suggestion that these are psychological investigations, pointing instead to the ways in which identity, thought, and subjectivity form themselves upon the movements of the phantasm. As such, Foucault's reflections on Michals are part of the effort to develop a form of thought that does not cut itself off from the differences that are its constitutive possibility. Michals' work is well suited for this project inasmuch as it is marked by hybridity, internal dissimilarities, and complexities that break representation.

Through a series of techniques, traps, and reversals, Michals alters the photographic medium to mix the orders of thought and sensation together in the image. His photos supplant their own identities as photographs in order to present the phantasms that exceed representational photography. Foucault quotes Michals: 'Everything can be photographed, most of all the difficult things in life: anxiety, the sorrows of childhood, desire, nightmares' (PE, 1063). As Foucault explains, this is accomplished only on the condition that photography abandon its pretension to capture and instead serve as a thoroughfare for these thought-emotions. Continuing with the quote from Michals, 'The things that one cannot see are the most meaningful. One cannot photograph them, only suggest them' (PE, 1063). Through a series of interventions, his photographs allow reality to escape, recording evidence of passage, transition, and disappearance. Foucault divides these procedures into four more or less distinct categories: paint added to finished photographs; the employment of photography to capture disappearance; the addition of words to images; and the deployment of a series of ironies—evasion of what should have been recorded, the frustration of normal sequential ordering, focuses on tangential objects, and an ironic timing that avoids a central action.

The first game takes place on the borders of photography and painting. Foucault explains of a series of prints which Michals painted over: 'I cannot prevent myself from seeing these painted photos as a laugh addressed to hyperrealism, an ironic reference to all attempts to bring reality before the photographer's eye with the incandescence of painting' (PE, 1064). If hyperrealists employ photographs in the construction of paintings, that is, if 'underneath' the hyperrealist's brush there lurks a photo, Michals, painting over actual photos, makes visible the interdependency of the two media. While hyperrealists trespass into photography, hoping to liberate the event with painting's intervention, Foucault and Michals meet this presumption with an amused smile: 'As if it were not the photo which allowed the real to escape' (*PE*, 1065). For Michals, photography is the source of the initial flight, one facilitated by our assumption that, with photography, what we see is what we get. His gesture mocks painting's claim that it alone provides access to the phantasm. And his work renders volatile our relationship with the real, supplying only the intimation of something passing or, for Foucault, 'haunting' these images.

In the series *Man Going to Heaven* (1967), five sequential photographs record a man ascending a staircase. In the first image, the figure is barely distinguishable from the darkness pervading the scene. Traces of light at the top of the photo shape the stairway; still one wonders how much is visible in this image, and how much supplied by its connection with the others. In the next frame, a bright light emanates from the doorway at the top of the stairs, flooding the scene. The figure of the man is illuminated and the perspective has changed slightly as he begins his ascent. The third image continues this momentum: he has passed into the center of the image and the stairway appears longer as the man traverses it. The man has nearly reached the summit in the fourth image; only his naked legs are visible, with his white flesh enveloped by the light. All that remains in the final image are the soles of the man's feet, a visual quip about the locus of personal immortality. Despite our knowledge that these are separate images, the sense of continuity and movement is unmistakable. Although these images are static, the action is palpable and the disappearance real. For Foucault, this amounts to a reversal of the ethic of photography, whereby evanescence itself is the subject of this series. A vanishing resists visual capture, but nevertheless serves as the series' guiding premise. Michal's contradictory undertaking 'creates the narrative of disappearance,' in order to generate the thought-emotions that accompany the presentiment of death and the hope of transcendence (*PE*, 1065).

The image is also lifted into the realm of thought through a series of 'Magrittean' processes. Michals had unusual access to the somewhat reclusive painter, convincing him in August of 1965 to pose for a number of photographs.[46] Magritte's paintings were important to Michals' conception of photography, instilling him with the conviction that visual art should be more than representation. As Michals explains the result of the encounter: 'I was freed from just looking.'[47]

The images Foucault classifies as Magrittean are not the portraits of Magritte, but those that Michals crossed with language. Michals began to experiment with this technique in the early 1960s, just prior to their meeting. For Michals, the inclusion of language was an attempt to break with the photo's essentially static nature, as Foucault has it, to remove all that is 'stifling' (*étouffant*). Michals recounts: 'I began to write for my photographs, not because I thought it was clever but because I was so frustrated with the photograph . . . . I began to write because I was trying to talk about what you cannot see in the photograph.'[48] As explained in Chapter 3, only by certain conventions do we anticipate that the words surrounding an image clarify it. Magritte's work exploited this expectation, deploying language to demonstrate the folly inherent in collapsing the visual and linguistic orders. These gestures do not stabilize images but have the opposite effect, and Michals' brief texts inevitably raise more questions than they answer. Not only are they elliptical but, as Foucault reminds us, they are composed such that it is unclear whose thoughts we are encountering. Do they belong to the people populating these photos? The viewer? Duane Michals? And if they belong to the latter, are they the thoughts that occupied him as he composed the photograph or those that occurred sometime afterwards? Foucault multiplies these questions, forcing us to admit we know not where these words originate, nor what they might signify.

This process is Magrittean, for linguistic indeterminacy undermines high levels of visual clarity. The images that Foucault focuses on are crisp presentations that eschew techniques, such as double exposure, which blur the image. They are opposed to those 'Baconian' images in Michal's repertoire, ones that, deriving inspiration from the painter Francis Bacon, efface and distort figures. These Magrittean photos, which ostensibly stake the greatest claim on the real, have been 'drained of all reality' (*vider de toute réalité*) not through the image's effacement, but the ceaseless shifts in context imported by language. These texts do not hold the image in any sort of finality, but destabilize it, 'exposing it to invisible breaths' (*PE*, 1066). With the same movement as *Ceci n'est pas une pipe*, a once-familiar object becomes uncanny in encountering language. The texts wrapping these photos thus allow them to take on a new life and to escape the confines of the photographic identity. Michals' images thus circulate between sensation and thought—in that space between seeing and saying.

Foucault also describes a series of ironies that Michals deploys to thwart the photographic medium's propensity for representation. In staging actions that ultimately evade capture, Michals' works evoke experiences necessarily absent from the space of representation. In contrast to the photographic tradition where the sequence relates a narrative or presents an action over time, Michals' serials belong, in Foucault's words, to a 'completely different economy' (*PE*, 1068). He explains: 'Instead of approaching an event (*événement*), a scene, or a gesture step by step in order to capture it, he lets them escape, as if by clumsiness or powerlessness' (*PE*, 1068). In works exploiting an 'irony of timing,' central actions are merely hinted at through the interplay of titles, words, and images. What surpasses representation is precisely what is thought-felt. In *The Moments Before The Tragedy* (Figure 6) a man and woman exit the subway, observed by a somewhat sinister-looking man—bald and clad in leather. As they reach the street, the couple part ways, with the respectable-looking man completing his exit by the fifth and final frame. The series ends with the woman walking away from the camera, presumably being followed by the menacing-looking man. Since we are indeed *before* the tragedy, we are never certain what the catastrophe consists of. Upon reflection, we realize we have been tricked by Michals, who leads us to believe the event involves the woman being accosted by the man in the leather jacket. This conclusion is, of course, unjustified by the photographic evidence and relies upon a plethora of assumptions. Where is the tragedy? Perhaps it involves the respectable-looking man's passing from the frame. Did he see that oncoming truck? Perhaps the man taken for a perpetrator will be visited by tragedy. Did the construction crew above adequately secure that girder? Through this irony of timing something essential about tragedy is expressed: events are tragic precisely because they befall us when we least expect and because they arise in unknown quarters.

Other ironies exploit the narrative conventions that inevitably attach themselves to the serial form. In what Foucault terms the 'irony of linking,' Michals joins images in unconventional ways. Rather than following a linear narrative, these series are driven by logics of free association, emotions, desire, and sensation. Likewise, traditional order is contested through the 'irony of side-issues' (*ironie de l'à-côté*). Instead of focusing on a narrative's central figures and actions, the camera becomes distracted by details surrounding the scene. Peripheral elements continually displace one another in a game

Figure 6 Duane Michals, *The Moments Before the Tragedy*, 1969. © Duane Michals. Courtesy of Pace/MacGill Gallery, New York.

of visual hyper-metonymy that perpetually shifts the focus of the series. The logic here follows from the obscure passions that attach us to objects; following this train invariably removes us from conventions of narrative and compels thought to unfold according to the experimental relationship that Michals creates.

Michals' employment of the serial is not, therefore, the attempt to represent movement, time, or proceedings in a story. His sequences are deliberately distorted to evoke the timeless thought-emotions that could never reside in representation. The series is the place where photography's identity can be fractured and divided. Echoing his contention that seeing and saying belong to different realms, Foucault explains that experience and time, although intermingled, are never reducible one to another.

If Duane Michals has often made recourse to sequences, it is not because he sees them as a form capable of reconciling the instantaneous of the photograph with the continuity of time in order to tell a story. It is rather to show, through photography, that even if time and experience do not cease to play together, they are not part of the same world. (*PE*, 1069)

Even though time and experience are brought together in Michals' series, they are never fully reconciled, with both escaping capture. This disjuncture of temporal experience is an invitation or, in Michals' words, a 'gift' to the viewer. This space is the opening where the thought-emotion circulates and becomes active. In causing these forces to pass between viewers, these images restore a freedom to seeing, thinking, and feeling. They make it possible to be otherwise.

CONCLUSION

All these processes, techniques, and games that fascinated Foucault are attempts to do the same thing: transform the ethic of photography so that it might yield an intimation of the invisible events forming human life. Love, desire, fear, and death are the subject matter of Michals' photographs, but only inasmuch as he is willing to contest their identity as photographs. As we saw in Chapter 2, one aspect of Manet's modernism consisted of the fact that he bent the painting medium and forced it to present the invisible. For Foucault, Michals belongs to this trajectory. Through a series of interventions, his photographs allow to escape the reality they were supposed to represent. Thus filmed are traces of transition, disappearance, and indefinable sentiments. Refusing the traditional orientation toward the visible is a necessary step in creating an event, the means by which force passes from image to viewer, providing him or her with a thought-emotion. The crucial difference between Michals and Manet, however, is that Michals does not simply indicate that there is something not seen, something occurring outside of representation; he restores phantasms to thought, thus moving the viewer emotionally and intellectually.

In Foucault's discussion of Gérard Fromanger's hyperrealist compositions, we saw his celebration of the power of images to disclose new possibilities of relating to others and ourselves. Fromanger's paintings were championed by Foucault quite simply because they taught us how to take pleasure in looking. This analysis of the ethical relationships inherent in the modern image is, as we have seen, predicated upon challenging thought's Platonic constrictions. To chart the surface, the effects, and the nexus of image-events, it was necessary to conceive of thought as something produced by the encounter with differences, rather than practice it as that which contains them. Even in Foucault's discussions of figurative art, his thought refuses the categories of representation, moving in the field announced by archaeology. This allows him to describe the ways in which images move, differ from period to period, along with the ways in which they continue to resonate as events. The anti-Platonic characteristics of modern art announced in Foucault's essay on Deleuze are carried through into his final course at the *Collège de France*. There, the concern will be to explain more fully the anti-Platonic character of modern art, consider the grounds for the artwork's traditional claim to truth, and to reinsert it within the practices of life from which it springs. The account that Foucault gives is nothing short of cynical.

CHAPTER 5

THE CYNICAL LEGACY

INTRODUCTION

The final facet of Foucault's genealogy of modern art must be understood on the basis of a certain paradox: the type of truth the work of art maintains in modernity is not at all modern and is in fact the reactivation, within modernity, of a classical form of truth. As we will see, this is paradoxical, because modernity, in particular philosophical modernity, is characterized by the decoupling of truth and *askēsis*, whereas the modality of truth that is at work in modern art is a redeployment of an ancient form of truth, i.e., *parrhēsia* (frank speech). If, as we are wont to believe, the modern work of art plays the role of a critical, truth-speaking device, on what basis does it do so? Where does the guarantee of its truthfulness come from? Foucault suggests that it is the relationship between the stylization of existence (*askēsis*) and a highly idiosyncratic form of truth (*parrhēsia*) that sustains the modern work of art. *Parrhēsia* is an ancient modality of speech that maintains a precise epistemological connection between truth and belief on the basis of a few essential characteristics that will be discussed below. For Foucault, the work of art manifests truth, despite the anti-Platonic proclivities for dissimulation we explored in Chapters 3 and 4, because of its intimate connections with the critical self-stylizations of the artist. Accordingly, the work of art cannot maintain its links with truth unless there is a corresponding exercise (*askēsis*) or ethical labor performed by the would-be subject of such a discourse, which enables him or her to become worthy of the truth. In this, Foucault sees the legacy of Hellenistic Cynicism and its strategy for securing *parrhēsia* on the basis of a life already become truth-disclosive. Just as the Cynic's *parrhēsia* is secured by ethical work, so too with modern art: critical, frank, and true 'speech' is the product of a life fashioned as critical, frank, and true. These reflections are presented throughout Foucault's final series of lectures at the *Collège de France* during the winter of 1984. As such, they are intimately bound up with his final investigations into the history of the rapport between subjectivity and truth. More specifically, these lectures form part of the historical analysis of the various ways in which people constitute themselves as subjects of truth by means of a relationship with themselves. This problematic emerges through a shift away from the trajectory announced in the first volume of the *History of Sexuality*. It is therefore necessary to consider briefly the contours of this project.

5.1 MODIFICATIONS TO THE *HISTORY OF SEXUALITY*

As we have seen, concerns with identity and subjectivity inform Foucault's writings on art in the 1970s and early 1980s. We saw, for example, in Foucault's analysis Duane Michals' hybrid images that in the aesthetic-cognitive encounter, thought could be freed from itself to experience sentiments which are not its own. This viewpoint corresponds with Foucault's understanding of the ways in which subjects are produced in and through deployments of power/knowledge. That is, in such analyses, the subject is considered as a position implied by movements of force in a given historical period. Through his study of the Christian practice of confession, however, Foucault felt it necessary to broaden his analysis to include the ways in which individuals, by means of taking up relationships with themselves, seek to constitute themselves as subjects capable of articulating the truth, either about themselves or the world around them. This is what occupied Foucault from the late 1970s until his death in June of 1984: the different historical ways in which men and women have undertaken to transform their beings in order to become either the subject or object of truth. Taking up a relationship with oneself is the domain Foucault calls ethics. 'I think we have to distinguish between the code that determines which acts are permitted or forbidden . . . and the kind of relationship you ought to have with yourself, *rapport à soi*, which I call ethics.'[1] Foucault contends that while the Western moral code—the rules governing what is forbidden and permissible—is relatively constant, the ways in which individuals constitute themselves as subject to morality's coded truths is variable. Following the obligations to truth inherent in the practice of confession, along with the modifications or practices of self required for the articulation of these truths, Foucault undertook to write the history of the ways in which people have taken up relationships with themselves in order to put themselves in the position to speak the truth.

In his 1983 lectures at the University of California, Berkeley, Foucault, echoing the distinction between the two critical positions he located in Kant, again highlighted two different orientations toward questions of truth within the philosophical tradition. The first tradition poses questions of truth by concerning itself with formalizing the criteria for true statements and principles of sound reasoning. The second direction, also inaugurated by Greek philosophy, raises questions of truth by investigating the truth-teller him- or herself. That is, it problematizes the activity of speaking the truth, reflecting upon the ethical, political, and spiritual conditions that must be fulfilled before someone can be considered a truth-teller. In short, the second form of analysis is distinguished by its insistence on posing the question, what price must be paid before one can attain the truth?[2]

This second vantage point, hinted at in the analyses of Christian confession in the first volume of the *History of Sexuality* and the 1974–1975 lecture course *Abnormal*, became the primary focus of Foucault's research and thus redirected the *History of Sexuality* project.[3] What is referred to as the 'Final Foucault' corresponds to the work undertaken after the completion of the first volume in 1976. Although in the years following its completion, Foucault would move away from the project's initial formulation, supplementing it with a history of the techniques of the self, we should not overplay this as a negation of the project's initial outline. We can say that the study of the construction of sexuality as a discourse, announced by the first volume, was replaced with a genealogy of ethics, 'understood as a history of the forms of moral subjectivation and of the practices of the self . . . meant to ensure it.'[4] During this time, Foucault turned to the techniques, developed in ancient philosophical schools, by which men sought to transform themselves. Practically, this means that throughout the early 1980s, Foucault pursued key moments in the history of subjectivity by means of their textual articulations. He attempted to isolate the practical transformations the *rapport à soi* underwent in Greek and Roman philosophy, the Christian faith, and the human sciences with an eye toward our modern sense of selfhood.

5.2 THE MODERN SENSE OF SELF

While this project is tragically incomplete, we can perhaps conclude—given the outline of the *History of Sexuality*, as well as various hints in lectures and interviews—that Foucault was primarily interested in determining how our modern sense of self is formed and how this subjectivity comes to be linked to a particular form of self-knowledge. That is, Foucault sought to unearth the historical accidents by which our identities became wedded to the project of discovering and articulating the truth of our individual natures. Why is it that our deepest truths are thought to reside in sexual desire, and why is desire taken as the truth of identity? Among many scattered references there is the suspicion that practices of self-discovery, this hermeneutics of desire, are part of the machinery that constructs obedient subjects and founds the human sciences. Foucault:

> I think that if we do not take up the history of the relationship between the subject and truth from the point of view of what I call, roughly, the techniques, technologies, practices, etcetera, which have linked them together and established their norms, we will hardly understand what is involved in the human sciences . . . and in psychoanalysis in particular.[5]

Partly in order to unearth the historical soil for this submissive subjectivity, and to disrupt processes of unreflective subjectivation, Foucault turned to early Christian, Roman, and Greek technologies of the self to see 'to what extent the effort to think one's own history can free thought from what it silently thinks, and so enable it to think differently' (*UP*, 9).

Such a perspective allows Foucault to call attention to the ways in which subjectivity itself differs from period to period. Schematically, we can say that in Christianity, the relationship of the self to itself is one of decipherment, discovery, and renunciation. In Greek ethics, the task was to create or transform the self, with the aim of constituting a self that has mastery over itself. In Hellenistic and Roman ethics, this tendency was taken to the extreme, with the achievement of self constituting the goal of assiduous labor. Christian practices of the self attempt to achieve purity, purging the self of any desires that obstruct a direct relationship with God. Pagan practices endeavor to transform the subject, performing the modifications that enable the practitioner to play an active role in civic life: the Greek must learn to govern himself before he can govern others. The Christian's task, however, is to realize that the real self exists elsewhere.

At the heart of these different practices of self is the notion of *askēsis*. In this Greek term, Foucault finds a common root for the Christian practices of austerity and pagan practices of self-stylization. For Foucault, the term *askēsis* encompasses a broad number of exercises (meditations, memorizations, abstinences, examinations of conscience, relationships with others, the keeping of notebooks) that aim at training and transforming the self. This perspective allows Foucault to explain how certain practices of the self are carried over from one epoch to the next. A number of his final lectures trace the appropriation of Greek and Roman exercises by early monastic communities, and highlight the different inflections they were given within a theological framework. In the texts of John Cassian (360–435 C.E.), Foucault finds a theoretically refined formulation of the Christian soul and the obligation for the examination of conscience. For Cassian, confession is not merely a listing of wrong actions, but a continuous verbal activity that attempts to put the obscure depths of desire into words, thus expelling it from consciousness. As Foucault points out, Cassian uses the image of a money-changer to explain the task of sorting pure from impure bits of consciousness. '[T]he moneychanger . . . to whom one goes to change coins of one currency into . . . another, does not accept just any money. He checks and tests each coin, examines what he is given and accepts only those he thinks are good' (*HER*, 299; The translation has been modified). The examination of consciousness is thus an *askēsis* designed to engender a state of intellectual purity. The moneychanger of thought is not, however, the invention of the Christian monastery. If, for Cassian, the moneychanger's task is to distinguish between pure and impure coins of thought, the Stoic moneychanger must recall a day's events and measure them against his philosophical precepts. For Epictetus (55–135 C.E.), 'We have to be moneychangers of our own representations . . . vigilantly testing them, verifying them, their metal, weight, effigy,' not to root out hidden desires, but with the aim of 'recalling principles of acting.'[6] The aim in Stoic ethics, therefore, is not purity, but a presence of self that enables the philosopher to put into practice Stoicism's theoretical tenets. The *askēsis* ensures that the theoretical lessons become active within the subject, hence forming the basis for action.

By highlighting the links between *askēsis* and truth, differences between the modern and classical periods come to light. Whereas Hellenistic philosophy never ceased to occupy itself with questions about how a subject must be modified before he or she could attain the truth, modern philosophy has dedicated itself to avoiding this question. Foucault:

> I think that the modern age of the history of truth begins when knowledge itself and knowledge alone gives access to the truth. That is to say, it is when the philosopher (or the scientist, or simply someone who seeks the truth) can recognize the truth and have access to it in himself and solely through his activity of knowing, without anything else being demanded of him and without him having to change or alter his being as subject. (*HER*, 17)

The 'Cartesian moment' is this severing of the rapport between truth and what Foucault understands as spirituality, that is, the work that one must perform on the self to make oneself worthy of the truth. In philosophical terms, the Cartesian moment is the revaluation of two principles, the *gnōthi seauton* (know yourself) and the *epimeleia heautou* (care for yourself). While the former is much more familiar to us today, the latter, according to Foucault, is essential for understanding ancient philosophy. Throughout the ancient world, self-care serves as a type of ethical bridge that moves one from philosophy, understood as 'the form of thought that asks what . . . enables the subject to have access to the truth,' to spirituality, i.e., 'the search, the practice, and experience through which the subject carries out the necessary transformations on himself in order to have access to the truth' (*HER*, 15). The care of the self thus designates the 'ensemble of transformations of self . . . that enable one to have access to the truth' (*HER*, 17; The translation has been modified slightly). Knowledge of the self, loosely understood, was one form that this care took. It was, for example, necessary to know the self—its limitations, strengths, relations—in order to effectively care for it. Self-knowledge was, however, destined to eclipse other forms of care, becoming the dominant mode of subjectivity in the modern period.

As such, the links between self-knowledge and *askēsis* are forgotten. With philosophy's entry into modernity, it is no longer necessary to alter the self in order to attain truth. 'Before Descartes, one could not be impure, immoral, and know the truth. With Descartes, direct evidence is enough. After Descartes, we have a nonascetic subject of knowledge.'[7] The modern experience of subjectivity is precisely this forgetting of the spiritual pursuit of truth.

Throughout the 1982 lecture course *The Hermeneutics of the Subject*, Foucault insists upon the broader field of practices that our modern experience denies. Within the tradition where truth is attained only by means of an *askēsis*, philosophy determines possible relationships between a subject and truth, while spirituality undertakes the exercises necessary for cementing those relationships. Foucault mentions three characteristics of philosophical spirituality: (1) Truth is never given directly to the subject. '[Spirituality] postulates that for the subject to have right of access to the truth he must be changed, transformed, shifted, and become . . . other than himself' (*HER*, 15). (2) The movement by which this transformation takes place is a work of *erōs* and *askēsis*. The subject must transform itself; it engages in a work of the self upon the self, the basis of which is a love for the truth. (3) Spirituality holds that truth illuminates the subject. Truth is not simply recompense for labors undertaken, but the completion of the subject, which brings tranquility of soul. Foucault explains, 'The truth enlightens the subject; the truth gives beatitude to the subject' (*HER*, 16).

Essential for our purposes is the recognition that, traditionally conceived, truth has a spiritual price. That is, truth was something that required a certain action on the part of the subject, who hoped to become worthy of incorporating and articulating the truth. Foucault explains:

> In European culture up to the sixteenth century, the problem remains: What is the work I must effect upon myself so as to be capable and worthy of acceding to the truth? To put it another way: truth always has a price; no access to truth without ascesis. In Western culture up to the sixteenth century, asceticism and truth are always more or less obscurely linked. (*OGE*, 279)

It is this intersection of truth and the practices of the self that is contrasted with the modern paradigm of truth as self-evidence.

Within modern philosophy, it is no longer necessary to work toward something that promises a reward. Instead, the subject is capable of attaining the truth by virtue of being a subject. The criteria of self-evidence suffices as an epistemological guarantee, and the subject is therefore no longer required to undergo the lengthy process of incorporating truth into his or her *bios*. Foucault explains that 'we enter the modern age (I mean, the history of truth enters its modern period) when it is assumed that what gives access to the truth . . . is knowledge (*connaissance*) and knowledge alone' (*HER*, 17). Consequently, truth is no longer conceived as something desirable, precious, and capable of rendering the subject beautiful. In the modern period, truth becomes knowledge, where the fulfillment once attained is transformed into the indefinite accumulation of facts and figures.

5.3 SUBJECTIVITY AND BEAUTY

To combat the sway of this disinterested pursuit of knowledge, Foucault unearths an alternative path out of the ancient period, one that allows us to rethink the relationships between subjectivity, truth, and beauty. In his 1984 course, *Le Gouvernement de soi et des autres: le courage de la vérité*, Foucault presents the fragments of a neglected tradition in Western thought, the aesthetics of existence. These practices of subjectivity are those 'actions by which men . . . seek to transform themselves, to change themselves in their singular being, and to make their life into an *oeuvre* that carries certain aesthetic values and meets certain stylistic criteria' (*UP*, 10–11). According to Foucault's reading of the history of philosophy, these practices of the self are obscured by two factors: first, the history of metaphysics that construes the self as an ontological unity distinct from the body, designated by the term *psuchē*; secondly, the relegation of aesthetic considerations to the domain of objects.[8] Both factors—the first, which holds that the self is something different from the lived life and the second, which limits the application of aesthetic values to the world of inanimate objects—leave ethics in a state of paucity. In a late interview, Foucault explains the consequences of this effacement, 'We have hardly any remnant of the idea in our society that the principal work of art which one must take care of, that main area to which one must apply aesthetic values, is oneself, one's life, one's existence' (*OGE*, 271). As these comments demonstrate, Foucault's research was not the disinterested pursuit of a historian, but that of a thinker attempting to provide new resources for living in the present. Foucault diagnoses and challenges our compartmentalization of aesthetics:

> What strikes me is the fact that, in our society, art has become something that is related only to objects and not to individuals or to life. That art is something which is specialized or done by experts who are artists. But couldn't everyone's life become a work of art? Why should the lamp or the house be an art object but not our life? (*OGE*, 261)

This suggests that Foucault's genealogy is tantamount to an intervention, inasmuch as it seeks to effectively change the way we relate to a given field of experience. And Foucault often spoke of his histories as attempts to uncover the treasury of cultural innovations— procedures, ideas, practices, and techniques—that, while not permitting a simple reactivation, could constitute a point of departure for the analysis, critique, and transformation of our present (*OGE*, 261). This consists of expanding the notion of aesthetics to include reflection on life, and as we will see, the consideration of the ways in which art and life have been linked throughout modernity.

5.4 BEAUTY AND TRUTH: THE CASE OF SOCRATES

The preoccupation with creating a shining and beautiful existence is very ancient and by no means the exclusive province of philosophy. Foucault explains that the theme can be found, in a relatively well-developed form, in Homer and Pindar. The Socratic moment, however, is an essential turning point, for it links the project of composing a beautiful existence with speaking the truth. This is a key point in the history of subjectivity, marking the place where the aesthetic project of self-transformation is inserted into games of truth and falsity. Foucault explains his interest in this Socratic intervention:

> [W]hat I would like to recapture is how truth speaking (*dire vrai*), in this ethical modality that appeared with Socrates at the beginning of Western philosophy, how this truth speaking (*dire vrai*) interfered with the principle of existence as a work to be fashioned in all its possible perfections. How the care of the self, that a long

time before Socrates had been commanded by the principle of a dazzling (*éclatant*) and memorable existence . . . was not replaced, but taken up again, inflected, modified, re-elaborated by the principle of truth speaking (*dire vrai*), by which one must confront oneself courageously. How the objective of a beautiful existence and that task of giving an account of oneself combined themselves in that game of truth. That art of existence and true discourse; the relation between the beautiful existence and the true life, the life in the truth, the life for the truth—that's a little of what I would like to try to recapture. (*GSA2: 29 Feb.*, 13–14)

For Foucault, the true life (*vraie vie*) that results from this encounter between the aesthetic tradition and the Socratic requirements of truth-speaking has four distinct facets, all derived from the Greek word *aletheia*: un-hidden (*non-dissimulé*), without mixture (*non-mélangé*), right or straight (*droit*), and immutable and incorruptible (*immuable et incorruptible*).[9] The true life is, in the first place, a life that hides nothing and is not afraid to show itself before others. This life does not recede into the shadows, precisely because there is nothing shameful about it (*GSA2: 7 Mar.*, 51–54). Secondly, it is a life that is unified and without superfluous or distracting elements. The opposite of this form of life, of course, is the man enslaved by his desires and carried off in many directions at once (*GSA2: 7 Mar.*, 54–56). Thirdly, the true life is right because it follows established laws and customs. There is thus a demonstrable rectitude in the life of the person who has respect for order and *nomos* (*GSA2: 7 Mar.*, 56–58). Finally, the true life is consistent, insulated against rapid change, corruption, or perturbation. In this consistency, and the resulting sovereignty, the philosophical practitioner thereby learns to take pleasure in himself (*GSA2: 7 Mar.*, 58–60).

The Socratic project of speaking the truth on ethical and political matters finds its condition of possibility in this life fashioned as true. In such cases, it is the harmony between the speaker's *bios* and *logos* that serves as a guarantee for his truthfulness. Foucault: 'The basis of *parrhēsia* is, I think, this *adaequatio* between the subject who speaks, and who speaks the truth, and the subject who conducts himself as this truth requires' (*HER*, 406). In this sense, Plato's dialogue *Laches* is of special interest for the way in which Socrates' manifestation of courage endows his words with added force when applied to ethical/educational matters. Socrates is justified, in the eyes of his interlocutors Nicias and Laches, to speak about ethical matters, because of the demonstrable harmony between his discourse and actions.[10] Within the Socratic conception of the true life, this harmony between *bios* and *logos* guarantees the truthfulness of speech.

5.5 THE CYNICAL REVERSAL

In these investigations into the relationships between truth and subjectivity, the Cynics occupy a privileged position, for they carry this theme of the true life to its breaking point, making its reversal (*retournement*) the essential condition for speaking the truth. In the Cynical *askēsis*, we find the scandalous return of the true life, inasmuch as the Cynical life is designed to serve as the visible reminder of their unbreakable hold upon the truth, as well as the inadequacy of other philosophical schools. Cynicism takes these themes, as they are articulated in the Platonic tradition, to their very limits, issuing philosophy a defiant challenge: put up or shut up. For Foucault, Cynicism appears as a scandal within ancient philosophy precisely because it has the courage to realize itself most directly in a form of life and to challenge philosophy on those grounds.

Cynicism would, to some extent, play the role of the broken mirror for ancient philosophy. The broken mirror where all philosophers can and must recognize themselves, in which one can and must recognize the same image of philosophy, the reflection of what it is and of what it should be; the reflection of what he is and of what he would like to be. And then at the same time, in this mirror, he perceives a grimace, a violent, ugly (*laide*), unsightly (*disgracieuse*) deformation, in which he would in no way recognize himself or philosophy.[11]

The form of life Cynicism espouses thus surpasses and reverses the true life, insisting that the real philosophical life is a life lived at the limits. In posing the question of the true life, Cynicism does philosophy one better, contending that the true life is really, as Foucault has it, the other life (*vie autre*). Cynicism's other life is a life lived as a rupture with traditional forms of existence. Its transgression occurs through the addition of a fifth principle, 'change the value of money,' the Cynical invention that undoes the traditional conception of the true life.

This cornerstone of the Cynical tradition is based upon a series of events in the life of Diogenes of Sinope (400–325 B.C.E.). Diogenes' father was a moneychanger. After counterfeiting charges were brought against him, both father and son were exiled. The young Diogenes traveled to the Oracle at Delphi, where he received this command: 'Change the value of money.' Foucault, highlighting the similarity between the Greek words for money (*noumisma*) and law (*nomos*), suggests: '"Change the value of money," it is also "take a certain attitude with regard to what is convention, what is rule, what is law"' (*GSA2: 7 Mar.*, 62). We thus see the Cynical variation on the image of the moneychanger, common to both Stoic and Christian ethics. For the Cynics, however, the project is not simply to test and evaluate the movements of thought, but to evaluate and change the customs, habits, and laws of society at large. For Foucault, it is a principle that commands the Cynic to 'break the rules,' and constitute a life that ruptures conventions. The ethical project the Cynic sets himself is not simply the devaluation or destruction of currency. He is instead, as Foucault interprets it, faced with the task of erasing all the false effigies unnecessarily built up upon the currency. The Cynic's work is reductive, seeking to put a coin back into circulation only after restoring its true value (*GSA2: 7 Mar.*, 63–64).

The addition of this principle effectively destabilizes the four facets of Platonism's true life. It takes them from within, carries them to the extreme and reinterprets them in a 'carnivalesque' fashion. We are dealing here with much the same movement by which the artistic rules of formation are called into question by a work or artist. The addition or subtraction of a given element operates a work of destructuring upon the regularity of an artistic practice, at the same time as it contains the rules for a new formation. Foucault thus understands the addition of the Cynical economic principle in much the same way as the work of Manet. It is an active extrapolation that carries the regularity of a practice to its limits and exposes those limits.

The Cynical reinterpretation of the true life is best grasped by looking at the *askēsis* by which the Cynic stylized his existence. The dog's life (*bios kunikos*) is the dramatic staging of the true life inspired by Socrates, in which all tendencies therein are put on display and turned against the true life to disclose its limitations. Foucault explains that this involves the Cynic's resolve to, in all senses of the word, '*expose* his life' (*GSA2: 14 Mar.*, 7). The Cynical life is at once on display and at risk. This exposure and risk occur not simply in the discourses the Cynic delivers but in the very exercise of his life. The life of a dog is, first of all, a life that is without shame or modesty. Like the Socratic life, this life seeks to hide nothing; however, the Cynic's life is actually lived in public view. 'It is the *mise en forme*, it is the *mise en scène* of life in its material and quotidian reality . . . . The life of the Cynic is un-hidden in the sense that it is really, materially, physically public' (*GSA2: 14 Mar.*, 39). Living in the streets, the Cynic thus 'dramatizes' the principle of un-hiddenness, making possible its 'transvaluation' (*GSA2: 14 Mar.*, 39). Through its unwavering application of this principle to life, the Cynic 'argues' that if nothing needs to be hidden it is precisely because nothing natural is bad.

Secondly, the dog's life is indifferent to the false needs occupying other men. Finding contentment in himself, the Cynic has no need of external attachments and is fulfilled without making commitments that constrain freedom. Cynical indifference is thus the physical dramatization of the life without mixture. Concretely, this takes the form of an active and deliberate poverty, one more extreme than the passive poverty that seems to be part and parcel of the philosophical life. Active poverty is an *askēsis*, an exercise of the self upon the self, which searches for new forms of renunciation. It is not the hypothetical poverty found in Stoic meditations, but a physical exercise designed to produce hardiness. 'Cynical poverty must be an operation that one performs on oneself to obtain the positive results of courage, resistance and endurance . . . . It is an elaboration of oneself in the form of visible poverty' (*GSA2: 14 Mar.*, 49–50). The Cynic's poverty, however, is also an indefinite labor, one that must continually find new means of renunciation. As such, the faithful application of this principle leads to the reversal of the life without mixture. Under this *askēsis,* the Cynic's life becomes one of humiliation, dependence, and ugliness. Foucault points out that by following the life of purity and autonomy to its limits, the Cynic ends up promoting dirtiness, ugliness, dependence, and abasement—values completely at odds with the Greek espousal of physical beauty.[12] We should note here that despite Foucault's obvious sympathy for the Cynic's insistence upon posing the question of the philosophical life, he is apprehensive about this legacy, this neglect of beauty in philosophical ethics. Of the Cynical adoption of poverty, ugliness, and slavery, he explains, 'And this, I think, is important and introduces at the same time in ethics, in the art of conduct and unfortunately also in philosophy, the values of ugliness which they still have not abandoned' (*GSA2: 14 Mar.*, 52). Such a valorization is seemingly at odds with the aesthetic-ethics Foucault was cultivating, even if, as we have seen, in other contexts he praised Manet's aggressive deployment of ugliness in the destructuring of aesthetic conventions. The Cynic's resolve to live life as a dog also overturns the notion of a right and straight life. Within the philosophical tradition, the straight life was the life in which there was a consistency between an individual's *logos* and *bios*. Thus, incumbent upon the philosopher of the true life was the task of conforming his being to nature, as well as to customs and laws. On the one hand, the true life is committed to living in accordance with nature and espouses the values of naturalness. On the other hand, philosophy demonstrates a respect for human conventions and social laws, often at odds with the natural world. It is this latter tendency that Cynicism will not cease to repudiate in its unflinching affirmation of animality. Foucault thus describes the dog's life as 'barking' and 'diacritical' or, simply, capable of distinguishing good from bad, virtue from vice, and, most importantly, natural from unnatural (*GSA2: 14 Mar.*, 26). The Cynic must be capable of making distinctions, if he is to live free of superfluous additions. As was the case with the Cynic's poverty, this is not simply a neutral affirmation of the fact of animality, but a challenge to be accepted and an obligation to be lived. Within the Cynical *askēsis*, the principle of conformity tends exclusively toward a life in accordance with nature. Neither conventions nor human prescriptions are to be obeyed, hence the Cynic's endorsement of incest and cannibalism.[13] In a philosophical context where the animal provides the point of refraction by which the human being can be differentiated and defined, as we witness in Aristotle's thought, the Cynic's positive valuation of animality not only overturns accepted customs but also reverses the direction of thought. Animality is thus an exercise of the self and a scandal for philosophical thought.

The dog's life is, finally, a life for the protection of others. Foucault's Cynic is also a guard dog whose life is lived in service. Epictetus once described the Cynic in military terms, as a 'scout' (*kataskopos*), explaining that he is a watchdog for humanity, sent in advance to determine what is favorable and what harmful (*GSA2: 29 Feb.*, 23). For Foucault, this function should be understood as the reversal of the true life, considered as the immutable or sovereign life.

Traditionally, sovereignty is construed as a relationship of self-mastery, whereby the practitioner at once takes care of himself and as a result is beneficial to others. The Cynics point to the folly of having numerous such sovereigns running about. Within the Cynical framework there is only one king, and he is, of course, the Cynic. In the famous encounter between Diogenes and Alexander of Macedonia (356–323 B.C.E.), as presented by Dio Chrysostom (*c.*A.D. 40–110), the young king became aware of his inferiority before the true king, Diogenes. On Foucault's reading, Alexander is brought to the realization that 'the only way to be a real king is to adopt the same type of *ethos* as the Cynic philosopher' (*FS*, 132). The belligerent nature of this exchange reveals that the Cynic is a sovereign who attacks, not out of any sort of weakness, but, in Foucault's words, as an 'aggressive benefactor.'[14] The Cynic bites, it is true, but the real victim is vice. Thus, Foucault can claim that the Cynic's combat is above all 'spiritual.' His actions and words are barbs directed 'against a certain state of humanity' (*GSA2: 21 Mar.*, 24). As such, his intentions are genial, urging humanity to change its ways. The Cynic is therefore the 'king against the king' (*le roi anti-roi*), 'who fights at once for himself and for others' (*GSA2: 21 Mar.*, 25). By dramatizing the life of sovereignty, the Cynic overturns this life, transforming it into something like the modern militant life.[15] Thus, the Cynical *askēsis* recognizes that sovereignty does not come without a fight, and the Cynic takes this fight to himself, before carrying it to others. In his struggles over vice he is indeed the king, but given the state of humanity the Cynic is destined to wander through this world unrecognized, with his actions misunderstood.

These practices of Cynicism are, for Foucault, somewhat paradoxical in that they are at once completely familiar—drawn almost entirely from traditional philosophical themes—and at the same time the scandalous fulfillment of the philosophical life. Cynicism, as Foucault conceives of it, is a performative reversal of the true life. Through its staging, the true life (*vraie vie*) returns as the other life (*vie autre*), a life completely heterogenous with everyday existence. This life's alterity does not simply suggest to those who behold it that there exists a choice to be made at the level of existence. The radically different subjectivity of the Cynic testifies, in its being, to the possibility of a different world (*monde autre*). The life of the Cynic has, under the direction of its *askēsis*, become a vehicle for disclosing the truth.

Another life for another world. It is necessary to say that we are . . . very far from many of the themes of . . . the ancient true life; however, I think that one has there the core of an ethical form that is completely characteristic of the Christian world and the modern world. To that extent, Cynicism as the movement by which the theme of the true life became the principle of the other life and the aspiration for another world, it seems to me that one has in Cynicism the matrix, or in any case the germ of an ethical experience that is fundamental in the Occident. (*GSA2: 21 Mar.*, 38–39)

The Cynic's life is at once a complete rupture with ordinary existence and the manifestation of the truth of existence. According to Foucault, what the Cynics transmit, across Western culture, is the idea that an ethical form of life can be a vehicle for disclosing truth. For this reason, the burgeoning monastic communities in Christian Europe quickly absorbed its practices.[16] The startling and visual display of truth, in the body of the Cynic, is why this ethical category has maintained such a hold on the Western imagination. This way of relating to oneself as something with the potential to ground and disclose truth is also, for Foucault, modern inasmuch as this link between truth as *parrhēsia* and *askēsis* is rediscovered in modern art.

5.6 CYNICISM AS A TRANSHISTORICAL ETHICAL CATEGORY

Modern art is, for Foucault, unique in that it is the place within modernity where the ancient rapport between truth and *askēsis* is redeployed. At nearly the same time as the spiritual tradition is being disqualified in philosophy, it is being rediscovered as the ground of artistic practice. The type of truth operative in modern art is one obtained by means of an ethical labor in which the subject who announces the truth must first undergo a series of modifications. Artistic practice is so intimately joined with *askēsis* that it even provides Foucault with a means of describing the notion more generally. 'This transformation of one's self by one's own knowledge is, I think, something rather close to the aesthetic experience. Why should a painter work if he is not transformed by his own painting?'[17] For Foucault, modern art is similar to the strategies of the Hellenistic Cynics in that it maintains a very precise relationship with truth, understood as *parrhēsia*, within a limited theoretical framework.

The distinctly performative quality of Cynical *parrhēsia* ensures that this is not simply another effort to reduce the functioning of art to a linguistic model. It is instead an attempt to highlight the relationships that artistic work maintains with truth, ethics, and life. The critical function art performs in contemporary life, along with its tendency to investigate its own bare essentials is, for Foucault, proof that Cynicism is not extinct with the ancient world. In fact, he claims that modern art is one of the vehicles by which Cynicism has persisted throughout Western culture.

The second half of Foucault's 29 February 1984 lecture at the *Collège* is, by his own admission, a bit of intellectual wandering. In this promenade Foucault explores how, far from being extinct with ancient philosophy, Cynicism might be understood as a 'historical category that traverses—under diverse forms and with varied objectives—all of Western history' (*GSA2: 29 Feb.*, 38). This should give us pause, for the thinker who pointed to the great ruptures in Western thought is now attempting to highlight 'the permanent existence of something that can appear as Cynicism across all of European culture' (*GSA2: 29 Feb.*, 45). Foucault even goes so far as to reject several studies of Cynicism that mark strong discontinuities between ancient and modern Cynicism. Foucault's 'transhistoric Cynicism' presupposes that we do not look for any sort of doctrinal fidelity or even the same styles of existence within different periods. The isolation of this Cynical transmission requires that we construe it as an ethical category, as a way of relating to oneself, that is, as an attitude. This way of life is one which links, in a very precise fashion, life and truth. Cynicism is, above all, 'the putting in contact a form of existence and the manifestation of the truth' (*GSA2: 29 Feb.*, 45). Foucault thus rejects the common characterization of Cynicism as a philosophy of extreme individuality. For him, the heart of Cynicism is this ethical relationship which makes the stylization of existence truth's essential precondition. With this understanding of Cynicism as an ethical-aesthetic category, Foucault thus isolates three main movements that make life the means of transmitting truth, or which construe '*le bios comme aléthurgie*' (*GSA2: 29 Feb.*, 46).

First, Christian culture is one of the ways that Cynicism is transmitted across Europe. Foucault admits that the textual references to the Hellenistic Cynics are sparse, but insists that the mode of comportment in certain Christian communities warrants the comparison. With the Franciscans, for example, practices of poverty, begging, and wandering (*errance*) strip life down to its essentials, and are designed to facilitate ministry. For St. Gregory of Nazianzus (325–389 C.E.), Cynical philosophers are to be emulated inasmuch as they devote their entire lives to the relentless pursuit of truth. Gregory praises the Christian ascetic Maxim: 'I compare you to a dog, not because you are impudent, but because of your *parrhēsia*.' Greogory continues: '[Y]ou are the best and most perfect of philosophers—*martyron thes aletheias*—being the martyr, the witness of the truth' (*GSA2: 29 Feb.*, 35). For Gregory, Cynical *parrhēsia* is not simply an instance of speech; it is an active witnessing which fashions life as truth-disclosive. This is an essential component of Foucault's portrait of the Cynic, for truth and life are immediately linked in a scandalous manifestation.

The second way Cynicism is transmitted across European culture is through revolutionary political movements. Militant organizations, from the beginning of the nineteenth century onward, cease to be solely political projects. They instead necessitate a specific form of life, one that testifies to the truth of the revolution's goals, thus reactivating the Cynical ideal of a life fashioned as witness to truth. According to Foucault, implicit in these movements is an ethics which holds that life, in the very form that it takes, must be wholly consecrated to the revolutionary project, and thus a demonstration of revolutionary values. Life is thus lived as a rupture with the ideals of a society, in order to 'manifest the concrete possibility and the evident value of another life' (*GSA2: 29 Feb.*, 54). For Foucault, the tendency toward *gauchisme* that is part and parcel of the European revolutionary project is a resurgence of the Cynical life, where life, practiced as a 'scandal of the truth,' functions as the grounds for critique (*GSA2: 29 Feb.*, 56). It would be interesting, Foucault contends, to track how beginning in the 1920s the French Communist Party began to replace the revolutionary life with an existence stylized in conformity with traditional values (*GSA2: 29 Feb.*, 57).

The final vehicle of Cynical transmission that Foucault considers is modern art. For him, the notion of the 'artistic life' that develops at the end of the eighteenth century, the idea that the life of the artist must be constituted as a testimony to what art is in its truth, is one of the ways in which the Cynical mode of life is carried forward and given a new form within modernity. According to Foucault, life itself serves as a foundation for art's traditional claim to truth, just as the Cynic's claim to *parrhēsia* is cemented by *askēsis*. This conception of

truth is given a decidedly Foucaultian inflection when it is explained
that the truth at play in the work of art is, like the Cynic's life, an
anti-Platonic search for existence's bare essentials.

5.7 THE CYNICAL TRUTH OF MODERN ART

In order to understand more precisely what Foucault has in mind, it
is important to note that the Cynical tradition he isolates is an ethical
category that sustains the artwork and not simply any Cynical themes
contained within specific works. In this second category, for example,
we could place the satires and comedies of Antiquity that expressed
ideas inspired by the Cynic school. Foucault also considers and
dismisses the existence, in the medieval world, of fables and other
literary expressions that deployed Cynical motifs. Despite a thematic
resonance with Hellenistic philosophy, neither forges the direct links
between life and art that is the hallmark of this ethical category.
It is above all in modern art—which Foucault here dates with the end
of the eighteenth and beginning of the nineteenth century—that
Cynicism, understood as a certain way of relating oneself to truth, is
reactivated and transmitted throughout culture. As Foucault explains:
what is distinctive about art in modernity is that it 'places in connection (*rapport*) a style of life and the manifestation of truth,' thereby
making life the essential condition for the manifestation of truth
(*GSA2: 29 Feb.*, 60).

The idea of the artistic life, as Foucault explains, is born in the
Renaissance with biographical projects such as Giorgio Vasari's
(1511–1574) *Lives of the Artists*. Implicit in such undertakings is the
idea that the life of an artist must in some way be eminent, or 'not
wholly commensurable with those of others' (*GSA2: 29 Feb.*, 60).
Within modernity, however, this idea is radicalized such that the
artist's life must not only be singular, but also 'constitute in the
very form that it takes a certain witness to what art is in its truth'
(*GSA2: 29 Feb.*, 60). In much the same way that the Cynic's *bios* was
devoted to securing the grounds for *parrhēsia*, the artist—inasmuch
as he or she purports to be a truth-teller—must also style a life
which could serve as 'authentification for the work of art' (*GSA2:
29 Feb.*, 61). Distinguishing modernity's demands from those of the
Renaissance, Foucault explains, 'Not only must the life of the artist
be sufficiently singular so that he may create his work (*oeuvre*), but
his life must be, in someway, a manifestation of art itself in its truth'

(*GSA2: 29 Feb.*, 60). That is to say, the artist's life must itself become a work of art and bear witness—much like the Cynic's body, doubled cloak, and staff—to the creation and transmission of truth. What is thus essential for construing modern art as a form of Cynicism is the way in which life, under the rigors of an *askēsis*, secures the work's claim to truth. From this perspective, the practices behind the artwork must also be considered when assessing its merits. This is perhaps reflected in the twentieth century's obsession with artists' biographies, the conditions under which works are produced, and the processes, i.e., practices by which they are created. If Foucault is correct, then what lies behind the impulse of this strand of modernist criticism is the will to discover the conditions for the possibility of an art object's relationship with truth.

Modern art is also a type of Cynicism inasmuch as its search for truth takes the form of an anti-Platonic reduction to the elementary truth of existence. As we saw in Chapter 4, the anti-Platonic products of modernity refuse to investigate the essence of things and to remain self-identical, instead circulating phantasmatic products to complicate thought and identity. Foucault himself demonstrated a preference for those works that unfold as obscure experiences, rather than those designed to solicit definitive thoughts. In these final lectures, anti-Platonism is expanded to include a third refusal, that of imitation and ornamentation. Foucault contends that, within modernity, art is such that it 'must establish a real rapport with that which is no longer the nature of ornamentation . . . [and] imitation' (*GSA2: 29 Feb.*, 61). The anti-mimetic direction art opens up can be understood as a 'stripping naked,' an 'excavation,' and a 'violent reduction to elementary existence' (*GSA2: 29 Feb.*, 62). This excavation of the elemental is characteristic of both literary and visual modernity, and a tendency Foucault contends is increasingly prevalent from the nineteenth century onward. In this context he cites Baudelaire, Flaubert, and Beckett as well as Manet and Francis Bacon (1909–1992). These are artists whose products find ways to contest what is deemed to be unnecessary in what has come before. Their works interrogate the practices governing artistic production and endeavor to shed these trappings. Again, this is more than Greenberg's thesis on modernity translated into a French idiom. It will be recalled that Greenberg ultimately retains a form of *mimēsis* by defining modern art as the 'imitation of imitating,' a move that allows him to isolate the processes of each art and remove them from the broader cultural sphere.[18]

'Anti-Platonic' designates more than the reductive function by which art investigates its own formal conditions; for Foucault it encapsulates art's capacity to move from a narrowly defined aesthetic sphere to impact society at large. It is that tendency of art to 'constitute itself as a place of eruption . . . from what in culture is not right, or at least does not have the possibility of expression' (*GSA2: 29 Feb.*, 62). Whereas for Greenberg, artistic modernity is a rather insular affair, with art engaged primarily in a dialogue with itself, modern art, for Foucault, constantly transgresses its own boundaries, impacting the broader culture. We should recall that these comments appear in a context where Foucault was attempting to think through the links between works of art understood as forms of critical truth and the processes of subjectivity sustaining them. To claim, as Foucault does, that the work of art is reductive and anti-Platonic is not to grant special privilege to the work's material elements, but to recognize that each work is potentially unstable and capable of overturning what has come before it, both in the world of art and culture at large.

In Chapter 2, we saw that Foucault understood Manet's art as a rupture with the established distributions of painting's formal elements. The key word in the 1984 course is eruption. The 'eruption' of the elementary is the means by which art establishes a polemical role with previous artistic conventions and the complacency of culture. Foucault is here calling attention to the movement by which an aesthetic challenge moves into the more general sphere of culture. For Foucault, this is one of the ways of understanding the scandal produced by Manet's work: it bursts upon the scene, overturning established conventions. He explains:

[T]here is an anti-Platonism of modern art, which was the great scandal of Manet, and which is, I believe, the profound tendency . . . that you find again from Manet up to Francis Bacon if you like, that you find from Baudelaire up to Beckett or up to Burroughs, etc. Anti-Platonism of art as the place of eruption of the elementary, the stripping nude of existence (*mise à nu de l'existence*); and by that, art establishes in culture, establishes with social norms, with values and aesthetic canons a polemical relation of reduction, of refusal and aggression. And it is what makes modern art since the nineteenth century this incessant movement by which each rule that is posed, or each rule that is deduced, induced, or inferred from each of the preceding acts, finds itself rejected and refused by the following act. There is a sort of permanent Cynicism regarding all established art in all new forms of art. (*GSA2: 29 Feb.*, 62–63)

These comments on the essentially polemical role that art plays with respect to aesthetic conventions and social values reiterate Foucault's claim from 1975 that the aggressiveness found in Manet's work was its 'systematic indifference to all aesthetic canons' (*QRP*, 1574). Further, it is the same type of movement that Foucault attributed to the Cynical *askēsis*: the Cynical practice of life contests the ordinary philosophical conception of existence and, by reducing it to its essentials, transforms it. This Cynical conception of modern art highlights its general mistrust of aesthetic canons and culture more generally. Implicit, of course, in Foucault's analysis is a rejection of all theories of modernity that isolate art from history, culture, ethics, and life. Just as the Cynic did not limit his critique to the world of philosophy, modern art is not, for Foucault, an autonomous realm, cut off from the broader culture. As we have seen, the works Foucault was drawn to are ones that have ethical or political relevance. Manet's work is exemplary in this respect, because it is an instance where cynicism for aesthetic propriety translates into a critique of social norms. It should also be noted that Foucault here sees Manet's work as providing something of the essential energy for the modernist undertaking. It is therefore legitimate to think of this 'incessant movement' of modernity as emanating from the 'profound rupture' that Foucault isolated in Manet's work.

Foucault's insistence upon the reductive, anti-Platonic character of modern art is a concept drawn directly from life. That is, reduction is one of the specific functions Foucault discusses in his analysis of the Cynical *askēsis*. Like the Cynic's life, the type of truth operating within modern art is, for Foucault, a reduction to the most essential level of existence. As we have seen, one of the crucial tendencies of modern art, as Foucault understands it, is the embrace of lowness. Whether it is Manet's stubborn insistence upon the material properties of the painted canvas, or Rebeyrolle's avoidance of representative forms in favor of the immediacy of painted forces, there is a certain truth grasped, presented, and transmitted by the act of laying bare the elementary. Like the Cynic's truth, this type of truth is a reduction to the most essential. And, just like the truth of the Cynic's withered and naked existence, modern art continually appears as the scandal of truth.

Foucault thinks of this anti-cultural tendency within modern art as a courageous manifestation of truth. For Foucault, modern art is the 'courage of art in its barbarous truth,' much in the same way that the Cynic's life was itself lived at the limit in the hope of engendering truth (*GSA2: 29 Feb.*, 63). Thus, modern art is, for Foucault, *parrhesiastic* inasmuch as it entails risk for continually questioning the conditions under which it takes place.

> Modern art is Cynicism in culture, it is the Cynicism of culture turned back toward itself. And I think that if this does not take place only in art, it is especially in art that is concentrated, in the modern world, in our world, the most intense forms of truth speaking that has the courage to take the risk of wounding.[19]

Modern art risks wounding because it is a constant reproach to what has come before. It announces a truth that will no doubt be unpopular, thus courting danger. In much the same way that the Cynic's life pointed to the insufficiency of the traditional philosophical life, modern art forms itself through a polemical exchange with what is accepted in culture at large. Modern art, therefore, conducts itself *parrhesiastically* about where art has fallen short and where culture itself has gone wrong.

5.8 PARRHĒSIA AS VISUAL TRUTH

Foucault's last two courses are dedicated to tracking the various transformations of this form of speaking, so essential to his understanding of the type of truth operating within modern art. Roughly, *parrhēsia* moves from being a negative right within Athenian democracy—every man must be given his say, no matter how unpopular his position—to a form of discourse secured only on the basis of ethical transformation and mastery.[20] As we will see, the highly visible nature of this type of truth, particularly in its Cynical manifestations, makes it well suited for a discussion of modern art. In this section we explore Foucault's conception of truth as it is presented in his final courses in order to better situate his comments about modern art. We first develop a general account of *parrhēsia*, and then highlight the visual components of its practice. In the following section, we examine in more detail the Cynical deployments of this modality as anticipations of modern art.

Parrhēsia designates a specific relationship between the speaker and what is said. Through the action of *parrhēsia*, the *parrhesiast* opens his heart and mind completely, speaking his own opinion (*FS*, 12). The *parrhesiast*, as Foucault has it, '*acts* on other people's minds by *showing* them as directly as possible what he actually believes' (*FS*, 12; The italics are my own). *Parrhēsia* is thus characterized by a certain amount of *frankness* on the part of the speaker. Structurally, *parrhēsia* has two adversaries—flattery and rhetoric. Flattery is the moral opponent of *parrhēsia* in that it attempts to wield influence by keeping the person to whom it is directed 'impotent and blind' (*HER*, 376). The *parrhesiast,* on the other hand, attempts to speak the truth in such a way as to free the person thus addressed. 'The objective of *parrhēsia* is to act so that at a given moment the person to whom one is speaking finds himself in a situation in which he no longer needs the other's discourse' (*HER*, 379). Rhetoric is opposed to *parrhēsia* on technical grounds. Whereas rhetoric embellishes the truth, the action of *parrhēsia* contains nothing in excess of the truth. '*Parrhēsia* is the naked transmission . . . of truth itself' (*HER*, 382). As we have seen, Foucault found within the Cynical *askēsis* and the practices of modern art the force of a truth stripped of everything inessential. The act of *parrhēsia* depends upon this reduction. It is an 'instrument . . . that does nothing other than put to work the truth of true discourse in all its naked force, without adornment' (*HER*, 382). The *parrhesiast* attempts to find the most direct form of possible transmission, so that the person who receives it, who 'must be impregnated by it,' will be able to exploit it as an active principle of subjectivity. Thus, the refusal of both flattery and rhetoric endow *parrhēsia* with maximum efficacity, one which allows for it to be recognized as truth and absorbed into the life of its addressee.

In the 1984 course, Foucault contrasts the *parrhesiast* with three other truth-tellers common to the ancient world: the prophet, technician, and sage. In each case, the modality of *parrhēsia* is distinct because of the highly specialized relationship between the speaker and the truth announced. The prophet does not speak the truth in his own name; the truth instead speaks through him. He is an intermediary between the gods and the world, or present and future. He is merely a messenger and as such does not guarantee the truth he announces with his own subjectivity. The technician speaks on behalf of a tradition, enabling the transmission of truth as *technē*. Like the prophet, he is an intermediary, representing a tradition, but not his own relationship with the truth. The sage, whose modality is wisdom, speaks of *his* wisdom and is, like the *parrhesiast,* closely linked with truth. The sage, however, is silent about specific matters, those involving risk and requiring courage, speaking instead about that which *is* most generally (*GSA2: 1 Feb.,* 27–46).

In contrast, the *parrhesiast* speaks on specific, contemporary matters, relevant to lives of individuals and the community. Moreover, in *parrhēsia* there is an ever more intimate relationship with truth, such that in the very act of announcing it, the speaker commits him or herself to a course of action and a way of life. *Parrhēsia* 'is speech that is equivalent to commitment, to a bond, and which establishes a certain pact between the subject of enunciation and the subject of conduct' (*HER,* 406). This commitment, however, cannot be assimilated to a speech act whereby a pledge or promise is made by the act of articulating it. It is, in the language of the 1984 course, an action by which the *parrhesiast* 'in some way signs himself to the truth that he announces' (*GSA2: 1 Feb.,* 20). Not every annunciation of truth, therefore, is an act of *parrhēsia,* but only those in which some sort of price is paid. This cost ensures the epistemological correspondence between the *parrhesiast's* belief and the truth communicated. One might well ask, does the *parrhesiast* say what he *thinks* is true, or what *really is* true? For Foucault, the *parrhesiast* says what in his opinion is true, because he really believes it to be true, and he believes it true because it really is true. Foucault explains, 'In the Greek conception of *parrhēsia* . . . there does not seem to be a problem about the acquisition of the truth since such truth-having is guaranteed by the possession of certain *moral* qualities' (*FS,* 15). These moral qualities are purchased through the performance of an *askēsis,* one ensuring that someone has the requisite moral qualities, the proof, that what first appears as an opinion is indeed true. In announcing that a specific path is the correct way of life, the *parrhesiast* makes reference to his own existence, holding up as evidence that he lives by what he claims as truth. He offers his conduct as proof that the truth he seeks to impart is based upon principles governing his life. Like an artist, he guarantees his discourse with his subjectivity. In *parrhēsia,* therefore, there is a correspondence between the speaker's opinion and the truth of the situation, and this adequation is guaranteed by the stylization of life. The *parrhesiast* speaks in his own name, but because of the utterance's roots in *askēsis* it can be verified and accepted as true.

The critical speech of the *parrhesiast* thus requires a change in the subject who hopes to be capable of articulating it. The Cynics avoided the development of knowledge for its own sake, instead directing their philosophical labors into the production and transformation of subjectivity. Knowledge, for the Cynical school, is valuable only when capable of producing a change in the knowing subject.[21] Hence, philosophical knowledge is instrumentalized and spiritualized, with the aim of weaving theoretical truths into prescriptions for thoughts, gestures, and actions. Simply put, the goal of the Cynical *askēsis* is to close the gap between the *logos* and *bios* so that the *logos* becomes operative in life as a permanent and active principle. For the Cynics, '*parrhēsia* is directly linked to a certain mode of life,' and the Cynic philosopher makes existence the 'essential condition for the speaking of truth' (*GSA2: 29 Feb.*, 27). The Cynic therefore becomes a credible subject on the basis of a life stylized according to a strict set of principles. In Foucault's presentation, the Cynical life provides a 'framework,' 'support,' and 'justification' for the use of *parrhēsia* (*GSA2: 29 Feb.*, 28). It enables philosophical Cynicism to exist with a relatively small theoretical component, because the Cynic secures a critical social function, not by recourse to epistemology or the elaboration of a system of ethics, but through the stylization of existence. Credibility is ensured by the ethical labor that instantiates the principles of the Cynical school into the lives of its practitioners. This *askēsis* allows the Cynic to function as a demonstration of where humanity has gone wrong and how its priorities, habits, and customs might be corrected.

The harmony between life and discourse was one of the guiding themes of Foucault's courses throughout the 1980s, where the truth of a *parrhesiastic* discourse could be guaranteed by the harmony between what is said and the life of the individual articulating it. As we saw in Foucault's reading of the *Laches*, Socrates' manifestation of courage permitted him to speak with *parrhēsia* on ethical matters. With the Cynics, however, the being of the subject itself, not simply a harmony between what he does and says, guarantees the exercise of *parrhēsia*. While the Cynic fulfills the general criteria of *parrhēsia*, his radical *askēsis* goes one step further, forging an unbreakable relationship with truth. Cynicism is not content with mere adequation; it fashions a much closer link, making the Cynical life itself the vehicle of truth's transmission. The Cynic's existence does not simply correspond to the discourse he proclaims, as in the case of Socrates, but itself becomes 'truth-disclosive' through the reductive operations that strip life down to its essentials. Whereas for Socrates it is a question of manifesting virtue, for the Cynics it is a question of revealing the very truth of life. As we saw, in reversing the true life, Cynicism constituted a life which was itself the manifestation of truth. It is this attempt to cut right to the naked truth of existence that distinguishes Cynicism from other philosophical schools, and justifies its use of the *parrhesiastic* modality. For Foucault, the Cynics managed to lead a life that was simultaneously a true life and the truth *of* life. Life, in Cynicism, presents itself as the immediate and scandalous presence of truth. Foucault thus contends, 'to exercise in and by life the scandal of the truth, that is . . . the core of cynicism' (*GSA2: 29 Feb.*, 37). For him, this means that in taking common philosophical principles and radicalizing them in life, the Cynic turns his *askēsis* into a constant challenge; one that constitutes a life more immediately truthful than those lived by other philosophers. The Cynic thus attempts to manifest, in his being, the simple, elementary truth of existence in all its fragility, brutality, and nakedness. It is this life, already fashioned as true, which ensures the ancients that the Cynic is the one with the most immediate right to true speech. Truth is something written upon the Cynic's body, palpable in his gestures, verifiable in his dress, in short, *visible* in his life, before critical words are articulated.

It is important to recognize that in Foucault's various presentations, *parrhēsia* is always something more than speech logically constructed or corresponding to given state of affairs. It is, one might say, a complicated intertwining of the discursive and the visible, one that allows for discourse to be recognized as true through reference to its sensible, visual instantiation. For the Cynics, speech is itself secondary to the truths first witnessed in their lives. They take the harmony between word and life farther than any of the other ancient schools, converting it into a visible relationship. Indeed, these visual dimensions of the Cynical *askēsis*—the scandalous actions, lives lived in public, and the shunning of all material comforts—form an essential part of the picture that Foucault draws, for through these practices the Cynic stakes a claim on *parrhēsia*. The appropriateness of Foucault's description of modern art in terms of the Cynical *askēsis* will become more evident if we understand their practices as performances designed to sustain speech and secure a critical social function. Visual immediacy is the goal of *parrhēsia* for other philosophical schools, and an essential piece of Foucault's presentation. The Cynics can be viewed as an extension of this problematic, one in which the ambitions of *parrhēsia* transform it from mere utterance into an event. We have already seen how flattery and rhetoric are the enemies of *parrhēsia* because they interfere with truth's direct conveyance. Both devices cloud transmission, employing extraneous and distracting elements. *Parrhēsia*, on the other hand, is effective precisely because it is stripped of all that is inessential for truth to become active upon a group or individual. When attempting to speak *parrhesiastically*, one seeks to relay the truth needed in the most direct manner possible. Here, language's limitations push *parrhēsia* into the sphere of a visual practice. In the letters of Seneca (5 B.C.E.–65 C.E.), Foucault finds a curious expression, which for him seems to encapsulate something essential about *parrhēsia*. In describing *libertas*, the Latin translation of *parrhēsia*, Seneca explains that he would like his own discourse to be unadorned and characterized by visual clarity. Seneca:

> Now who thinks of polishing his style except lovers of the pretentious? If we were sitting alone with each other or taking a walk together, my conversation would be unaffected and easygoing (*inlaboratus et facilis*). I should like my letters to be like that; they have nothing studied or artificial about them. If it were possible, I should prefer to show you my thoughts rather than translate them into language.[22]

Foucault marks this final line and returns to it later in his lecture, asking, 'What does it mean "to show one's thoughts rather than speaking?"' (*HER*, 404). In the first instance, he answers, it is the 'pure and simple transmission' of thought such that embellishments are kept to a minimum. More significantly, however, this showing of thought consists of demonstrating that these thoughts belong intimately to the person conveying them. To constitute an act of *parrhēsia*, one must find a way to mark his or her own personal relationship with what is announced, in the way it is announced. In *parrhēsia*, 'what must be shown is not just that this is . . . the truth, but . . . that I who am speaking am . . . also the person for whom they are true' (*HER*, 405). Further still, this relationship with truth must be shown to be constitutive of subjectivity. This means, as Foucault explains, that the *parrhesiast* must demonstrate that 'not only do I feel and consider the things I say to be true, but I even love them, am attached to them and my whole life is governed by them' (*HER*, 405). One must, therefore, introduce a bit of one's existence into discourse to make manifest its truthfulness. Foucault:

> What seems to me the crucial element in this conception of *libertas* and *parrhēsia* . . . is that in order to guarantee the *parrhēsia* (the frankness) of the discourse delivered, the presence of the person speaking must be really perceptible (*effectivement sensible*) in what he actually says. (*HER*, 405)

The proliferation of visual metaphors in the ancient sources and in Foucault's redeployments points away from an exclusively discursive situation and places *parrhēsia* within the realm of sensible experience. The Cynics were no doubt the most successful of the ancient schools in claiming the right of *parrhēsia*, because their *askēsis* moved the farthest beyond simple locutions to the visual performance of their relationship with the truth. Indeed, more than anything that they thought, taught, or wrote, the figures these ancient Cynics stylized are what secured their hold on the Western imagination. Even for Seneca, who disapproved of certain Cynical strategies, the ideal remains a relationship between *bios* and *logos* such that both are available for inspection—independently of language. It is for this reason that the Cynics linked the exercise of *parrhēsia* to beauty. Not only, as Foucault explains, is truth beautiful, but truth itself is something that must be linked to a beautiful existence. Cynical *parrhēsia* thus takes the classical pairing of truth and beauty to the extreme limit, making a carefully stylized existence the precondition for truth's possession (*GSA2: 29 Feb.*, 21). As we have seen, however, Foucault has reservations about the Cynic's paradoxical affirmation of ugliness and physical debasement. Nevertheless, we can say that it is the *relationship* between existence and truth that is, for the Cynics as well as Foucault, beautiful. Without a doubt, what was appealing to Foucault, as he sought out ways to disrupt our complacent forms of subjectivation, is the idea that life itself, in becoming the object of an aesthetic preoccupation, could become a vehicle for the manifestation of truth.

5.9 CYNICAL STRATEGIES AND THE ANTICIPATION
OF MODERN ART

As opposed to the elitist forms that truth-speaking and philosophical practice took in other philosophical schools, the Cynics took their message to the public. During a period in which *parrhēsia* came to be increasingly confined to interpersonal relationships, primarily between government officials and philosophical advisors, the Cynics moved the game into the open. '[T]hey thought that their teachings had to consist in a very public, visible, spectacular, provocative, and sometimes scandalous way of life' (*FS*, 117). As Foucault explains, the Cynics' self-understanding stems from a certain interpretation of the Socratic legacy, whereby the philosopher is a public figure who engages all people, regardless of social position, in conversation. This means that the site and style of their discourse was shifted away from conversations with the well-positioned, toward the public arena where it was accessible to all.

Within the Cynical tradition, *parrhēsia* was gradually transformed into what Foucault terms 'critical preaching' (*FS*, 119). These public invectives were directed against institutions, laws, ethical conventions, superfluous cultural additions or anything else that placed limits on freedom and self-sufficiency. Cynical preaching exhorted a form of self-care grounded in simplicity and naturalness. The public form of this preaching is historically significant for two reasons: it anticipates Christian proselytization, both in terms of its practice and themes, and it extends to the people at large the philosophical theme of the care of the self. The Cynic's preaching is thus one of the ways in which the concern for truth was removed from the exclusive grasp of the philosophical elite and transferred to the public. Preaching is a key moment in the history of the relationship between truth and subjectivity because it 'involves the idea that the truth must be told and taught not only to the best members of the society, or to an exclusive group, but to everyone' (*FS*, 120). This means that the *parrhesiast's* public persona had to be carefully stylized and interventions carefully planned. That is, his existence and discourse had to take on certain aesthetic qualities.

Scandalous behavior, understood as gestures designed to challenge collective habits and opinions, is one of the forms this Cynical *parrhēsia* took. These actions, as Foucault points out, come down to us mainly by legend and are an extension of the Cynical position that the philosopher must cultivate an emblematic life. Within the Cynical movement in which there are very few recognizable doctrines and canonical texts, reflection begins with the consideration of a 'philosophical hero,' real or mythical persons who achieved great things in life and action. Cynicism is thus transmitted through an analysis of key events and actions in the lives of its adherents. This happens at once through the stylization of life and the provocative insertion of this subjectivity into the public imagination. Diogenes, as recounted by Dio Chrysostom, once challenged the folly inherent in the Isthmian festival's athletic contests. After bothering the organizers and spectators, Diogenes proceeded to crown himself with pine as though he had been victorious in the games. Just before he could be removed, Diogenes explained that he alone was victorious in defeating the much more fearsome foes of vice, desire, and poverty. Later, after witnessing a fight between two horses, Diogenes placed a crown upon the head of the horse that had effectively stood its ground. For Foucault, these gestures show how the distribution of prizes is, at bottom, arbitrary: If awards are to be doled out for moral battles, then no one is more deserving than Diogenes; however, if the distribution of prizes depends simply on feats of physical strength, then horses too ought to be crowned (*FS*, 121–122). Within the Cynical tradition, therefore, the gesture, the action, and the public intervention formed an essential starting point for philosophical reflection. It was, as Foucault's interpretative reconstruction attests, one of the primary ways in which Cynical thought could be transmitted.

Provocative dialogue was another Cynical technique designed to move interlocutors to truth by means of hostile exchanges. Foucault contrasts this form of dialogue with the Socratic, explaining:

> Whereas the Socratic dialogue traces an intricate and winding path from an ignorant understanding to an awareness of ignorance, the Cynic dialogue is much more like a fight, a battle, or a war, with peaks of great aggressivity and moments of peaceful calm—peaceful exchanges which, of course, are additional traps for the interlocutor. (*FS*, 130)

In all the accounts of the encounter between Diogenes and Alexander, it is significant that the Cynic continually strikes at the vanity of the King. During the exchange, it is not, for Foucault, a matter of leading Alexander to recognize his ignorance, but an all-out offensive where Diogenes wounds his interlocutor's pride, mocking his political aspirations, casting doubt upon his courage and calling him a bastard (*FS*, 124–133). In Foucault's analyses of the situations in which these frank conversations took place, there is always a tacit agreement that allows one party to speak openly, without fear of retribution.[23] The Cynic's *parrhēsia* 'borders on transgression' since it continually challenges the contractual relationship within which truth is relayed (*FS*, 127). The Cynics tested the boundaries of this covenant with the ways they initiated conversations, the aggressiveness of their discourse and the directness of their gestures. Thus, much in the way that the modern artist interrogates the received codes of artistic practices, the Cynics stretched *parrhēsia* to the point at which the limits of its transmission became bare. When they were successful, the Cynics were able to take the game to a new stage, thereby transforming its rules. As we have seen, this is the transition that, in Foucault's analysis of Manet, is referred to as a rupture. What motivates these practices is the desire to alter the rules of discursivity, to strip them of anything that impedes truth's direct transmission. In order to achieve this, however, Cynical *parrhēsia* must constitute itself as an event, one that questions the very rules of the discursive situation in which it finds itself.

It is this movement—this tendency to transgression and this tendency to reduce the game to its essentials—that, for Foucault, characterizes the movements of modern art. Like the Cynics whose truth is initially unacceptable, the products of modern art create the conditions under which they can be recognized as true by first contesting the products that have come before. Faced with a set of received rules and practices, the modern artist finds himself or herself in the position of the Cynic who must 'change the value of money.' As we saw, this critical role, whereby truth is transmitted directly and frankly, presupposes the Cynical way of life. That is, it is the Cynical *askēsis* that guarantees the subject's worthiness of attaining and announcing the truth. For Foucault, the truth at stake in the art of modernity presupposes this same type of transformation on the part of the subject who would be its originator. It requires that some sort of price be paid, whether it is the refusal of material comforts, the rigors of an apprenticeship, or the struggle to compose a beautiful existence, before the aesthetic challenge can be seen for what it is, and communicated to culture at large. And if scandal and risk are such an integral part of modern art, it is because its preconditions are found in this form of truth according to which truth is never simply given, but discovered through provocation.

CONCLUSION

What is especially scandalous for contemporary readers, no doubt, is the reactivation of this spiritual understanding of truth within the modern era of technical, scientific knowledge. In philosophy, we are accustomed to relegating the problem of art to that nebulous realm known as aesthetics where we then, with all the trappings of a science, pursue false problems, while treating art and vision as if they had no history and little connection with life. The addition of the Cynical vocabulary highlights the intimate connections between artistic practice and those of life. The combination, within modernity, of a way of life and the privileged access that it grants to the truth should be seen as a challenge to the post-Cartesian paradigm of subject-neutral knowledge, itself a position marked out by the contours of modernity. If, on certain readings, the modern project was to separate the aesthetic from the realms of moral and cognitive knowledge, Foucault shows how, when compared with the actual practices of art, such theories are disingenuous. He does this on the basis of a reading of modernity—of who we are and what we have come to expect from life and work. In the language of philosophical aesthetics: Foucault rejects those efforts to think of artistic products as separate from human contexts, and especially those other arts, known to him as ethics, by which men and women attempt to transform themselves for the better. As he explained in conversation with Werner Schroeter: 'I do not draw a distinction between people who make of their existence a work and those who make a work during their existence. An existence can be a perfect and sublime work.'[24] This insistence upon the fundamental similarity between these two modes of creation is exactly what we see in Foucault's deployment of concepts borrowed from the ethical stylizations of the Hellenistic Cynics. The expanded conception of aesthetics this gives us does not neglect what is unique about modern art. Quite the contrary, by means of its genealogical approach, it isolates the moments where art and life sustain each other. For Foucault, the spiritual relationship with truth at work within the modern art object necessitates the production of a corresponding subjectivity worthy of announcing that truth. This is not an effort to romanticize the life of the artist, nor is it a blanket endorsement from the thinker who was so suspicious of philosophical anthropology, biographical criticism, and the 'author function.' It is the recognition of the distinctly modern way in which the cultural spheres we inhabit make demands upon our subjectivity. To neglect this functioning of art would be to pose the aesthetic question merely from the perspective of the spectator.

NOTES

INTRODUCTION

1 Michel Foucault, 'What is Enlightenment?,' in *Ethics: Subjectivity and Truth: Essential Works of Foucault, 1954–1984, Volume One* (henceforth cited as *EST*), ed. Paul Rabinow (New York: The New Press, 1997), 305. Henceforth cited as *WE*. The 1983 course distinguishes between two relations with modernity: the 'longitudinal rapport' compares modernity with the ancient period, asking if it is a period of ascendance or decline; and Kant's 'sagittal rapport' that forges a direct, 'vertical' relationship with the present. See, Michel Foucault, *Le gouvernement de soi et des autres: Cours au Collège de France (1982–1983)* (Paris: Seuil/Gallimard, 2008), 15. Henceforth cited as *GSA1*. All translations of this text are my own.

2 Charles Baudelaire, *The Painter of Modern Life and Other Essays*, trans. Jonathan Mayne (New York: Phaidon Press Inc., 2005), 41. Henceforth cited as *PMLO*.

3 Baudelaire describes the need to establish a 'rational and historical theory of beauty, in contrast to the academic theory of an unique and absolute beauty.' Such a theory would show how 'beauty is always . . . of a double composition,' and how the circumstances of everyday life, when beheld in the right way, can be made to offer up the invariable element of the beautiful. *PMLO*, 3.

4 Throughout, I quote Donald F. Bouchard and Sherry Simon's translation 'Nietzsche, Genealogy, History,' in *Language, Counter-Memory, Practice: Selected Essays and Interviews* (henceforth cited as *LCMP*), ed. Donald F. Bouchard (Ithaca, New York: Cornell University Press, 1977), 154. Henceforth cited as *NGH1*. In places where the translation has been modified, I have made reference to the version 'Nietzsche, la généalogie, l'histoire,' in *Foucault: Dits et écrits I, 1954–1975* (henceforth cited as *DE1*), ed. Daniel Defert, François Ewald, and Jacques Lagrange (Paris: Éditions Gallimard, 2001), 1004–1024. Henceforth cited as *NGH2*.

5 Michel Foucault, 'La force de fuir' (1973), in *Foucault: Dits et écrits I, 1954–1975*, 1269. Henceforth cited as *FF*. This essay first appeared as Michel Foucault, 'La force de fuir,' *Derrière le miroir: Rebeyrolle* no. 202

(March, 1973), 1–8. *Derrière le miroir* was a publication of the Maeght Gallery, Paris. It was a slender publication that usually included a brief essay as well as color reproductions of works from an exhibition. This issue devoted to Rebeyrolle accompanied an exhibition in March of 1973. All translations of this text are my own; however, I was aided throughout by James Bernauer's unpublished translation.

6 Benjamin H. D. Buchloh, 'The Group that Was (Not) One: Daniel Buren and BMPT,' *Artforum* XLVI, no. 9 (May 2008), 313.

7 Gary Shapiro, *Archaeologies of Vision: Foucault and Nietzsche on Seeing and Saying* (Chicago: The University of Chicago Press, 2003), 271. Henceforth cited as *AV.*

8 *AV*, 338. See, Chapter Eleven, 'Pipe Dreams: Recurrence of the Simulacrum in Klossowski, Deleuze, and Magritte,' 325–346.

9 Michel Foucault, *The Order of Things: An Archaeology of the Human Sciences* (1966) (New York: Vintage Books, 1994), 387. Henceforth cited as *OT.* See also, Michel Foucault, *Les mots et les choses: Une archéologie des sciences humaines* (Paris: Éditions Gallimard, 1966), 398. Henceforth cited as *LMC.* The hesitant tone that I am here calling attention to is present in the French original.

10 This essay first appeared as Michel Foucault, 'Ceci n'est pas une pipe,' in *Les Cahiers du chemin*, 15, no. 2 (1968): 79–105. Additions were made to the 1973 book version and serve to clarify greatly Foucault's analyses; I therefore give priority to this edition. Foucault also deleted a few passages from the 1968 text. None of these changes, however, significantly alter the diagnosis of modern painting that this work holds. Throughout, I refer to the 1973 edition of this text. Michel Foucault, *Ceci n'est pas une pipe* (1968) (Paris: Fata Morgana, 1973). Henceforth cited as *CP.* Citations refer to the English translation: Michel Foucault, *This is Not a Pipe* (1968), trans. James Harkness (Berkeley: University of California Press, 1983). Henceforth cited as *TNP.* Modifications have been made to this translation and are noted. It is the 1968 version of this essay that is collected in *DE1*, 663–678. The same is true of the English translation found in *Aesthetics, Method, and Epistemology: Essential Works of Foucault, 1954–1984, Volume Two*, ed. James D. Faubion (New York: The New Press, 1998), 187–203. Henceforth cited as *AME.* For this passage see, *TNP*, 54. Also, *CP*, 78.

11 One could cite many sources here. I confine myself to what is perhaps its most eloquent philosophical articulation. Arthur C. Danto, *After The End of Art: Contemporary Art and the Pale of History* (Princeton, New Jersey: Princeton University Press, 1997). Danto conceives of Warhol as a postmodern artist—though he prefers to use his own neologism of 'post-historical art' to refer to art produced after the end of modernism—and frequently cites his *Brillo Boxes* as an essential turning point in the history of art. For Danto, this work is indicative of the closure of a specific era of art, one that predicated art's identity upon its difference from quotidian objects.

12 Michel Foucault, 'Structuralism and Post-Structuralism,' in *AME*, 448. Henceforth cited as *SP.*

CHAPTER 1

1 Didier Eribon, *Michel Foucault*, trans. Betsy Wing (Cambridge: Harvard University Press, 1991), 155. Henceforth cited as *MF*.
2 Michel Foucault, *History of Madness* (1972), trans. Jonathan Murphy and Jean Khalfa (London: Routledge, 2006), 17. Henceforth cited as *HM*.
3 *HM*, 16. The divergence of word and image is of the utmost significance for the first part of Foucault's history in that it is the source of two radically different conceptions of madness. In the morality tales of Brant and Erasmus is found a 'critical consciousness of man,' a conception of madness that attempts to erase its more wide-ranging and troubling characteristics. On the other hand, in fifteenth-century painting—Foucault mentions Bosch, Breugel, Thierry Bouts and Dürer—there is a different experience, that of the 'tragic madness of the world.' This is the vision that reveals that the world is itself delirious. The former conception is an essential step in the Classical age's conversion of madness into unreason, and it is this critical consciousness that is 'increasingly brought out into the light, while its more tragic components retreated further into the shadows . . . .' The tragic experience, however, is not completely effaced, and madness is not completely mastered, for it is this tragic experience that bursts forth in the works of Sade, Goya, Artaud, Nietzsche's last works, and Van Gogh's final paintings. See, *HM*, 24–28 and 530–538.
4 Gary Shapiro offers a stunning reading of Foucault's analysis of *Las Meninas* by thematizing the way in which Foucault's discourse continually reflects upon the heterogeneity of the discursive and the visual. See, *AV*, 247–263.
5 Michel Foucault, *The Birth of the Clinic: An Archaeology of Medical Perception* (1963), trans. A. M. Sheridan Smith (New York: Vintage Books, 1994), xii. Henceforth cited as *BC*.
6 Michel Foucault, *Death and the Labyrinth: The World of Raymond Roussel*, trans. Charles Ruas (New York: Doubleday & Company, Inc. 1986).
7 In his essay on Magritte, Foucault draws a crucial distinction between resemblance and similitude. Both terms refer to relations based on similarities, but only resemblances are governed by a prior thought, image, or model. Similitude, on the other hand, is usually termed simulacrum. In the space of Magritte's art, Foucault finds relationships of resemblance that do not affirm anything, that is, his similitudes are empty forms of resemblance. This distinction will be made more explicit in Chapter 3; however, in this chapter I follow Foucault's usage in *OT*, treating similitude as descriptive of resemblance.
8 Foucault devotes a chapter to each of these empiricities. He demonstrates the essential rapport these disciplines maintain with the Classical project of representation as well as the fundamental heterogeneity between these fields and those that supercede them in modernity: philology, biology, and political economy. Throughout this chapter we draw primarily upon

the discussions of natural history and biology, as these fields are the most explicitly visual.

9 Apparently unbeknownst to Foucault, only volumes I–IV were completed by Aldrovandi, while volumes V–XIII were compiled by his students from notes left behind at the time of his death. Foucault refers to Vol. X *Serpents and Dragons* (1640). See, *OT*, 39–40 and 128–129. Also: Sherman C. Bishop, 'Aldrovandi's Natural History,' *University of Rochester Library Bulletin*, vol. V, no. 2 (Winter 1950). It is anachronistic to refer, as Bishop does, to Aldrovandi's project as 'natural history.' The term belongs to Jonston's *Natural History of Quadrupeds* of 1657.

10 Ana Martín Moreno, *Las Meninas*, trans. Nigel Williams (Madrid: Aldeasa, 2003), 28. Henceforth cited as *LM*.

11 Quoted in John Rupert Martin, *Baroque* (New York: Harper & Row, Publishers, 1977), 167.

12 Michel Foucault, 'Pierre Boulez, Passing Through the Screen,' in *AME*, 243. Henceforth cited as *PB*.

13 Comte de Lautréamont is the pseudonym of Isidore Lucien Ducasse (1846–1870), the author of *Les Chants de Maldoror* (1868–1869). The line to which Foucault refers is found in the sixth and final canto of *Maldoror*. The narrator is describing the charms of a 16-year-old boy, Mervyn, who is about to become Maldoror's victim: 'He is as handsome as the retractibility of the claws of birds of prey; or again, as the uncertainty of the muscular movements of wounds in the soft parts of the posterior cervical region; or rather as the perpetual rat-trap, re-set each time by the trapped animal, that can catch rodents indefinitely and works even when hidden beneath straw; and especially as the fortuitous encounter upon a dissecting-table of a sewing-machine and an umbrella!' Comte de Lautréamont, *Les Chants de Maldoror*, trans. Guy Wernham (New York: New Directions Publishing Corporation, 1966), 263.

14 Martin, *Baroque*, 12–13 and 39–41.

15 Foucault, 'The Father's "No,"' in *LCMP*, 74. Henceforth cited as *FN*. This essay is collected as Michel Foucault, 'Le <<non>> du père,' in *DEI*, 217–231. Throughout I refer to Bouchard's translation.

16 Completed in 1967, Nauman used a neon light sign, like one would find advertising a product in a store window, to reflect upon the occupation of the artist, spelling out the message quoted above. See: Joan Simon, ed., *Bruce Nauman*, (Minneapolis: Walker Art Center, 1994), 124.

17 Michel Foucault, 'Qui êtes-vous, professeur Foucault?,' in *DEI*, 635. Henceforth cited as *QV*.

CHAPTER 2

1 Foucault, 'A Preface to Transgression,' in *LCMP*, 35.

2 See Note 1 above.

3 Michel Foucault, 'An Ethics of Pleasure,' in *Foucault Live* (henceforth cited as *FL*), ed. Sylvère Lotringer (New York: Semiotext(e), 1996), 372.

4 Michel Foucault, 'La philosophie structuraliste permet de diagnostiquer ce qu'est "aujourd'hui,"' in *DE1*, 612. The translation is my own. For a more detailed account of Foucault's time in Tunisia, see David Macey, *The Lives of Michel Foucault: A Biography* (New York: Pantheon Books, 1993), 183–208. Henceforth cited as *LMF*.

5 For accounts of Foucault's political involvements in Tunisia, see: Rachida Triki, 'Foucault en Tunisie,' in *La Peinture de Manet* (henceforth cited as *PM*), ed. Maryvonne Saison (Paris: Éditions du Seuil, 2004), 61–63. Also, *LMF*, 190–193 and 203–208. Also, *MF*, 192–195.

6 Gilles Deleuze, *Foucault*, trans. Seán Hand (Minneapolis: University of Minnesota Press, 1988), 58.

7 Maryvonne Saison, 'Introduction,' in *PM*, 11.

8 This lecture was delivered on 20 May 1971 at the Tahar Haddad Cultural Club in Tunis.

9 Michel Foucault, *The Archaeology of Knowledge and The Discourse on Language*, trans. A. M. Sheridan Smith (New York: Pantheon Books, 1972), 192.

10 The other two analyses outlined are: (1) The archaeology of sexuality, termed 'ethical,' aimed at showing how manifestations of sexuality, verbal and nonverbal alike, are governed by practices that control, limit and proscribe its appearance. (2) An archaeology of political knowledges describing how discourses, actions, and theories gain enunciability. *AK*, 192–195.

11 Michel Foucault, 'Les mots et les images,' in *DE1*, 649. Henceforth cited as *LMI*. All translations of this text are my own. The italics reflect those found in Foucault's original text.

12 Michel Foucault, 'The Discourse on Language' appears as an appendix to *AK*, 231.

13 *AK*, 40–70. Foucault devotes a chapter to each of these domains of the discursive formation.

14 Michel Foucault, 'Fantasia of the Library,' in *LCMP*, 90. Henceforth cited as *FLib*. The essay is collected as Michel Foucault, (Sans titre), in *DE1*, 321–353. Henceforth cited as *ST*. Throughout, I refer to Bouchard's translation, making reference to *DE1* where I have modified the translation.

15 Robert Rosenblum and H. W. Janson, *19th-Century Art* (New York: Harry N. Abrams, Inc., 1984), 282. Henceforth cited as *19CA*. In this collaborative endeavor, Rosenblum is responsible for the essays on painting and Janson sculpture.

16 Georges Bataille, *Manet* (Paris: Éditions d'Art Albert Skira S. A., 1994), 38. Translations of this text are my own.

17 Bataille contrasts the discursive function of traditional art with Manet's autonomous painting. 'Previously painting was anything but autonomous, being only part of a majestic edifice, offering to the masses an intelligible totality. . . . Manet turned away from all that.' Bataille, *Manet*, 28. He compares Manet's *The Execution of Maximilian* with Goya's *The Third of May*, arguing the essential difference is that Manet's

composition demonstrates no concern for the event it recounts: 'Manet paints the death of the condemned with the same indifference as if he had chosen to depict a flower or a fish.' Bataille, *Manet*, 45. This work's indifference emblematizes Manet's negation of 'eloquence.'

18 Gilles Néret, *Édouard Manet: The First of the Moderns* (Los Angeles: Taschen, 2003), 16.

19 Michel Foucault, 'À quoi rêvent les philosophes?,' in *DE1*, 1574. Heceforth cited as *QRP*. All translations of this text are my own.

20 Triki, 'Foucault en Tunisie,' in *PM*, 57.

21 Quoted in *MF*, 46. I am grateful to Catherine Soussloff for calling my attention to this passage.

22 John T. Paoletti and Gary M. Radke, *Art in Renaissance Italy* (New York: Harry N. Abrams, Inc., Publishers, 1997), 205. Henceforth cited as *ARI*.

23 Representational light renders possible the modeling of the human form. Modeling is the technical term for the illusion of weight and volume created through the manipulation of light and shading. Some speculate linear-point perspective was precipitated by the need to keep pace with this technique's life-like presentation of the body. See, *ARI*, 204. For Foucault, Caravaggio (1573–1610) is its undisputed master.

24 Foucault analyzes the 1868 version in the collection of the Städtische Kunsthalle, Mannheim.

25 Ernest Chesneau, for example, wrote admiringly: 'Manet does not immobilize his forms; he surprises them in their affective movement.' Quoted in Pierre Courthion, *Manet* (New York: Harry N. Abrams, Inc., 2004), 124.

26 Daniel Defert, 'Chronologie,' in *DE1*, 49. Defert's chronology suggests Foucault's November 1970 lecture in Florence dealt more extensively with this work than the Tunis lecture.

27 James W. Bernauer, *Michel Foucault's Force of Flight: Toward an Ethics for Thought* (Amherst, New York: Humanity Books, 1990), 2.

28 Foucault, 'The Discourse on Language,' 219. '[T]he penal code started out as a theory of Right; then, from the time of the nineteenth century, people looked for its validation in sociological, psychological, medical and psychiatric knowledge. It is as though the very words of the law had no authority in our society, except in so far as they are derived from true discourse.'

29 Throughout this section I have made use of Macy's history of G.I.P.'s activities and his discussion of Foucault's role in the group. For a more detailed history, see his chapter 'Intolerable,' in *LMF*, 257–289.

30 Michel Foucault, 'Je perçois l'intolérable,' in *DE1*, 1072. The translation is my own.

31 Michel Foucault and Gilles Deleuze, 'Intellectuals and Power,' in *FL*, 76. Henceforth cited as *IP*.

32 Michel Foucault, 'Enquête sur les prisons: brisons les barreaux du silence,' in *DE1*, 1042. The translation is my own.

33 Foucault, 'Je perçois l'intolérable,' 1072.

CHAPTER 3

1 Let there be no misunderstandings: many fine essays take Foucault's reflections on Magritte as their starting point. There is simply a great diversity of opinion about what are its important points. Two outstanding treatments were helpful in composing this chapter: *AV*, 325–346. In this section, Shapiro traces the Nietzschean heritage of Foucault's reflections, bringing them into dialogue with Pierre Klossowski and Gilles Deleuze. And, Scott Durham, 'From Magritte to Klossowski: The Simulacrum, between Painting and Narrative,' *October* 64 (1993), 17–33. This imaginative presentation of the different functions of the simulacrum in art and literature provides a remarkably clear analysis of both Magritte and Klossowski. I have not followed these authors in discussing Foucault's treatment of Magritte in terms of his essay on Klossowski for the simple reason that it would direct us away from the historical analysis of painting Foucault develops in this essay. The connections with Deleuze are developed in Chapter 4.

2 Defert, 'Chronologie,' in *DE1*, 41.

3 See Note 2 above.

4 *TNP*, 53. *CP*, 77–78. The translation has been modified. I translate '*lieu commun*' as 'common place' and not 'common ground,' as part of Foucault's analysis shows how by depriving objects and words of their meeting place, Magritte moves everyday objects from the domain of the commonplace into the mysterious. I do not wish to suggest that James Harkness is not sensitive to this play. In other places he has rendered '*lieu commun*' as 'common place,' and even explains the pun in a footnote. For the reasons mentioned, I contend that it should be employed in this passage as well.

5 René Magritte, 'Letter to Michel Foucault,' reproduced in *TNP*, 57.

6 See *TNP*, 57. On the use of resemblance and similitude throughout *OT*, the correspondence with Magritte, and an account of the multiple senses of each word in French, see: Dominique Chateau, 'De la ressemblance: un dialogue Foucault-Magritte,' in *L'Image: Deleuze, Foucault, Lyotard*, ed. Thierry Lenain (Paris: Librairie Philosophique J. Vrin, 1998), 95–108.

7 Magritte, 'Letter to Michel Foucault,' in *TNP*, 57.

8 Silvano Levy, 'Foucault on Magritte on Resemblance,' *The Modern Language Review* 85, no. 1 (1990), 50–56. Levy is critical of what he considers Foucault's misinterpretations of Magritte's distinction. He shows that similitude is, for Magritte, a broader notion than for Foucault in this essay, encapsulating both what the latter terms resemblance and similitude. Resemblance, on the other hand, designates the process by which the mind is 'exercised on visible entities.' Levy demonstrates the integral role of resemblance in Magritte's conception of the creative process.

9 *TNP*, 44. *CP*, 61. The translation has been modified. This important and complicated passage was added to the 1973 version of this essay. The French reads: '*Il me paraît que Magritte a dissocié de la ressemblance la similitude et fait jouer celle-ci contre celle-là. La ressemblance a un*

<<*patron*>> : *élément original qui ordonne et hiérarchise à partir de soi toutes les copies de plus en plus affaiblies qu'on peut en prendre. Ressembler suppose une référence première qui prescrit et classe.*' I translate '*patron*' as 'pattern,' largely because of the context in which it occurs and to preserve the reference to a generative element. The French has many senses, compounded by Foucault's placing it within quotation marks. With '*patron*,' the reader should hear 'owner' and 'boss,' as well as 'patron,' as in 'patron of the arts,' and of course 'pattern,' in the sense above. I prefer this to Harkness's 'model,' reserving that word for '*modèle*,' which Foucault uses in other places.

10 Palpable in the 1973 version is the influence of Deleuze's discussions of the simulacrum. These exchanges are considered in Chapter 4.

11 H. H. Arnason, *History of Modern Art*, 3rd edn. Revised and updated by Daniel Wheeler (New York: Harry N. Abrams, Inc., Publishers, 1986), 127. Henceforth cited as *HMA*.

12 Jacques Meuris, *René Magritte*, trans. Michael Scuffil (Los Angeles: Taschen, 2004). Henceforth cited as *RM*. See in particular the chapter, 'Magritte the Realist—Imagination and Inspiration' where Meuris discusses the relationship between Magritte's art, the tradition of nineteenth-century French Realism, and the twentieth-century currents of Pop Art and Hyperrealism.

13 Arnason offers one possible source for these arrows: 'Teaching gave Klee much of his iconography. As he used arrows to indicate lines of force for his students, these arrows began to creep into his works.' *HMA*, 329.

14 Michel Foucault, 'L'homme est-il mort?,' in *DE1*, 572. Henceforth cited as *HEM*. All translations of this text are my own.

15 *QV*, 642. In another interview from this period, dedicated to the work of André Breton, Foucault distinguishes between 'two great families of founders,' those who build and those who excavate. He places Klee in the latter camp: 'Perhaps we are, in our uncertain space, closer to those who excavate: to Nietzsche (rather than Husserl), to Klee (rather than Picasso).' See, 'C'était un nageur entre deux mots,' in *DE1*, 582.

16 Foucault describes Magritte's calligram in three main ways: *défait* (undone), *dénoué* (unraveled), and *décomposé* (decomposed). These are relatively easy to translate, with the exception of the first. It is employed in the subtitle for the second section of Foucault's essay: '*Le Calligramme Défait.*' In addition to having the sense of being undone or unmade, Foucault's usage suggests the calligram is tormented and defeated. The subtitle could therefore be translated as 'The Defeated Calligram,' in place of Harkness's 'The Unraveled Calligram.' My argument in this section is that Magritte's defeated calligram, the one 'come undone,' is the first to successfully efface the distinction between word and image.

17 For Foucault, the traditional calligram has three primary functions: to *augment* the alphabet, making it delimit in visual form what it describes; to *repeat*, without the aid of rhetoric, what is given by words; to *capture* its object by means of a double movement, one visual, the other linguistic. See, *TNP*, 20–21.

18 *TNP*, 54. Foucault, *CP*, 79. The translation has been modified slightly. 'Campbell, Campbell, Campbell, Campbell,' obviously refers to the work of Andy Warhol, who in the early 1960s incorporated imagery from Campbell's Soup cans into his own iconography. Foucault, as we see in Chapter 4, develops this analysis of the simulacrum and his meditation on Warhol in: Michel Foucault, 'Theatrum Philosophicum,' in *LCMP*, 189. Henceforth cited as *TP*.

CHAPTER 4

1 Gilles Deleuze, *Difference and Repetition*, trans. Paul Patton (New York: Columbia University Press, 1994), 150. Henceforth cited as *DR*. On the exclusion of stupidity see, Chapter Three, 'The Image of Thought,' 129–167.

2 *TP*, 169. Foucault inserts this phrase, he tells us, perhaps against the letter of Deleuze's thought.

3 Gilles Deleuze, 'The Simulacrum and Ancient Philosophy,' appendix to *The Logic of Sense*, trans. Mark Lester and Charles Stivale. (New York: Columbia University Press, 1990) 256–257. Henceforth cited as *SAP*.

4 *SAP*, 256. Deleuze: 'It is in this sense that Plato divides in two the domain of images-idols: on the one hand there are *copies-icons*, and on the other there are *simulacra-phantasms*.'

5 Jacques Rancière has recently shown how, through Feuerbach's influence, a type of Platonism entered Debord's conceptualization of the spectacle. See, Jacques Rancière, 'The Emancipated Spectator,' *Artforum* XLV, no.7 (2007), 271–280.

6 *TP*, 188. Foucault: '[C]ategories silently reject stupidity . . . . Thus, we court danger in wanting to be freed from categories; no sooner do we abandon their principle than we face the magma of stupidity.'

7 *TP*, 187. Foucault: 'Differences would revolve of their own accord, being would be expressed in the same fashion for all these differences, and being would no longer be a unity that guides and distributes them, but their repetition as differences.'

8 On this point, see the section 'Lucretius and the Simulacrum,' in Deleuze, *The Logic of Sense*, 266–279.

9 Deleuze also cited Warhol's 'serial' paintings as a process that converted the copy into a simulacrum. For Deleuze, modern art should not be understood as imitation, but as repetition. 'Art does not imitate, above all because it repeats; it repeats all the repetitions, by virtue of an internal power (an imitation is a copy, but art is simulation, it reverses copies into simulacra).' This is an action that, for Deleuze, breaks with the banality of the modern world 'in order that Difference may at last be expressed.' See, *DR*, 293–294.

10 *TP*, 189. Foucault, 'Theatrum Philosophicum,' in *DE1*, 961. The translation has been modified.

11 Hans Belting, *Art History After Modernism*, trans. Caroline Saltzwedel, Mitch Cohen, and Kenneth Northcott (Chicago: The University of

Chicago Press, 2003), 44–53. For Belting, the two ways in which this movement was narrated is an example of his guiding thesis: the fundamentally fragmented nature of modern art poses difficulties for art history's traditional goal of constructing a coherent, unified story of Art.

12 Andy Warhol, *The Philosophy of Andy Warhol* (New York: Harcourt Brace & Company, 1977), 149.

13 This is quoted in: Kristine Stiles and Peter Selz, eds., *Theories and Documents of Contemporary Art: A Sourcebook of Artist's Writings* (Berkeley: University of California Press, 1996), 340.

14 Stiles and Selz, *Theories and Documents*, 344. This was quoted by Nicholas Love at a Memorial Mass for Andy Warhol, St. Patrick's Cathedral, New York, April 1, 1987.

15 There are three haircut films: *Haircut No. 1*, *Haircut No. 2* and *Haircut No. 3*. All were filmed in 1963.

16 Dave Hickey, 'The Delicacy of Rock–And–Roll,' in *Air Guitar: Essays on Art & Democracy* (Los Angeles: Art issues. Press, 1997), 99.

17 Andy Warhol and Pat Hackett, *POPism: The Warhol '60s* (London: Pimlico, 1980), 39–40.

18 Foucault's title is a reference to William Henry Fox Talbot's (1800–1877) 'Photogenic Drawing,' a process of creating contact prints by exposing sheets of paper covered in photo-sensitive materials.

19 Richard Kostelanetz, ed., *Moholy-Nagy: An Anthology* (New York: Da Capo Press, 1970), 56–57.

20 Michel Foucault, 'Photogenic Painting' (1975), in *Gérard Fromanger: Photogenic Painting*, ed. Sarah Wilson and trans. Dafydd Roberts (London: Black Dog Publishing Limited, 1999), 84. Henceforth cited as *PP*. Foucault's essay originally appeared as 'La peinture photogénique,' in *Le désir est partout* (Paris: Galerie Jeanne-Bucher, 1975). It is collected in *DE1*, 1575–1583. Throughout, I have made reference to Roberts' translation, offering alternative renderings where appropriate.

21 Adrian Rifkin, 'A Space Between: On Gérard Fromanger, Gilles Deleuze, Michel Foucault and Some Others,' in *Gérard Fromanger: Photogenic Painting*, 39.

22 Michel Foucault, 'Le jeu de Michel Foucault,' in *Foucault: Dits et écrits II, 1976–1988* (henceforth cited as *DE2*), ed. Daniel Defert, François Ewald, and Jacques Lagrange (Paris: Éditions Gallimard, 2001), 299. Henceforth cited as *LJF*. All translations of this text are my own.

23 Michel Foucault, 'Des supplices aux cellules,' in *DE1*, 1588. The translation is my own.

24 For example, the reform discourses following the deployment of the nineteenth-century penal network were immediately reabsorbed because they were themselves inscribed by the *dispositif*. Likewise, in the first volume of the *History of Sexuality*, the political critique of sexual repression is shown to unfold within '*Le dispositif de sexualité,*' not outside and against it.

25 The history of this case is recounted in Aaron Scharf, *Art and Photography* (London: Allen Lane The Penguin Press, 1968), 113–117. Henceforth

cited as *AP*. The complete statement of the petition, from which Foucault quotes only a phrase, reads: 'Whereas photography consists of a series of completely manual operations which no doubt require some skill in the manipulation involved, but never resulting in the fruits of intelligence and the study of art—on these grounds, the undersigned artists protest against any comparison which might be made between photography and art.' Quoted in *AP*, 116.

26 For a brief history of the discovery of this technique, see *AP*, 32–34.

27 The reference here is to Foucault's lecture 'The Subject and Power,' in which he argues that resistance to the 'double bind' of biopower, at once totalizing and individualizing, might proceed through the promotion of new forms of subjectivity. 'Maybe the target nowadays is not to discover what we are but to refuse what we are.' Michel Foucault, 'The Subject and Power,' in *Power: Essential Works of Foucault, 1954–1984, Volume Three*, ed. James D. Faubion (New York: The New Press, 2000), 336.

28 *QRP*, 1574–1575. Clovis Trouille (1889–1975) was what one might term a 'Sunday painter.' He was a marginal figure in the Surrealist movement, exhibiting with them periodically, while earning a living by working for Pierre Imans, a mannequin manufacturer in Paris. In 1963, he had his first solo exhibition at the *Galerie Raymond Cordier*. It was an invitation-only affair, as a scandal was feared. Trouille's canvases contain anticlerical themes as well as the admixture of the erotic and religious. Several render homage to the Marquis de Sade in day-glo colors. For a selection of works see: Clovis Trouille, *Clovis Trouille* (Paris: Editions Filipacchi, 1972).

29 Alain Jouffroy, 'Boulevard des Italiens,' in *Fromanger: Boulevard des Italiens* (Paris: Editions Georges Fall, 1971), 32–57.

30 Gilles Deleuze, 'Breaking Things Open,' in *Negotiations: 1972–1990*, trans. Martin Joughin (New York: Columbia University Press, 1995), 89.

31 Michel Foucault, 'La pensée, l'émotion' (1982), in *Foucault: Dits et écrits II, 1976–1988*, ed. Daniel Defert, François Ewald, and Jacques Lagrange (Paris: Éditions Gallimard, 2001), 1065. Henceforth cited as *PE*. Foucault's essay originally appeared as 'La Pensée, L'Émotion,' in *Duane Michals: Photographies de 1958 à 1982*, (Paris: Paris Audiovisuel/ Direction des Affaires Culturelles de la Ville de Paris, 1982). This catalogue accompanied the first international retrospective of Michals' work, held at the *Musée d'Art Moderne de la Ville de Paris* (9 November 1982 through 9 January 1983). Throughout I cite the version contained in *DE2*. All translations of this text are my own.

32 Foucault exploits the dual sense of the word '*expérience*,' which means both experience and experiment. This provides the basis for Shapiro's reading of this essay as a type of methodological statement. 'Most of all, Foucault is saying something about his own working method; he would like to be seen as an experimenter' (376). See, *AV*, 375–390. I depart from this interpretation, reading this piece in terms of Foucault's late investigations into the practices of the self, that is, his analyses of the procedures by which the self is formed and transformed. In my discussion, I attempt

to bring this together with his interest in the artistic-technical ways in which visual expectations are thwarted. It is my hope that this approach captures the ethical significance Foucault attributed to these images.

33 For an account of the scandal created by Guibert's publication, see: *LMF*, 478–480.

34 Michel Foucault, 'Non au sexe roi,' in *DE2*, 261–262. The translation is my own.

35 When asked what he reads for pleasure, Foucault responded: 'The books and the authors which produce in me the greatest emotion: Faulkner, Thomas Mann, the novel by Malcom Lowry, *Under the Volcano*.' Michel Foucault, 'Vérité, pouvoir et soi,' in *DE2*, 1599.

36 Maria Malibran (1808–1836), the mezzo-soprano upon whom this film is loosely based, was one of the most famous opera performers of the early nineteenth century.

37 *LMF*, 341. Macey cites as his source an interview with Daniel Defert.

38 Foucault, 'Sade, sergent du sexe,' in *DE1*, 1690. Henceforth cited as *SSS*.

39 Walter Benjamin, 'The Work of Art in the Age of Its Technological Reproducibility,' in *Selected Writings, Volume 3, 1935–1938*, trans. Edmund Jephcott, Howard Eiland, et al. Edited by Howard Eiland and Michael W. Jennings (Cambridge, Massachusetts: The Belknap Press of Harvard University Press, 2002), 115–116.

40 Michel Foucault, 'Conversation avec Werner Schroeter,' in *DE2*, 1070. All translations of this text are my own.

41 Foucault, 'Conversation avec Werner Schroeter,' 1075.

42 *AK*, 17. The quotation marks are Foucault's own as this paragraph appears in the context of an interview with himself.

43 Michel Foucault, 'The Masked Philosopher,' in *EST*, 321.

44 Duane Michals in *Inside the Studio: Two Decades of Talks with Artists in New York*, ed. Judith Olch Richards (New York: Independent Curators International, 2004), 66–69.

45 See, for example, Roland Barthes' distinction between the *studium* and *punctum* in *Camera Lucida: Reflections on Photography*, trans. Richard Howard (New York: Hill and Wang, 1982).

46 Duane Michals, *A Visit With Magritte* (Providence, Rhode Island: Matrix Publications Inc., 1981).

47 Michals, *A Visit With Magritte*.

48 Michals in *Inside the Studio*, 67.

CHAPTER 5

1 Michel Foucault, 'On the Genealogy of Ethics,' in *EST*, 263. Henceforth cited as *OGE*.

2 Michel Foucault, *Fearless Speech*, ed. Joseph Pearson (Los Angeles: Semiotext(e), 2001), 169. Henceforth cited as *FS*.

3 I do not wish to suggest that Foucault was posing the question in the same terms as he would throughout the 1980s, only that the different

modifications of self required by confession are present in Foucault's discussions of these texts and practices. See, for example, the analyses in the 19 February 1975 lecture in Michel Foucault, *Abnormal: Lectures at the Collège de France, 1974–1975*, ed. Valerio Marchetti and Antonella Salomoni, trans. Graham Burchell (New York: Picador, 2003), 167–194.

4 Michel Foucault, *The Use of Pleasure: Volume 2 of The History of Sexuality* (1984), trans. Robert Hurley (New York: Vintage Books, 1990), 29. Henceforth cited as *UP*.

5 Michel Foucault, *The Hermeneutics of the Subject, Lectures at the Collège de France, 1981–1982* (2001), ed. Frédéric Gros and trans. Graham Burchell (New York: Palgrave Macmillan, 2005), 188. Henceforth cited as *HER*.

6 Michel Foucault, 'Technologies of the Self,' in *EST*, 240.

7 *OGE*, 279. The Cartesian paradigm of self-evidence is, for Foucault, not the culmination of Renaissance science, but of a scholastic theology, which tacitly posits a universal subject able to have knowledge of God without first undergoing a process of transformation. See, *HER*, 25–28.

8 Michel Foucault, 29 February 1984 Lecture at the Collège de France, 11–12. Henceforth cited as *GSA2: 29 Feb.* I am quoting from an unpublished transcript of Foucault's final course, '*Le Gouvernement de soi et des autres: le courage de la vérité.*' Each lecture is paginated individually and the citations refer to numbered pages within each lecture. Michael Behrent prepared this transcript. All translations of this text are my own. I am grateful to James Bernauer for making this material available to me. A copy is available for consultation in the O'Neill Library at Boston College.

9 Foucault, 7 March 1984 Lecture, 46–48. Henceforth cited as *GSA2: 7 Mar.*

10 This dialogue is analyzed in at least two places. See: *FS*, 91–104 and the 22 February 1984 Lecture, 9–69.

11 Foucault, 14 March 1984 Lecture, 3. Henceforth cited as *GSA2: 14 Mar.*

12 *GSA2: 14 Mar.*, 51–53. Foucault also notes how the Cynic's practice of humiliation informs the practices of humility within Christian monastic communities. See, *GSA2: 14 Mar.*, 53–58.

13 On these themes see, Farrand Sayre, *Diogenes of Sinope: A Study of Greek Cynicism* (Baltimore: J. H. Furst Company, 1938), 44–46.

14 Foucault, 21 March 1984 Lecture, 22. Henceforth cited as *GSA2: 21 Mar.*

15 *GSA2: 21 Mar.*, 31–33. Foucault argues that this somewhat anachronistic comparison is justified, for the idea that one must have a certain type of being before one could speak the truth politically is one of the ways in which Cynicism is transmitted across Western culture. It is obviously a theme that interested Foucault. In the 1982 course he remarked, 'One day the history of what could be called revolutionary subjectivity should be written.' *HER*, 208. In the same course he follows the development of the notion of conversion, within the practices of ancient philosophy and Christianity. It is, he contends, fundamental for understanding the

revolutionary experience of the nineteenth century. In the 1984 course, Foucault highlights certain Cynical practices and teachings because they anticipate the ethical comportment of nineteenth-century radicals. The Cynics were not, of course, the only school to espouse a type of philosophical militancy; however, for Foucault, they are distinct in that the means they employed were often 'violent and drastic.' Their preaching did not simply aim to educate people, as much as to startle them and to convert them to a way of life. See, *GSA2: 21 Mar.*, 33.

16 Foucault, 28 March 1984 Lecture, 17–55.
17 Michel Foucault, 'Michel Foucault: An Interview by Stephen Riggins,' in *EST*, 131.
18 Clement Greenberg, 'Avant-Garde and Kitsch,' in *Art and Culture* (Boston: Beacon Press, 1989), 7.
19 *GSA2: 29 Feb.*, 63. This difficult passage reads: '*L'art moderne c'est le cynisme dans la culture, c'est le cynisme de la culture retourné vers elle-même. Et je crois que si ce n'est pas simplement dans l'art, c'est dans l'art surtout que se concentre[nt] dans le monde moderne, dans notre monde à nous, les formes les plus intenses d'un dire vrai qui a le courage de prendre le risque de blesser.*'
20 *Parrhēsia* first presented itself to Foucault in his analysis of relationships of governance, guidance and practices of confession. In the 1982 lecture course, Foucault explains how *parrhēsia* moves from being a desirable quality in a philosophical master, i.e., a virtue that combines speech and courage so as to make him capable of giving frank advice to someone in his charge, to an obligatory state of openness whereby the subject of the enunciation also becomes the referent of his own discourse. In the first case, the guide who is to give advice must not seek to influence those under his care by means of flattery or rhetoric. He must instead calibrate his words carefully to ensure that they bring about the necessary change of life. The master's discourse 'must not be a discourse of seduction. It must be a discourse that the disciple's subjectivity can appropriate and by which . . . the disciple can reach his own objective, namely himself.' *HER*, 368. In the Epicurean communities, where friendship and the mutual correction of faults were essential parts of philosophical practice, the obligation to speak freely (*parrhēsia*) was transferred to the students. This obligation for frank speech on the part of the one guided is an essential component in the construction of Western mechanisms of confession. Of this shift in the location of *parrhēsia* within the relationship of guidance, Foucault explains: 'It seems to me that it is the first time that we find this obligation that we will meet again in Christianity, namely: I must respond—I am encouraged, called upon, and obliged to respond—to the words of truth that teach me the truth and consequently help me in my salvation, with a discourse of truth by which I open the truth of my own soul to the other, to others.' *HER*, 391. Historically, however, *parrhēsia* first appeared not in a spiritual context, but in a political one. Foucault's *Fearless Speech* lectures, given at Berkeley in 1983, trace the crisis surrounding political *parrhēsia* in Greek thought and practice at the end of the fourth and beginning of the fifth centuries, B.C.E. The 1983 course

at the Collège de France, *Le Gouvernement de soi et des autres* considers *parrhēsia* as political practice and the 1984 course *Le Gouvernement de soi et des autres: le courage de la vérité* traces its transformation into an ethical practice. In the 1 February 1984 lecture Foucault explains that he was surprised by the political history of this form of speech and how its analysis has indeed taken him afield from his initial problem: the history of the ancient practices of speaking the truth about oneself. See, Foucault, 1 February 1984 Lecture, 14. Henceforth cited as *GSA2: 1 Feb.* He thus proposes to examine how, by means of its problematization in the political realm, it migrates into the ethical realm of subjectivity. On this point, see Foucault, 8 February 1984 Lecture. Henceforth cited as *GSA2: 8 Feb.* Such an approach, Foucault explains, has the benefit of allowing him 'to pose the question of the subject and truth from the point of view of the practices one can call "the government of oneself and others."' *GSA2: 8 Feb.*, 15. That is, by means of *parrhēsia*, Foucault intends to join the history of the practices of the self with the theme of governmentality and the questions of truth that were posed in his courses during the late 1970s. Thus, Foucault intends to consider 'the relations (*les rapports*) between truth, power and the subject' not as collapsible into one another, but as constitutive of each other. *GSA2: 8 Feb.*, 16. The history of the ethical transformation of *parrhēsia* is both complicated and incomplete. Roughly, Foucault's thesis is that as *parrhēsia* is disqualified as a dangerous practice in Greek democracy, it is secured on the basis of techniques of ethical differentiation. Foucault: 'what one could call, a little pretentiously, the crisis of democratic *parrhēsia* in Greek thought of the fourth century . . . makes us immediately bump into the problem of *ēthos* and of ethical differentiation.' *GSA2: 8 Feb.*, 40. This is the origin of what Foucault, in 1983, termed the second critical tradition. Distinct from the tradition of philosophy that concerns itself with principles of sound reasoning and criteria for true statements, the other critical tradition focuses on the activity of truth-telling as such and concerns itself with the ethical characteristics of the would-be truth-teller. Accordingly, Greek philosophy 'raised questions like: Who is able to tell the truth? What are the moral, the ethical, and the spiritual conditions which entitle someone to present himself as, and to be considered as, a truth-teller?' *FS*, 169.

21 *HER*, 231–238. Foucault, following various ancient sources, describes this type of knowledge as 'ethopoetic,' or capable of producing a change in an individual's mode of being.

22 Seneca, *Letters*, LXXV, quoted in *HER*, 401–402.

23 'It is . . . this pact between the one who takes the risk of speaking the truth and the one who accepts to listen to it which is at the heart of what one could call the *parrhesiastic* game.' *GSA2: 1 Feb.*, 23.

24 Foucault, 'Conversation avec Werner Schroeter,' *DE2*, 1075.

BIBLIOGRAPHY

Ariès, Phillipe, ed. *Michel Foucault, la littérature et les arts.* Paris: Éditions Kimé, 2004.

Arnason, H. H. *History of Modern Art,* 3rd edn. Revised and updated by Daniel Wheeler. New York: Harry N. Abrams, Inc., Publishers, 1986.

Barthes, Roland. *Camera Lucida: Reflections on Photography.* Translated by Richard Howard. New York: Hill and Wang, 1982.

Bataille, Georges. *Manet.* Paris: Éditions d'Art Albert Skira S. A., 1994.

Baudelaire, Charles. *The Painter of Modern Life and Other Essays.* Translated by Jonathan Mayne. New York: Phaidon Press Inc., 2005.

Belting, Hans. *Art History After Modernism.* Translated by Caroline Saltzwedel, Mitch Cohen, and Kenneth Northcott. Chicago: The University of Chicago Press, 2003.

Benjamin, Walter. *Selected Writings, Volume 3, 1935–1938.* Translated by Edmund Jephcott, Howard Eiland, et al. Cambridge, Massachusetts: The Belknap Press of Harvard University Press, 2002.

Bernauer, James W. *Michel Foucault's Force of Flight: Toward an Ethics for Thought.* Amherst, New York: Humanity Books, 1990.

Bernauer, James W., Edward F. McGushin, and Joseph J. Tanke, eds. *Philosophy and Social Criticism* 31, no. 5–6 (2005). Special issue commemorating the 20th anniversary of Foucault's death.

Bishop, Sherman C. 'Aldrovandi's Natural History.' *University of Rochester Library Bulletin* V, no. 2 (1950), 32–34.

Buchloh, Benjamin H. D. 'The Group that Was (Not) One: Daniel Buren and BMPT.' *Artforum* XLVI, no. 9 (May 2008), 311–313.

Courthion, Pierre. *Manet.* New York: Harry N. Abrams, Inc., 2004.

Danto, Arthur C. *After The End of Art: Contemporary Art and the Pale of History.* Princeton, New Jersey: Princeton University Press, 1997.

Deleuze, Gilles. *Foucault.* Translated by Seán Hand. Minneapolis: University of Minnesota Press, 1988.

—*The Logic of Sense.* Translated by Mark Lester and Charles Stivale. New York: Columbia University Press, 1990.

—*Difference and Repetition.* Translated by Paul Patton. New York: Columbia University Press, 1994.

—*Negotiations: 1972–1990*. Translated by Martin Joughin. New York: Columbia University Press, 1995.

Dreyfus, Hubert L. and Paul Rabinow. *Michel Foucault: Beyond Structuralism and Hermeneutics*. 2nd edn. Chicago: University of Chicago Press, 1982.

Durham, Scott. 'From Magritte to Klossowski: The Simulacrum, between Painting and Narrative.' *October* 64 (1993), 17–33.

Eribon, Didier. *Michel Foucault*. Translated by Betsy Wing. Cambridge: Harvard University Press, 1991.

Foucault, Michel. *Les mots et les choses: Une archéologie des sciences humaines*. Paris: Éditions Gallimard, 1966.

—'Ceci n'est pas une pipe.' *Les Cahiers du chemin* 15, no. 2 (1968), 79–105.

—*The Archaeology of Knowledge and The Discourse on Language*. Translated by A. M. Sheridan Smith. New York: Pantheon Books, 1972.

—*Ceci n'est pas une pipe*. Paris: Fata Morgana, 1973.

—'La force de fuir.' *Derrière le miroir: Rebeyrolle*, no. 202 (1973), 1–8.

—*Language, Counter-Memory, Practice: Selected Essays and Interviews*. Edited by Donald F. Bouchard. Ithaca, New York: Cornell University Press, 1977.

—*This is Not a Pipe*. Translated by James Harkness. Berkeley: University of California Press, 1983.

—'*Le Gouvernement de soi et des autres: le courage de la vérité.*' Unpublished transcript of course at the Collège de France, prepared by Michael Behrent, 1984.

—*Death and the Labyrinth: The World of Raymond Roussel*. Translated by Charles Ruas. New York: Doubleday & Company, Inc., 1986.

—*The Care of the Self: Volume 3 of The History of Sexuality*. Translated by Robert Hurley. New York: Vintage Books, 1988.

—*The History of Sexuality: Volume 1: An Introduction*. Translated by Robert Hurley. New York: Vintage Books, 1990.

—*The Use of Pleasure: Volume 2 of The History of Sexuality*. Translated by Robert Hurley. New York: Vintage Books, 1990.

—*The Birth of the Clinic: An Archaeology of Medical Perception*. Translated by A. M. Sheridan Smith. New York: Vintage Books, 1994.

—*The Order of Things: An Archaeology of the Human Sciences*. New York: Vintage Books, 1994.

—*Discipline and Punish: The Birth of the Prison*. Translated by Alan Sheridan. New York: Vintage Books, 1995.

—*Foucault Live*. Edited by Sylvère Lotringer. New York: Semiotext(e), 1996.

—*Ethics: Subjectivity and Truth: Essential Works of Foucault, 1954–1984, Volume One*. Edited by Paul Rabinow. New York: The New Press, 1997.

—*Aesthetics, Method, and Epistemology: Essential Works of Foucault, 1954–1984, Volume Two*. Edited by James D. Faubion. New York: The New Press, 1998.

—*Power: Essential Works of Foucault, 1954–1984, Volume Three*. Edited by James D. Faubion. New York: The New Press, 2000.

—*Fearless Speech*. Edited by Joseph Pearson. Los Angeles: Semiotext(e), 2001.

—*Foucault: Dits et écrits I, 1954–1975*. Edited by Daniel Defert, François Ewald, and Jacques Lagrange. Paris: Éditions Gallimard, 2001.

—*Foucault: Dits et écrits II, 1976–1988*. Edited by Daniel Defert, François Ewald, and Jacques Lagrange. Paris: Éditions Gallimard, 2001.

—*Abnormal: Lectures at the Collège de France, 1974–1975*. Translated by Graham Burchell. New York: Picador, 2003.

—*La Peinture de Manet*. Edited by Maryvonne Saison. Paris: Éditions du Seuil, 2004.

—*The Hermeneutics of the Subject, Lectures at the Collège de France, 1981–1982*. Translated by Graham Burchell. New York: Palgrave Macmillan, 2005.

—*History of Madness*. Translated by Jonathan Murphy and Jean Khalfa. London: Routledge, 2006.

—*Le gouvernement de soi et des autres: Cours au Collège de France (1982–1983)*. Paris: Seuil/Gallimard, 2008.

Fromanger, Gérard. *Gerard Fromanger: Le désir est partout*. Paris: Galerie Jeanne-Bucher, 1975.

Greenberg, Clement. *Art and Culture: Critical Essays*. Boston: Beacon Press, 1989.

Hickey, Dave. *Air Guitar: Essays on Art & Democracy*. Los Angeles: Art issues Press, 1997.

Jouffroy, Alain and Jacques Prévert. *Fromanger: Boulevard des Italiens*. Paris: Editions Georges Fall, 1971.

Kostelanetz, Richard, ed. *Moholy-Nagy: An Anthology*. New York: Da Capo Press, 1970.

Lautréamont, Comte de. *Les Chants de Maldoror*. Translated by Guy Wernham. New York: New Directions Publishing Corporation, 1966.

Lenain, Thierry, ed. *L'Image: Deleuze, Foucault, Lyotard*. Paris: Librairie Philosophique J. Vrin, 1998.

Levy, Silvano. 'Foucault on Magritte on Resemblance.' *The Modern Language Review* 85, no. 1 (1990), 50–56.

Macey, David. *The Lives of Michel Foucault: A Biography*. New York: Pantheon Books, 1993.

Martin, John Rupert. *Baroque*. New York: Harper & Row, Publishers, 1977.

McGushin, Edward F. *Foucault's Askesis: An Introduction to the Philosophical Life*. Evanston, Illinois: Northwestern University Press, 2007.

Meuris, Jacques. *René Magritte*. Translated by Michael Scuffil. Los Angeles: Taschen, 2004.

Michals, Duane. *A Visit with Magritte*. Providence, Rhode Island: Matrix Publications Inc., 1981.

—*Duane Michals: Photographies de 1958 à 1982*. Paris: Paris Audiovisuel/ Direction des Affaires Culturelles de la Ville de Paris, 1982.

Moreno, Ana Martín. *Las Meninas*. Translated by Nigel Williams. Madrid: Aldeasa, 2003.

Néret, Gilles. *Édouard Manet: The First of the Moderns*. Los Angeles: Taschen, 2003.

Paoletti, John T. and Gary M. Radke. *Art in Renaissance Italy*. New York: Harry N. Abrams, Inc., Publishers, 1997.

Rancière, Jacques. 'The Emancipated Spectator.' *Artforum* XLV, no.7 (2007), 271–280.

Richards, Judith Olch, ed. *Inside the Studio: Two Decades of Talks with Artists in New York*. New York: Independent Curators International, 2004.

Rosenblum, Robert and H. W. Janson. *19ᵗʰ-Century Art*. New York: Harry N. Abrams, Inc., 1984.

Sayre, Farrand. *Diogenes of Sinope: A Study of Greek Cynicism*. Baltimore: J. H. Furst Company, 1938.

Scharf, Aaron. *Art and Photography*. London: Allen Lane, The Penguin Press, 1968.

Shapiro, Gary. *Archaeologies of Vision: Foucault and Nietzsche on Seeing and Saying*. Chicago: The University of Chicago Press, 2003.

Simon, Joan, ed. *Bruce Nauman*. Minneapolis: Walker Art Center, 1994.

Soussloff, Catherine M. *The Absolute Artist: The Historiography of a Concept*. Minneapolis: University of Minnesota Press, 1997.

Stiles, Kristine and Peter Selz, eds. *Theories and Documents of Contemporary Art: A Sourcebook of Artist's Writings*. Berkeley: University of California Press, 1996.

Trouille, Clovis. *Clovis Trouille*. Paris: Editions Filipacchi, 1972.

Warhol, Andy. *The Philosophy of Andy Warhol*. New York: Harcourt Brace & Company, 1977.

Warhol, Andy and Pat Hackett. *POPism: The Warhol '60s*. London: Pimlico, 1980.

Wilson, Sarah, ed. *Gérard Fromanger: Photogenic Painting*. Translated by Dafydd Roberts. London: Black Dog Publishing Limited, 1999.

INDEX

INDEX